Praise for *Proclaim Peace*

In *Proclaim Peace*, Mason and Pulsipher invite readers along on a "theological journey" in pursuit of peacemaking. Such a vital treasure hunt! Using scriptural texts of the Restoration and insights born of faithful commitment and gospel study, they demonstrate that pursuing peace is godly, foundational, muscular, and not for the faint of heart. The book is sparkling, deep, and radiant!

—LINDA HOFFMAN KIMBALL,
a founding member of Mormon Women for Ethical Government
and editor of *The Little Purple Book: MWEG Essentials*

Proclaim Peace provides readers an intelligent, faith-promoting perspective on how peace is central to the gospel and how the Book of Mormon can be read to think more critically about the justification of violence and the necessity of pursuing peace. Compared to many other faith traditions, The Church of Jesus Christ of Latter-day Saints is very new to exploring ethics of war and peace, and this book provides Latter-day Saint young adults some important tools for looking at their religion's scripture and doctrine more deeply and understanding war and peace more fully. There is a massive void when it comes to Latter-day Saint voices in peacebuilding, so this work represents a huge, important contribution.

—BENJAMIN COOK,
associate professor of law and director for the Center for
Peace and Conflict Resolution at BYU–Provo

A
Living Faith
Book

Living Faith books are for readers who cherish the life of the mind and the things of the Spirit. Each title offers an example of faith in search of understanding, the unique voice of a practicing scholar who has cultivated a believing heart.

OTHER LIVING FAITH BOOKS INCLUDE:

Samuel M. Brown, *First Principles and Ordinances: The Fourth Article of Faith in Light of the Temple*

Samuel M. Brown, *Where the Soul Hungers: One Doctor's Journey from Atheism to Faith*

James E. Faulconer, *Thinking Otherwise*

George B. Handley, *The Hope of Nature*

George B. Handley, *If Truth Were a Child*

Ashley Mae Hoiland, *One Hundred Birds Taught Me to Fly: The Art of Seeking God*

Patrick Q. Mason, *Planted: Belief and Belonging in an Age of Doubt*

Adam S. Miller, *Letters to a Young Mormon* (2nd ed.)

Steven L. Peck, *Evolving Faith: Wanderings of a Mormon Biologist*

Thomas F. Rogers, *Let Your Hearts and Minds Expand: Reflections on Faith, Reason, Charity, and Beauty*

Melissa Wei-Tsing Inouye, *Crossings: A Bald Asian American Latter-day Saint Woman Scholar's Ventures through Life, Death, Cancer & Motherhood (Not Necessarily in That Order)*

Charles Shirō Inouye: *Zion Earth Zen Sky*

PROCLAIM PEACE

THE RESTORATION'S ANSWER
TO AN AGE OF CONFLICT

PATRICK Q. MASON AND
J. DAVID PULSIPHER

The paper used in this publication meets the minimum requirements of the American National Standard for Information Sciences—Permanence of Paper for Printed Library Materials. ANSI Z39.48-19

ISBN: 978-1-9503-0416-5

Cover design: Grace Pulsipher, Heather Ward
Interior artwork: Grace Pulsipher
Book design: Emily V. Rogers

Printed in the United States of America

http://maxwellinstitute.byu.edu/

Library of Congress Cataloging-in-Publication Data

Names: Mason, Patrick Q., author. | Pulsipher, J. David (John David), 1967-
   author.
Title: Proclaim peace : the Restoration's answer to an age of conflict /
   Patrick Q. Mason & J. David Pulsipher.
Description: Provo, UT : Neal A. Maxwell Institute for Religious
   Scholarship, Brigham Young University, [2021] | Includes index. |
   Summary: "An extended meditation on what it means to follow Jesus Christ
   in a world of violence, this book invites readers, especially the rising
   generation, to reflect seriously on the interpersonal, ethical, and
   social dimensions of Christian discipleship. It is a spiritual journey
   by two Latter-day Saint scholars of peace--a journey of scriptural
   exegesis and hermeneutics that breathes new life into familiar and
   beloved texts from the Bible, Book of Mormon, Doctrine and Covenants,
   and Pearl of Great Price"-- Provided by publisher.
Identifiers: LCCN 2021027065 | ISBN 9781950304165 (paperback)
Subjects: LCSH: Peace--Religious aspects--Church of Jesus Christ of
   Latter-day Saints. | Peace--Religious aspects--Mormon Church. | Church
   of Jesus Christ of Latter-day Saints--Doctrines. | Mormon
   Church--Doctrines.
Classification: LCC BX8643.P43 M37 2021 | DDC 261.8/73--dc23
LC record available at https://lccn.loc.gov/2021027065

for our children,
and the rest of the rising generation

Contents

Contents

Acknowledgments

Paths of peace often feel circuitous, and the path of this book is no different. It has taken more than a decade from conception to completion, with the help of many friends, colleagues, and supporters along the way.

The genesis for the project came in March 2011, during a conference on Latter-day Saint perspectives on war and peace cosponsored by the Howard W. Hunter Chair of Mormon Studies at Claremont Graduate University—then occupied by Richard Bushman—and the Kroc Institute for International Peace Studies at Notre Dame. We are indebted to the scholars who gathered at Claremont to share their insights, and to Greg Kofford Books for publishing the resultant volume, *War and Peace in Our Time: Mormon Perspectives*. A deeply thoughtful review of that book by political theorist Benjamin R. Hertzberg encouraged us to think about the necessity of a more comprehensive, sustained treatment of the topic.

Acknowledgments

The project really got a kick start thanks to Andrew Bolton, whose commitment to nonviolence from his perspective as a member and leader in the Community of Christ is truly inspiring. The three of us met together for several intense and productive days, which resulted in creating the project's first working outline. While the book has evolved significantly since those initial efforts, we are indebted to Andrew's friendship and expert midwifery. We hope he will be pleased at our modest effort to articulate a Latter-day Saint vision of Jesus Christ's peaceable kingdom.

The manuscript developed in fits and starts over the subsequent years, but there were several key elements that moved it along. First, we were able to present our ideas and receive feedback at numerous conferences, symposia, and universities, including the American Academy of Religion, Sidney Sperry Symposium, Mormon History Association, J. Reuben Clark Society (Phoenix and Orange County chapters), National World War I Museum and Memorial, LDS National Security Professionals symposium, Miller-Eccles Study Group, Society for Mormon Philosophy and Theology, J. Reuben Clark Law School and Center for Peace and Conflict Resolution at Brigham Young University, University of Notre Dame, Claremont Graduate University, Utah Valley University, and Brigham Young University–Idaho. We are especially thankful to the Wheatley Institution at Brigham Young University, which sponsored a multiday seminar and subsequent conference on Latter-day Saint ethics of war and peace. Fred Axelgard spearheaded the effort and brought together a terrific group of Latter-day Saint and other scholars from around the world whose presentations significantly informed our thinking.

A second important factor in moving this book forward was opportunities for sustained thinking and writing. Here we are indebted to Dick and Sue Jacobsen and their family, who own and operate Sky Mountain Ranch near Victor, Idaho. Over several multiday retreats, we were able to disconnect from the world, read scripture, argue interpretation, and write our conclusions, all within view of the Tetons. If there is a place that consistently speaks peace, Sky Mountain is that place. Patrick even survived the hike to the top of the mountain.

Once we (finally) had a complete manuscript, Sky Mountain also served as the site for an important gathering of scholars and friends—Chad Ford, Fiona Givens, Elray Henriksen, Grace Kao, Hyrum Lewis, Jerry Powers, and Joe Spencer. Sponsored by the Neal A. Maxwell Institute for Religious Scholarship at Brigham Young University and the Leonard J. Arrington Chair of Mormon History and Culture at Utah State University, with additional assistance from the Department of History at Brigham Young University–Idaho, this two-day retreat was invaluable to further refining our ideas. It is impossible to adequately thank these friends for their incisive criticism, generosity, charity, and encouragement, which sent us back to the drawing board in certain regards but helped produce a much stronger book. One of their most important contributions was a unanimous suggestion to move away from addressing a primarily academic audience (our original intention) and focus instead on writing to our fellow Latter-day Saints. How grateful we are for that insight.

Along the way we have also benefited from the thoughtful readings of various drafts by our students. The graduate students at Claremont Graduate University and Utah State University, along with undergraduate students at Brigham Young University–Idaho and the Intercultural Peacebuilding Program at Brigham Young University–Hawaii have offered enormously helpful feedback about how our ideas play in the minds and hearts of the rising generation. Other scholars and friends, including Matthew Bowman, Amanda Hendrix-Komoto, David Howlett, Melissa Inouye, Jeannie Johnson, Laurie Maffly-Kipp, and Jana Riess also offered helpful suggestions. We likewise appreciate Dawn Durante, then editor at the University of Illinois Press (now at the University of Texas Press), for her enthusiasm and encouragement when the project still had primarily academic intentions, and for her generous understanding when we shifted our focus.

We thank the boards of the Maxwell Institute and Deseret Book for their faith in this project, and for the anonymous reviewers who helped us make yet further refinements. At every step, the book has only been improved by the efforts of others. In particular, we are deeply indebted to our able editors (and cheerleaders) Miranda Wilcox and Morgan Davis at Maxwell. At Deseret Book, Lisa Roper's effort, patience, and skill have also been invaluable. Thank you to everyone on these amazing editorial teams, as well as all those others who worked behind the scenes at Maxwell and Deseret Book to produce the actual book. As always, any errors of fact or interpretation are solely the responsibility of the authors.

Finally, while it is fairly standard practice for authors to thank their families, in our case they definitely deserve our heartfelt gratitude for their love, support, and (above all) patience. Both of us have been blessed with loving and peace-filled parents, spouses, children, in-laws, siblings, nieces, and nephews. Even when asking (again) when the book would be done, or pointing out our shortcomings when it comes to putting peace principles into practice (and they've had a lot of material to work with), our families have been a constant source of inspiration and encouragement. They have never stopped believing in us throughout our seemingly endless and quixotic peacebuilding journey, and we love them for that priceless gift.

More particularly, all our children—Finn, Rhett, Lucy, and Willa Mason, and Elizabeth, Andrew and Sara, Jonathan, Michael, Grace, and Katherine Pulsipher—and one grandchild (so far) have helped us to see the implications of peace and the enormous stakes of getting it right. This project is for them and the future they will both inherit and create. Already, they are building peace in ways that awe us, and their influence permeates these pages, extending even to its cover design and interior artwork (thanks to the talents of Grace).

Finally, we thank our practically perfect partners, Melissa and Dawn, for not giving up hope but seeing us through to the end. We may write about and yearn for peace, but they reach out and live it in ways we both hope to someday emulate. Their examples inspire us to continue to seek after the Prince of Peace, Jesus Christ, in whom we place our ultimate faith and to whom we express our deepest gratitude for being the Light, the Life, and the Way. May his peaceable kingdom come, on earth as it is in heaven.

Introduction

Peace I leave with you, my peace I give unto you.
—John 14:27

Therefore, renounce war and proclaim peace.
—Doctrine and Covenants 98:16

In a world that often feels rife with conflict—in our streets, between nations, on the internet, even in our homes—people can be led to cry out, as Emma Lou Thayne did in the first line of her moving hymn, "Where can I turn for peace?"[1] The ultimate answer, as embraced by Latter-day Saints around the world and articulated by Thayne, is simple—"He, only One." He, of course, is Jesus Christ, the healer of both souls and societies. Most Latter-day Saints are personally familiar with the myriad ways by which he "answers privately" and "reaches [our] reaching."[2] We regularly testify of the ways that Christ heals our individual souls. But what about our societies? How does Jesus speak to the violence in our communities and between nations? How can he mend our broken and oppressive institutions? In short, how can the gospel of Jesus Christ help to heal our fallen world and provide answers in an age characterized by "wars and rumors of wars," when "the love of men shall wax cold"?[3]

This book proposes that such peacebuilding is at the heart of the restored gospel of Jesus Christ. On one level, this is an unremarkable statement. All Christians believe in the Savior's teaching "Blessed are the peacemakers: for they shall be called the children of God."[4] And yet the peacebuilding potential of the Restoration, which began some two centuries ago when Joseph Smith had his first vision of God the Father and Jesus Christ, remains generally obscure to both insiders and outsiders. Most peacebuilding professionals have not been introduced to the Restoration as a wellspring of peace principles. Likewise, most Latter-day Saints themselves are not accustomed to applying Restoration principles as effective strategies to mitigate violence and transform conflict. Yet the Restoration's distinctive scriptures—the Book of Mormon, Doctrine and Covenants, and Pearl of Great Price—feature rich veins of peace and nonviolent theology. These scriptures and their insights into the human condition are not just beneficial or relevant to Latter-day Saints. In the same way the Torah inspires people outside Judaism and the sutras speak to others besides Buddhists, the Restoration's sacred texts contain wisdom that is applicable for a wider world.

At the heart of this wisdom are several core ideas: All humans are inherently divine and eternally interrelated. Enduring power can be achieved only through persuasion and love. Conflict is built into creation and can be constructively transformed for positive purposes. In rare instances violence may be justified, but only nonviolent responses based in love are truly sanctifying and efficacious in the long term. And "Zion"—the Restoration's term for the beloved community of those who collectively follow the principles taught by Jesus Christ—is not simply an otherworldly aspiration but rather an achievable aim for this world if individuals and societies embrace love, equality, justice, and peace as a way of life.

Thus, for anyone with questions about how to seek peace in an age of conflict, the Restoration has distinctive insights to contribute. Latter-day Saints can add our heretofore little-known but nonetheless significant flame to those luminaries already enlightening the paths of greater peace and human flourishing. We can sing, along with the nonviolent civil rights activists of the 1950s and 1960s, "This little light of mine, I'm gonna let it shine!"

A STRANGE THING

"There is a strange thing in the land; a wild man hath come among us."[5] So said the people who heard the ancient prophet Enoch preach. In the Bible, Enoch is a relatively obscure character mentioned in only four verses in Genesis and one passing reference in the New Testament. Yet these spare details are tantalizing: "Enoch walked with God; then he was no more, because God took him."[6] From this little nugget, Joseph Smith expanded the Enoch story into two sprawling chapters in his inspired revision of the Bible. As it turns out, Enoch, this "wild man" who pursued such a "strange" ministry, was a peacebuilder par excellence.

As with the later prophets Moses, Samuel, and Isaiah, Enoch's call came out of nowhere. He heard a voice from heaven directing him to urge the people to renounce their ungodly ways. In particular, God was upset because the people's "hearts [had] waxed hard," they had departed from his commandments, and they had "devised murder."[7] God's creation had fallen far afield from the peace and harmony that prevailed in the Garden of Eden, and needed repair.

Enoch's world was not a happy one. Communities were embroiled in constant conflict; "wars and bloodshed" prevailed. Raising his eyes from earth to heaven, Enoch saw a vision of the devil laughing and God weeping because the people were "without affection, and . . . hate[d] their own blood."[8] The violence in their hearts had culminated in a seemingly never-ending cycle of aggression and revenge.

But Enoch broke the cycle. He saw what the rest of the people could not. He realized that it didn't have to be this way. And so he went to work, preaching and persuading. Contrary to the militaristic culture that surrounded him, Enoch's power came not from the sword but from the word. In fact, "so powerful was the word of Enoch, and so great was the power of the language which God had given him," that his enemies were rendered powerless in their attempted attacks against him and his followers. Those who came to share Enoch's vision of a better, holier way eventually created a community that God called "Zion, because they were of one heart and one mind, and dwelt in righteousness; and there was no poor among them."[9] Enoch's people understood that it isn't enough to stem the tide of direct violence in their culture. They also had to create social and economic conditions that would allow all of God's children to flourish and maximize their full potential.

Zion didn't arise overnight. More than three and a half centuries passed between Enoch's call and when "God received [Zion] up into his own bosom."[10] Enoch built a people of peace patiently, steadily, and purposefully. Articulating a vision of hopeful possibility rooted in a deep conviction that God is on the side of love, peace, and justice, Enoch's message sounded "strange" in a world consumed with violence.

The story of Enoch offers both a cautionary tale and a beacon of hope for modern readers. As Martin Luther King Jr. perceived on the eve of his assassination, "it is no longer a choice between violence and nonviolence in this world; it's nonviolence or nonexistence."[11] The threats are manifest and multiple, ranging from weapons of mass destruction to ecological devastation and a new age of extinction.[12] Like Enoch, we too might bring ourselves to see a different path and build a more peaceful world, even if at first glance the nonviolent principles upon which such a society can be built might seem "strange."

READING RESTORATION TEXTS

The story of Enoch offers a taste of how the scriptures of the Restoration might meaningfully contribute to the theology and practice of peace. But to fully appreciate the insights of these Restoration scriptures, we have to see our sacred texts with new eyes. This goes for both believers and nonbelievers. Believers, of course, will approach Restoration scripture as the word of God revealed for our benefit in modern times. But one does not have to accept the Restoration's truth claims to seriously study, or even glean wisdom from, its scriptures. As Grant Hardy has demonstrated with his narrative analysis of the Book of Mormon, questions about the origins of sacred scriptures can be set aside for constructive dialogue about the intended (and even unintended) meaning of those texts.[13] In this context of curiosity and mutual engagement, believers and nonbelievers can come together to explore the principles of common concern that any sacred text might articulate. As authors we have learned much from the scriptures and wisdom of other religious traditions; here we invite both Latter-day Saints and our sisters and brothers of other faiths (or no faith at all) to consider how Restoration scripture can offer distinctive contributions to our united quest for peace.

Because the Restoration is such a deeply scriptural tradition, any peace theology must necessarily draw from and be responsive to its accepted canon. As theologian Adam Miller has affirmed, Latter-day Saint theology is "shaped by the centrality of scripture. . . . With immense care and patience, it reads and re-reads sacred texts with a keen eye for their latent patterns and defining details."[14] Thus, *Proclaim Peace* is at its heart a work of scriptural theology. Our method will be to read Restoration scripture closely to discern its possible meanings (what scholars call exegesis) and then to offer our own interpretations (what scholars call hermeneutics).

Why theology? For a problem as urgent and earthy as violence, isn't theology a little abstract? Wouldn't it be better to move straight to practice? Yes and no. We recognize the danger of being too theoretical when the suffering of victims of violence is all too real. But we also believe that right thinking precedes right action. This is a principle that apostle Boyd K. Packer frequently taught when he said, "True doctrine, understood, changes attitudes and behavior. The study of the doctrines of the gospel will improve behavior quicker than a study of behavior will improve behavior."[15] Reverend Otis Moss III, one of contemporary America's great preachers, also made a case for good theology when he wrote that "when you have no theology, then you have a messed-up psychology, and you cannot have the right sociology, and you will have a skewed anthropology."[16] Our hope is that the theological reflections here will enhance the development of Latter-day Saint psychology, sociology, anthropology, and community engagement, all rooted in revealed principles of the restored gospel. To be clear, we are not suggesting any changes to the doctrine of The Church of Jesus Christ of Latter-day Saints; only those called as prophets, seers, and revelators have the authority to do that. But we believe that all Church members can participate in the work of theology, by which we mean reasoned reflection on the doctrine received by the body of the Church. We therefore invite you, the reader, to join us on a theological journey, making your own reasoned reflections alongside us.

DEFINING PEACE AND VIOLENCE

Latter-day Saints have confronted the problem of violence from the founding of the restored Church of Jesus Christ. Early nineteenth-century America could be a notoriously violent place, with vigilantes and mobs often acting with impunity, especially in the types of frontier communities where the Restoration took hold. Western Missouri was one such place, and in the summer of 1833 mobs attacked Church members and drove them from their homes. Several hundred miles away, as Joseph Smith began to receive reports of the turmoil, he asked God what to do. The answer came in a revelation in which the Lord laid out divine principles regarding how his people should respond to violence. This remarkable revelation's basic advice can be encapsulated in one succinct phrase: "renounce war and proclaim peace."[17]

This raises the question, what exactly is *peace*? As with simple yet capacious terms like *love* and *democracy*, the word *peace* eludes a single definition. Restoration scriptures point to a wide range of meanings, all of which are instructive. Often they speak of *personal* or *inner peace*, achieved when a person lives in accordance with moral law and ethical principles. As the psalmist said, "Great peace have they which love thy [God's] law."[18] In other instances the scriptures refer to *interpersonal peace*, characterized by healthy, loving relationships with one's family, neighbors, and even strangers. This type of peace is signaled in Paul's advice to the saints in Rome: "If it is possible, so far as it depends on you, live peaceably with all."[19] Similarly, in the Book of Mormon King Benjamin taught his people that true followers of Christ "will not have a mind to injure one another, but to live peaceably."[20] Another type of peace portrayed in Restoration scripture is *intercommunal peace*, distinguished by harmonious relations between communities and nations. This ideal is described by Isaiah in his prophecy of some future day when the peoples of the world "shall beat their swords into plowshares, and their spears into pruning-hooks: nation shall not lift up sword against nation, neither shall they learn war any more."[21]

All of these aspects of peace are essential and should be pursued energetically. However, these definitions of peace are often framed negatively, in terms of what is *not* happening. Note that in Isaiah's vision, for instance, nations will *not* go to war with one another. Because it is expressed in negational terms, scholars refer to the absence of violence as *negative peace*.[22] Latter-day Saint apostle Dallin H. Oaks confirmed this definition when he taught that "peace is more than the absence of war."[23] *Positive peace*, then, refers to a state of affairs in which justice, equity, and an abiding commitment to the common good is built into the very structures of society. Positive peace corresponds with the Hebrew Bible's concept of *shalom*, which connotes harmony, wholeness, and shared prosperity for all. This more comprehensive notion recognizes that there is "no peace without justice."[24] With this sentiment in mind, scholars have recently coined the term *justpeace*, which speaks to "new relations characterized by equality and fairness according to the dictates of human dignity and the common good."[25] In Restoration scripture, the vision of positive peace is encapsulated simply and evocatively in the word *Zion*. Recall that in Enoch's city of that name, the people not only eschewed war but also eliminated economic inequality.

Understanding peace in this more expansive way also helps us recognize that the concept of violence may not be as simple as we often suppose. Usually we think of violence in terms of a variety of actions that cause physical harm and may result in death. Examples of this *direct violence* include hitting, shooting, bombing, sexual assault, and so forth. But there are other, more insidious ways in which individuals or entire societies also cause harm by limiting access to opportunities or goods that lead to human flourishing. Sometimes these forms of *structural violence* are formal, for instance in the apartheid regime in South Africa, but they can also be informal manifestations of injustice, discrimination, repression, exploitation, inequality, and abuse. As the peace scholar Johan Galtung explains, "When one husband beats his wife there is a clear case of personal violence, but when one million husbands keep one million wives in ignorance there is structural violence."[26]

Both direct and structural violence are often made possible because of the existence of *cultural violence*, which refers to the social attitudes, assumptions, and traditions that make various forms of violence seem legitimate and natural—or at least normal and acceptable. Cultural violence obscures the reality and harmfulness of direct and structural violence, in that we either do not see the violence clearly or do not see it at all.[27] For instance, the *cultural* violence of anti-Black racism rendered the *structural* violence of Jim Crow laws and the *direct* violence of lynching simultaneously invisible and acceptable for many Whites in nineteenth- and twentieth-century America. Painful traces of all three forms of violence—direct, structural, and cultural—continue to haunt modern American race relations, as was laid bare by the nationwide protests in the United States during the summer of 2020. In his joint response with the NAACP to America's festering racial divides, Russell M. Nelson, president and prophet of The Church of Jesus Christ of Latter-day Saints, acknowledged the importance of combating racism, not only through the transformation of personal prejudice, but also through the reform of "processes, laws, and organizational attitudes" that undergirded those individual beliefs and behaviors.[28]

Restoration scripture offers a prophetic critique of all three forms of violence—direct, structural, and cultural. The prophet Mormon's final counsel to his readers featured a strong renunciation of direct violence. "Know ye that ye must lay down your weapons of war," he pleaded, "and delight no more in the shedding of blood, save it be that God shall command you."[29] Jesus was even more direct, telling his disciples to "put away your sword . . . , for all who take the sword will die by the sword."[30] In addition, over and over the Book of Mormon demonstrates how inequality alienates people from one another and from God. Nephite prophets frequently call on the people of God to address this form of social sin.[31]

To "proclaim peace" is to renounce all forms of violence. More than that, however, it means to actively promote communities and conditions of peace, sustained across generations, that maximize opportunities for all of God's children to flourish without fear of unjust harm and oppression. In short, to proclaim peace is to build Zion. For the Restoration, as we will show, the individual and collective pursuit of positive peace is nothing more nor less than truly worshiping and following "the founder of peace," Jesus Christ.[32]

PEACE IS POSSIBLE

This book addresses a number of theological and ethical questions about living in and responding to an age of violent conflict. What is the nature of power, how does it operate, and how might it be used most effectively? How might the atonement of Jesus Christ—the central doctrine of the Restoration—inform our understanding of peace and violence? Is salvation only an individual and otherworldly concern, or might Christ's atonement have relevance for this world's social and political affairs? Given that conflict seems inevitable in a world populated by people with competing worldviews, experiences, and interests, how might we engage such tensions more constructively? Restoration scripture and history alike feature examples of godly people who fought in wars, along with others who avoided or rejected violence. Is there a preferred option, and how might we know what it is? Are there any circumstances in which the use of violence might be justified? What about examples in scripture where God either commands or perpetrates violence? What might that mean for us, and how might we best understand other examples of violence in scripture? For those who have covenanted to consecrate their lives to the kingdom of God, what obligations might they have as citizens in a secular nation-state, especially when it goes to war? What might a modern-day Zion look like, and what might we do now to build it?

Reasonable and faithful people can and will disagree on the answers to such difficult questions. Together we have spent decades studying and reflecting on matters of violence and peace and how they are related to the Restoration, and this book is the fruit of that effort. At the same time, we claim no special ecclesiastical authority for our conclusions. We offer this book as our best effort to understand how these issues relate to a life of sincere Christian faith and moral commitment. This is not the final word on the subject; our goal here is to make a case, then open the conversation.

This book operates simultaneously on two levels, with dual purposes and audiences in mind. Our primary aim is for Latter-day Saints to better appreciate the nonviolent life, mission, and saving work of Jesus Christ, the Prince of Peace, and to translate that understanding into a more "peaceable walk with the children of men."[33] It is not enough to merely *believe* in peace; disciples of Christ are called to put their living faith into action and *build* peace—in their homes, their communities, their nations, and the world. For those Latter-day Saints already committed to or engaged in nonviolent social change, we want them to recognize that they can do so from their deepest theological commitments, rather than in spite of them. Secondarily, we hope *Proclaim Peace* will join a growing library of books that outline distinctive approaches to peace and nonviolence from the world's diverse religious traditions.[34] Latter-day Saints have some catching up to do, but it's time for us to claim a seat at the peacebuilding table.

It is easy to become resigned about violence, to share the sentiment of the narrator in Bruce Springsteen's song "Nebraska," who flatly observes, "I guess there's just a meanness in this world."[35] Indeed there is, and has been since Cain killed Abel. As advocates of peace, we are neither naive nor blind to human depravity. But then, neither was Jesus—an innocent victim of violent hatred, torture, and execution. God sent his Son not to condemn us, but to shine a light into the darkness, to offer salvation for both our souls and our societies.[36] Jesus proclaims peace and calls his followers to do the same.

We believe, with President Russell M. Nelson, that "peace is possible" in *this* world and that all the heirs and "descendants of Abraham—entrusted with great promises of infinite influence—are in a pivotal position to emerge as peacemakers."[37] We affirm, along with Elder Dieter F. Uchtdorf, that Latter-day Saints are called to "clearly speak out for peace" and to become a "people of peace and reconciliation."[38] This begins as an individual quest but soon is magnified to have much broader impact. "What our Savior taught about peace in the life of a single person," President Dallin H. Oaks taught, "also applies to peace in a family, peace in a nation, and peace in the world."[39]

Our world is not so different from Enoch's, and each of us has the same choice set before us: will we choose the Word or the sword? Will we build the positive peace of Zion or remain wedded to our world's various forms of violence? As the poet Emma Lou Thayne wrote, it is time

> to calculate whether we peacemakers
> shall inherit or destroy
> this blessed earth. . . .
> It's time. It's time we said together
> Yes to life. To ashes, simply No.[40]

It is our hope that the Restoration's distinctive insights presented throughout this book may lead more of us to renounce our violent traditions and proclaim positive peace in a world that desperately needs it.

CHAPTER ONE

Power and Influence

. . . what if Earth
Be but the shadow of Heaven, and things therein
Each to other like, more than on Earth is thought?
—Milton, *Paradise Lost*

[My] honor . . . is my power.
—Doctrine and Covenants 29:36

During the winter months of 1838–39, Joseph Smith and five companions languished in the dungeon of a small but sturdy rock prison in the frontier—and, for them, ironically named—town of Liberty, Missouri. In a fourteen-by-fourteen-foot cell with a low ceiling, raw earth floor, and dirty straw for beds, the imprisoned men were fed food so filthy that one recalled, "We could not eat it until we were driven to it by hunger."[1] Even worse, they knew that their families, along with thousands of other Latter-day Saints, were being exiled from the state, trudging over the frozen ground and across the Mississippi River. It was perhaps the lowest point of Joseph Smith's life. And yet within this dark, damp chamber he received some of his most enlightening revelations. Owing to the potency and poetry of those inspired words, Liberty Jail is often remembered, even hallowed, by Latter-day Saints as "more temple than prison."[2]

One of the most poignant moments came near the end of the long winter. In a two-part letter to his beloved Saints, Joseph Smith cried in agony: "O God, where art thou?" Penning a lamentation reminiscent of the ancient Hebrew prophets, Joseph wondered how a God of such immense power could (or would) not come to the rescue of his beloved children:

> O Lord God Almighty, maker of heaven, earth, and seas, and of all things that in them are, and who controllest and subjectest the devil, . . . stretch forth thy hand; let thine eye pierce; let thy pavilion be taken up; let thy hiding place no longer be covered; let thine ear be inclined; let thine heart be softened, and thy bowels moved with compassion toward us. Let thine anger be kindled against our enemies; and, in the fury of thine heart, with thy sword avenge us of our wrongs.[3]

If God could "control" and "subject" the devil, surely he could employ his mighty power to rescue the Latter-day Saints from their persecutors. In response came divine reassurance and a gentle rebuke: "My son, peace be unto thy soul; thine adversity and thine afflictions shall be but a small moment."[4] God assured the prophet that his justice and power would ultimately prevail. In the meantime, Joseph Smith and the Latter-day Saints had some lessons to learn.

What followed was a sublime meditation on the peaceful nature of godly power—a constructive counterpoint to Joseph Smith's yearnings for a divine sword of vengeance to fall upon his enemies. In contrast with the fleeting influence of such coercive force, the revelation articulated a more expansive notion of enduring influence based on deep, unfailing love. On the heels of the Saints' persecutions in Missouri, as well as considerable dissension within the Church itself, the prophet's inspired words articulated a devastating diagnosis of human nature: "We have learned by sad experience, that it is the nature and disposition of almost all men, as soon as they get a little authority, as they suppose, they will immediately begin to exercise unrighteous dominion." This dim view of the human condition was capped by a brief but potent observation about the true nature of "authority" and "dominion" both in heaven and on earth: "No power or influence can or ought to be maintained by virtue of the priesthood, only by persuasion, by long-suffering, by gentleness and meekness, and by love unfeigned; by kindness, and pure knowledge, which shall greatly enlarge the soul without hypocrisy, and without guile."[5]

The full significance of this lesson requires some context to appreciate. In Restoration theology, "priesthood" is more than a clerical order or even the authority to act *for* God. Rather, Latter-day Saints understand priesthood as "the eternal power and authority *of* God."[6] A beneficent God shares his power and authority with his children, but with a caveat: "the powers of heaven cannot be controlled nor handled only upon the principles of righteousness."[7] God allows humans to exercise great power over one another and their natural and social environments. But there are rules, and consequences, inherent in the exercise of that influence.

The letter from Liberty Jail represents a distinctive Latter-day Saint contribution to the canon of great prison literature, such as Martin Luther King Jr.'s "Letter from a Birmingham Jail," offering poignant reflections on power by those who suffer its abuses. "No power or influence can or ought to be maintained . . . , only by persuasion, by long-suffering, by gentleness and meekness, and by love unfeigned." Joseph Smith's March 1839 revelatory letter did not simply offer wise counsel about how ecclesiastical authority *should* ideally be exercised in a particular Christian denomination. Rather, it exists as a meditation on how power in the universe *actually* works. It is not merely that power *ought not* be maintained through "unrighteous dominion," but more significantly that it *cannot*. To put it bluntly, there is no such thing as enduring coercive power. Not for God. Not for humans. Neither in heaven nor on earth. Enduring influence, for both gods and mortals, can be established only through love because, at its core, enduring influence can be built only through trust.

BEFORE THE BEGINNING

The foundations for Joseph Smith's Liberty Jail meditation on power and influence stretch way back, to the deepest corners of space and time. Joseph Smith's revelations describe a time before the creation of the earth when human spirits existed "also in the beginning with God."[8] Instead of creating other intelligent beings *ex nihilo*, or out of nothing as traditional Christian theology posits, at the outset of creation our Heavenly Father found himself in the midst of a multitude of self-existing "intelligences." God was and is "greater"—more intelligent, more advanced, more perfected in personality and character—"than they all." But at the most fundamental level, all intelligent beings, including women and men, were similar to God in one crucial respect—"they existed before, they shall have no end, they shall exist after, for they are . . . eternal."[9]

The startling implication of this "co-eternality" is a universe populated by human souls who are truly free. Humans are not mere creatures of a Creator, whom they might blame for their strengths and weaknesses, their predilections and idiosyncrasies. Rather, as independent personalities, they shoulder ultimate responsibility for what they become—a reality that is both liberating and terrifying. This freedom is not without constraints, however. Each soul chooses and acts within a universe populated with other free souls who are also choosing and acting, and all these personalities are constantly bumping up against and influencing one another. At first glance, the universe described in Joseph Smith's revelations might seem like a libertarian paradise of hyper-individualism. But it is in fact a web of profound interconnectivity and interdependence.

The first discernible and dramatic event in the Restoration's salvation history was a premortal argument held in a grand assembly. Drawing on potent imagery in the book of Revelation, Latter-day Saints often refer to this event as a "war."[10] Joseph Smith, however, preferred the more peaceable term *council*. This does not discount the danger nor the magnitude of the conflict. Upon the outcome hung nothing less than the nature of God's sovereignty and human destiny. But rather than invoking traditional iconography that depicted the archangel Michael slaying the beast with a sword, Joseph Smith's vision was more in line with Thomas Paine's observation that an actual "war" in heaven was impossible because "none of the combatants could be either killed or wounded."[11] The fundamental nature of this premortal council was thus not a battle between armies but rather a contest of ideas, an epic clash between two irreconcilable visions of human freedom.

At the center of the struggle was a benevolent Father seeking for the eternal progression and ultimate exaltation of his spirit children. The primary purpose of the council was to devise and implement a plan by which undeveloped intelligences might, under God's direction, advance in knowledge, power, and glory.[12] According to the Restoration's cosmology, the distinction between God and his spirit children—in other words, all of humanity—is one of magnitude rather than of kind. We humans are essentially the same species as God, differing only in our degree of perfection and glory.[13] Likewise, the earth that we live on is essentially similar in nature to heaven, though, again, far less refined. The upshot is that while divine power may seem mysterious and elusive, God's purpose for creating and populating this world was for it to become a laboratory in which we might learn to use and constructively harness the same power that he possesses and exercises.

Our efforts, both individually and collectively, are necessarily halting, messy, and imperfect. But here is the crucial fact: divine nature is the model for human nature. The way that God exerts power is, at base, the model for the way we should. As God declared to Joseph Smith, "If you will that I give unto you a place in the celestial world, you must prepare yourselves by doing the things which I have commanded you and required of you."[14] Patterns of divine power are designed to be knowable and largely replicable. Latter-day Saint scholars Terryl and Fiona Givens have noted that humans "may be in the infancy of moral development, as individuals and as a species," but we can nevertheless strive "toward a perfect model that God already embodies."[15] If we are to fulfill our divine destiny, then as both individuals and societies we must learn and practice the key attributes that define the heavens, beginning with those characteristics outlined in the Liberty Jail letter: persuasion, long-suffering, gentleness, meekness, kindness, knowledge, and most of all "love unfeigned."

HONOR = POWER

The lynchpin in the Father's plan for his children to progress and become like him was the condition that they must freely choose to do so. In keeping with the noncoercive principles of divine power, God would, in the words of the first hymn in the

Restoration's first hymnbook, "call, persuade, [and] direct aright, / And bless with wisdom, love, and light, / In nameless ways be good and kind, / But never force the human mind."[16] Of course, the unforced human mind would inevitably fail to always choose goodness. God fully foresaw this eventuality, so in the premortal council he announced that he would provide a savior who would reconcile the Father's fallen children to him and to one another and enable them to expand their capacities into the eternities. To the Father's query "Whom shall I send [as this savior]," the premortal spirits of both Jesus and Lucifer—not yet the devil Satan—each proffered the same reply: "Here am I, send me."[17] Lucifer proposed a plan whereby "one soul shall not be lost." "I will be thy son," he audaciously told the Father, "and surely I will do it; wherefore give me thine honor." Responding to this brazen bid to usurp God, Jesus countered by expressing support for the original plan and its author: "Father, thy will be done, and the glory be thine forever."[18]

In Restoration cosmology, this premortal face-off is a pivotal moment. Satan's gambit constituted a serious twofold threat. First, it represented an attempt to "destroy the agency of man."[19] Second, it constituted a nakedly ambitious attempt to dethrone God. These two threats were actually intertwined, coming together in the notion of God's "honor," which Lucifer sought to have for himself. As employed here, divine "honor" is more than credit, glory, or standing.[20] Rather, divine honor speaks to God's perfect character—his love, righteousness, compassion, and faithfulness. These qualities combine to make the Father inherently and completely trustworthy, which was precisely the grounds on which our premortal spirits entered into relationship with him. In other words, God's honor, or character, is the source of God's power and influence in the universe.

Any durable power or influence over independent moral beings requires their consent and participation. A free and intelligent mind must ultimately agree to obey and yield. Granted, this assent might be obtained through intimidation, deception, manipulation, or even chemical alteration. But influence obtained by any of these coercive methods cannot "be maintained" forever. The Liberty Jail revelation exposes the fragility of such influence: "When we undertake to cover our sins, or to gratify our pride, our vain ambition, or to exercise control or dominion or compulsion upon the souls of the children of men, in any degree of unrighteousness, behold, the heavens withdraw themselves; the Spirit of the Lord is grieved; and when it is withdrawn, Amen to the priesthood or the authority of that man." To the contrary, true power works "*only* upon the principles of righteousness"—"*only* by persuasion, by long-suffering, by gentleness and meekness, and by love unfeigned."[21] There is no other way.

Therefore, the essence of enduring power, in both heaven and earth, is trust. Such trust can be built only on (true) love and (loving) truth—"kindness" and "pure knowledge" that is "unfeigned" and "without guile."[22] Such love and truthfulness are two of God's defining characteristics.[23] His love is unfailing and eternal, which means he is always worthy of our love, trust, and worship. Thus, as independent premortal intelligences, we chose to enter into relationship with God precisely because of how perfectly he embodied love and truth, which therefore allowed us to trust that he would help us realize our inherent divine potential.

God's power is thus inseparable from and dependent on his character. This is not "soft" power, at least not if soft is considered secondary to hard force. In a universe of free agents, the ultimate and only enduring form of power is to invite (sometimes in the form of a command) and be freely obeyed.[24] The divine word has power and influence because of the sublime personality and perfect character behind the voice. Succinctly affirming this principle, God precisely declared that "[my] honor . . . is my power."[25]

Since God and humans are different in degree but not in kind, principles of godly power and influence simultaneously apply to the exercise of human power and influence. Endowed with freedom, human personalities must necessarily give their assent to be led or governed, and so enduring power in this world is likewise inseparable from character. The American founders intuited this principle in the secular realm, emphasizing the necessity of virtue and charity in public life.[26] But the principle goes far beyond secular politics. The Liberty Jail revelation invites human souls to develop the same principles of love, truth, and constancy that God embodies, and thereby achieve similarly divine and abiding authority:

> Let thy bowels also be full of charity towards all men, and to the household of faith, and let virtue garnish thy thoughts unceasingly; then shall thy confidence wax strong in the presence of God; and the doctrine of the priesthood shall distil upon thy soul as the dews from heaven. The Holy Ghost shall be thy constant companion, and thy scepter an unchanging scepter of righteousness and truth; and thy dominion shall be an everlasting dominion, and without compulsory means it shall flow unto thee forever and ever.[27]

Though speaking of love and virtue, this language is hardly the sentimental stuff of greeting cards. Rather, the epistle from Liberty Jail is a tutorial on how persuasion and love are the keys to accessing divine authority and everlasting dominion—and also how to maximize influence on earth in the meantime. It is all predicated on the exercise of power "without compulsory means."

TEMPORARY POWER AND ENDURING INFLUENCE

This is not to suggest there is no such thing as divine compulsion or that violence never works. Power and influence over free souls cannot "be maintained" through brute force or raw authoritarianism. But these forms of power can and often do have *temporary* influence. Myriad examples from scripture suggest that even God sometimes adopts a forceful approach (a topic we explore in depth in chapter 7), albeit with one important qualification. Noting that the exercise of power may involve "reproving betimes with sharpness, when moved upon by the Holy Ghost," the Liberty Jail revelation notes that such instances require "showing forth afterwards an increase of love toward him whom thou hast reproved, lest he esteem thee to be his enemy; that he may know that thy faithfulness is stronger than the cords of death."[28]

Divine chastisement hardly seems gentle, meek, or kind. Yet, even after issuing a "sharp" rebuke, our Father is never an "enemy" to his children, and his "faithfulness is stronger than the cords of death." God's application of "sharp" power and authority may command attention and hopefully prompt repentance, but even this divine show of force cannot, on its own, hold loyalty or sustain obedience. In a universe of intelligences coeternal with him, even God's fearsome power cannot "be maintained" without attendant love and faithfulness.

The Restoration makes an important distinction between *agency*—the power to choose, which is intrinsic to and inalienable from the soul—and *freedom*—the power to act upon our agency, which can be constrained in a variety of ways, including physical laws, a person's own actions, and the actions of others. As President Dallin H. Oaks explained: "Interferences with our freedom do not deprive us of our . . . agency. When Pharaoh put Joseph in prison, he restricted Joseph's freedom, but he did not take away his . . . agency."[29] This principle was similarly articulated by Holocaust survivor Victor Frankl when he observed that "everything can be taken from a man but one thing," namely, the ability "to choose one's attitude in any given set of circumstances, to choose one's own way."[30]

God may at times restrict certain freedoms, constraining the range of choices to an individual or group, but he can never totally eliminate their agency. Nor can such constraints ultimately win the loyalty of his children. At best restrictions might gain their attention. But once he has his children's attention, an enduring appeal to their hearts and minds can come only through love and faithfulness, all the while protecting the very agency that allows them to reject those appeals. God holds agency so inviolate that he will even allow people to misuse that agency in ways that hurt others. In Joseph Smith's vision of Enoch, a weeping Father pleads with his children to exercise compassion and choose happiness. Yet he never forces that choice, even when his beloved children choose (and inflict) violence and misery.[31]

Similar dynamics attend human attempts at power and influence. Parents may rebuke, threaten, or even physically restrain their children—for example, to keep them from running into busy streets—but cannot protect them indefinitely with such methods. Threats and compulsion, especially of a physical sort, cannot endure. Parental love, faithfulness, and example must be sufficient that children will trust their parents to freely and consistently obey their counsel to avoid playing in such dangerous places, especially when the children do not fully understand the reasons behind such words. Such principles also apply to governments and economies. Authoritarian states comprehend the essential value of securing at least the veneer of assent from their subjects, recognizing that brute force alone cannot long guarantee legitimacy and obedience. Leon Trotsky, one of the chief architects of twentieth-century communism, understood that command economies had a fatal flaw, in that the state's economic planning and decision making were imposed on workers rather than developed in consultation with them. Trotsky theorized that only a "reciprocal economic relation" between workers and the state would result in "the voluntary exchange" necessary for long-term stability.[32] Compulsion, no matter how powerful and seemingly total, can be merely temporary. Only trust, gained through persuasion and reciprocity, is enduring.

It is easy to discount trust and overestimate the effectiveness of brute force. Human history seems to attest to the primacy of aggression. It is true that violence does exert real power and influence, often in sudden and dramatic ways. But its immediate impact cloaks its inherent weakness. Raw force may win an individual's or even a society's compliance, but only persuasion provides a platform for long-term stability and loyalty, let alone authentic human flourishing. In a world saturated with the lazy premise that "might makes right"—a lesson frequently reinforced through video games, action films, and political theater—humans too often excuse their simple violent compulsions, whether on an intimate or national scale. Replacing our violence with more enduring principled alternatives, no matter how effective, seems less glamorous, less patriotic, less dramatic. It requires more time, more work, more imagination, more sacrifice, and more faith to follow the path of persuasion and love.

Thus, in the premortal council, Satan's plan was doomed to fail because it employed principles of power that could not "be maintained." Instead of "pure knowledge," Satan employed deception. Instead of an appeal to "love unfeigned," he appealed to self-interest and fear. So, whatever loyalty or obedience Satan managed to attract at the council, and whatever assent he continues to procure on earth through similar methods, can only be temporary. The "powers of heaven"—influence that is enduring and everlasting—"cannot be controlled nor handled only upon the principles of righteousness."[33] Satan could not and cannot wield enduring influence and command obedience without true "honor." And he could not and cannot achieve honor and trust without the requisite character, integrity, and love. In essence, Satan was asking to borrow (or steal) God's character—not realizing or appreciating that honor, like most personal qualities, is a nontransferable good.

FALLING FROM HEAVEN

Faced in the council with two volunteers to perform the role of redeemer, God chose Jesus. Or, as Joseph Smith clarified, "the grand council gave in for Jesus" and "the lot fell on him."[34] Satan did not retreat quietly, and "many followed after him"—as many as "a third part of the hosts of heaven."[35] But his heavenly rebellion was unsuccessful. Satan and his followers were "thrust down, and thus came the devil and his angels."[36]

In traditional Christian narratives—and even in some Latter-day Saint interpretations—the archangel Michael and his lieutenants, or even Christ himself, forcibly expel Satan and his followers from heaven. John Milton imagined the scene with expressions of divine "terror" and "wrath."[37] The Italian poet Dante Alighieri extended the image of Satan's forced banishment from heaven, placing a sign over the gates of hell that reads in part, "Divine power made me."[38] Seen this way, God's plan of salvation was brought about and guaranteed through the exercise of brute power, even violence. The ramifications of this view are significant. If violence was a legitimate, even godly, means of fulfilling the divine plan in heaven, then logically it is also a legitimate, even godly, means of doing so here on earth. By this reasoning, authorized agents of God's kingdom may resort to violence to establish and maintain the rule of righteousness, especially when dealing with unrepentant and recalcitrant opponents.

Restoration scriptures suggest other possibilities. The exact methods by which Satan and his followers left heaven are somewhat ambiguous. Certainly some scriptural language appears physically forceful, referring to Satan being "cast" or "thrust down."[39] But other relevant verbs—including *fall*—imply other, more subtle dynamics.[40] One can imagine that in the face of dwindling support as the heavenly host began to coalesce around Jesus's selfless character and leadership, Lucifer may have simply fled the scene with his rebellious supporters in tow. God may have commanded them to depart, but no one physically pushed them. They could not abide celestial glory and thus vacated it. They simply *walked* out of heaven.[41] In this view, Satan and his followers appear to have left of their own accord. God no more forced Satan out of heaven than he forces anyone in.

Tellingly, God and Jesus did not initiate a victory celebration after successfully defending both their honor and humanity's agency. To the contrary, Lucifer's defection caused them deep sorrow, to the point that "the heavens wept over him." One senses a lingering and heartfelt melancholy that even while Satan "maketh war with the saints of God"—utilizing the same tools of deception, intimidation, and seduction he employed in the council—our Father remembers a time when the devil was still "a son of the morning."[42]

In the long run, the powers of deception and coercion will fail, precisely because they cannot be maintained. The scriptures predict a future time in which divine influence will be ubiquitous, an era when "Christ will reign personally upon the earth."[43] In this millennial age, "Satan shall be bound," not with physical fetters or any other manner of coercion or violence, but rather because no one will pay him any heed nor allow him any influence in their lives.[44] Their hearts will be given to God instead. Drawn to the power of selfless sacrifice, perfect integrity to truth, and abiding love, the children of God will freely choose to follow the Father and his Beloved Son.

ON EARTH AS IT IS IN HEAVEN

Hard-bitten modern society tends to discount the strength of truth and love, seeing them as beautiful but impractical for the "real world," where force is considered to be the only language that is understood. But the power of love and truth—God's power—is anything but fragile. To the contrary, it is robust, very real, and yes, even practical. True love and loving truth are both moral imperatives and effective strategies that offer a real alternative path to gaining influence through coercion. They expose the fleeting influence and ultimate weakness of violence. In his letter from Liberty Jail, Joseph Smith wrote that the same evil spirit that inspires "lies" and "confusion" among God's children also leads to the "damning hand of murder, tyranny, and oppression" across the land, until "the whole earth groans under the weight of its iniquity." And Latter-day Saints, Joseph noted, have an "imperative duty" to widows, orphans, and victims of violence to "waste and wear out our lives in bringing to light all the hidden things of darkness, wherein we know them."[45]

Moroni, the last prophet and author in the Book of Mormon, was equally earnest in his effort to bring to light "the hidden things of darkness." In revealing the murderous "secret combinations" that plagued Nephite society and ultimately contributed to its ruin, Moroni observed that God does not desire "that man should shed blood, but in all things hath forbidden it, from the beginning of man."[46] As a former warrior who watched the genocidal destruction of his people, Moroni knew of what he spoke. But he was sure that "in the gift of his Son hath God prepared a more excellent way."[47] By exposing darkness, secrecy, and violence through the light of divine truth and love, Moroni believed

15

his words would hasten the time "that evil may be done away," when "Satan may have no power upon the hearts of the children of men, but that they may be persuaded to do good continually."[48] Moroni also points to the strength of seemingly weak things. "I [will] make weak things become strong,"[49] God told him. This is not a promise of some future fantasy fulfilment in which the powerless become dominant, but a realization that true strength and enduring influence are achieved through principles that are too often perceived as inconsequential. Things that appear weak are sometimes precisely the opposite. Contemporary philosopher Cornel West has observed that "intellectual power, moral power, spiritual power, those are the 'weak' and 'feeble' kinds of power, which in the end could be the most powerful."[50]

A world organized around and ruled through love and truth is thus neither unrealistic nor misty-eyed. It is not some purist alternative to either be practiced outside of current corrupt structures or preserved for some distant future. Rather, principles of love and truth can and should be practiced here and now, within existing structures and societal patterns. Such principles exert actual power in this world as they build trust, community, and enduring loyalty. All power, whether familial or national, is based on assent; if people remove their assent, the power fails. Those who exert the greatest influence, whether they are leaders of families or of nations, are those who engender the greatest trust and obedience and who lead through honor, character, persuasion, truth, and love. This is as true "on earth as it is in heaven."[51]

Divine power is indomitable because it is based on enduring principles. The God of the Restoration exercises power through persuasion, not compulsion; truth, not deception; compassion, not coercion; selflessness, not avarice; gentleness, meekness, kindness, and love unfeigned, not violence; reproving betimes with "sharpness," but afterward showing forth an increase of love. Because we are self-existent eternal beings, God's relationship with us, and the nature of his power in our lives, will always be based on love, trust, and free will. In the cosmic struggle for loyalty, obedience, and the assent of free souls, God continues to hold the field. Jesus fulfilled the task commissioned him by the Grand Council and provided the path to God through his incarnation, ministry, death, and resurrection—in short, his atonement. That atonement affirms that love's victory is already won.

CHAPTER TWO

This Perfect Atonement

. . . Jesus the mediator of the new covenant,
who wrought out this perfect atonement
through the shedding of his own blood.
—Doctrine and Covenants 76:69

Come, take up the cross, and follow me.
—Mark 10:21

Jesus Christ stands at the center of Restoration theology and devotion, not only as the ultimate source of spiritual salvation but also as the perfect exemplar for the moral life. In the Book of Mormon, Christ himself emphasized this essential fact by answering his own question—"What manner of men ought ye to be?"—with a simple yet challenging mandate—"even as I am."[1] This injunction to not only follow but also become like Christ is an invitation, in the words of Peter, to "be partakers of the divine nature," which means receiving a portion of, and thus sharing in, "divine power."[2] In the last chapter we discussed the principles on which power and influence operate, both in heaven and on earth. Now we will consider the power that God exemplifies—and wants us to emulate—through the ministry and atonement of Jesus Christ.

The term *atonement*, which literally means to become "at one," was coined by William Tyndale in his sixteenth-century English Bible translation. He captured in a single word Jesus's supernal work of reconciliation, enabling sinful humans to achieve both a vertical oneness with God and a horizontal oneness with one another. The meaning of Jesus's life, ministry, suffering, death, and resurrection is thus more expansive than cleansing personal sin, as unspeakably marvelous as that dimension is. Christ's "infinite atonement" also encompasses the collectivity of sin manifest in our communities.[3] In other words, his atonement is intended to purify our hearts *and* transform our communities, to save both souls *and* societies.

Contemporary Latter-day Saints are not generally accustomed to thinking about these dual dimensions of the atonement of Jesus Christ. Given our emphasis on individual accountability and agency, not to mention the enormity of the problem of personal sin and brokenness, we tend to focus our teaching on how Christ can forgive individual sins, heal the human heart, and lead us each to greater personal holiness. Readers of Restoration scripture are thus transformed, one by one, as they come to understand the powerful doctrines of personal redemption and healing contained therein. This is an indispensable aspect of Christ's atoning work for which each of us should "stand all amazed."[4]

But Restoration scripture makes clear that redemption is not *merely* an individual affair. God's children don't live in isolation, nor do we sin in isolation. In order to be truly "infinite," the Atonement must go wherever sin and brokenness exist, and must offer a path toward healing, reconciliation, and transformation in those same places. Latter-day Saint theologian Deidre Green has beautifully written about how Restoration scripture witnesses of "the integration, reconciliation, and wholeness that is possible only in and through the atonement of Jesus Christ for both individuals and societies who have been fragmented and disintegrated through traumatic experience or sin." Just as "all suffering and sin are inherently social," Green reflects, "so too is the work of redemption."[5] If Christ's atonement includes a social dimension, then so too must Christian discipleship. As Latter-day Saint scholar Daniel Becerra has observed, the Book of Mormon consistently affirms "that Christian discipleship should inform one's conduct in the public sphere."[6] The atonement of Jesus Christ epitomizes and charts this challenging path of socially engaged discipleship.

As with all forms of lasting influence, the heart of the Atonement's transformative power is love. On the eve of his death, Jesus taught his most intimate followers, "A new commandment I give unto you, That ye love one another; as I have loved you, that ye also love one another."[7] Selfless love is never easy, even among friends and family. But Jesus also encouraged his disciples to strive for something even more strenuous—loving their enemies. The most cited teaching of Jesus among early Christians came from the Sermon on the Mount: "Love your enemies, bless them that curse you, do good to them that hate you, and pray for them which despitefully use you, and persecute you."[8] This enemy-love has been foundational for dedicated Christians for two thousand years. Because both neighbor-love and enemy-love are outward facing, Christian love inherently takes on a social dimension. In its most expansive and creative forms, "love one another" has been a powerful means of social and even political transformation. Reflecting on how the civil rights movement ultimately triumphed, Martin Luther King Jr. asserted that "the Christian doctrine of love operating through the Gandhian method of nonviolence was one of the most potent weapons available."[9]

This love of friend and foe alike—a love that actually recognizes no such distinctions—therefore represents not simply a personal virtue but a sweeping social and political ethic as well. Love is at the heart of the "kingdom of God" that Jesus proclaimed throughout his mortal ministry. His insistent talk of a "kingdom" should immediately point us to the fact that God's work has a political dimension. Kingdoms are not a matter of people's hearts or homes—they refer to the social and political organization of society. What Jesus offered his followers, therefore, is more than a path to personal redemption, however important that is. God's kingdom is a stark alternative and thoroughgoing challenge to all existing social and political regimes. The ministry, suffering, death, and resurrection of Jesus—his atonement[10]—together offer both otherworldly salvation and this-worldly transformation. When it comes to choosing between personal and social redemption, Jesus is a both-and God, not an either-or one.

Both the Bible and Book of Mormon chronicle how people who were transformed by Christ's words and atoning love were not content with their own private salvation. Instead, they radically reordered their entire way of life along new principles. Jews fellowshipped with Gentiles. The church in Jerusalem, empowered by "great power" and "great grace," became "of one heart and of one soul" to the point that "they had all things common."[11] Nephites and Lamanites abandoned the dueling identities and violent wars that had gripped them for centuries. For two hundred years the descendants of Lehi lived together in peace, harmony, and justice. Why? "Because of the love of God which did dwell in the hearts of the people," which led them to understand that "they were in one, the children of Christ."[12] For the people who actually felt the prints of the nails in the resurrected Christ's hands and feet—and for those who later believed this witness—salvation was both individual *and* communal. They understood that Christ's "perfect" and "infinite" atonement, punctuated by his suffering in the Garden of Gethsemane and on the cross of Calvary, redeems and transforms both our personal and political worlds.

We have considered how the premortal Jesus modeled nonviolent power and influence during the Grand Council in Heaven. Now we will explore how the atonement of Jesus Christ—his earthly ministry, suffering in Gethsemane and on Golgotha, and triumphant resurrection—both enacted and empowered loving and nonviolent social transformation. Whereas most of this book draws primarily from the distinctive scriptures of the Restoration, here we focus especially on the scriptures that Latter-day Saints share with all Christians, namely the New Testament, and in particular the four Gospels.

A KINGDOM LIKE NONE OTHER

When Jesus commanded his followers to "come, take up the cross, and follow me," he was inviting them to adopt very different principles of power and influence than those typically employed in this fallen world.[13] Rather than embracing tyrannical "lordship" and coercive authority as worldly kingdoms do, the kingdom of God operates with a different dynamic.[14] Power and influence accumulate to those who absorb violence rather than inflict it, love their enemies rather than revile against them, and exert compassion rather than coercion.

Jesus taught and exemplified these principles of peaceful power during his journey to the cross, but they were so foreign to the way humans normally operate that even his closest friends and disciples did not immediately grasp them. Many Jews in first-century Palestine expected the Messiah to be a political deliverer—a new Moses, a second David—who would lead a traditionally violent revolution against their Roman occupiers. The Gospel writers insist that the people's political hopes were indeed realized in Jesus of Nazareth—just not in the way most people expected or longed for.

In Luke's account, Jesus's public ministry began in his hometown synagogue in Nazareth, where he stood one Sabbath day and read to the assembled audience from the writings of Isaiah. Specifically, he recited a prophecy announcing that the Messiah would bring political, economic, and social redemption to God's oppressed people:

> The Spirit of the Lord is upon me,
> Because he has anointed me to bring good news to the poor.
> He has sent me to proclaim release to the captives
> And recovery of sight to the blind,
> To let the oppressed go free,
> To proclaim the year of the Lord's favor.[15]

For a people saddled with debt, suffering from persistent intergenerational poverty, oppressed and often imprisoned by the Romans, such a proclamation would have been heard and understood in more than merely spiritual terms. For instance, "the year of the Lord" referred to the jubilee, a stipulation of the Mosaic law stating that every fifty years all the people's debts would be forgiven, thus leveling differences between the rich and the poor and providing for social and economic equality within Israel.[16]

Jesus's ministry thus contained social, political, and economic implications from the outset. Consider, for instance, his early miracle of feeding several thousand people with only five loaves and two fishes. This was early in his ministry, and so the assembled crowd consisted not of devoted disciples but rather curious onlookers. What might they have seen and heard? Here is a man who has announced a new kingdom—in obvious contrast to the current rule of Caesar and his legions. A man who provides food for the poor, starving, colonized masses. A man who offers liberation and fills our bellies. A man who will be our Provider, our Deliverer, our King!

Jesus sensed the feeling of the crowd. He knew "they would come and take him by force, to make him a king." But instead of leading them to violently overthrow their hated oppressors, he retreated to a nearby mountain to be alone.[17] When his disciples sought him out and testified of his messiahship, Jesus replied, for the first time, that his revolution would not be the one that the crowds—and perhaps even his closest disciples—had in mind. Rather, he taught them, he "must suffer many things, and be rejected . . . and be slain, and be raised the third day." Furthermore, anyone who would follow him should also be prepared to bear the cross. From this point forward, Luke reports, Jesus "steadfastly set his face to go to Jerusalem," thus orienting the remainder of his ministry to the inevitable crucifixion that awaited him.[18]

Many have read this episode as evidence that Jesus's ministry was in fact nonpolitical—that in walking away from the crowd he was also abandoning any form of social agenda. This has also been a common reading of the second temptation in the wilderness, when Christ rejected the devil's (false) promise to grant him "all the kingdoms of the world," with their power and their glory, if only he would worship Satan.[19] In both of these cases—and every other—Jesus did not turn his back on society and politics per se, but rather rejected the *particular* type of society and politics offered to him by the crowds and the devil. Jesus would establish a kingdom, but not on their terms. His kingdom would not correspond to their assumptions about the coercive, self-aggrandizing nature of power. Rather, the kingdom of God would reflect a political and socioeconomic reordering based on principles of love, justice, and peace.[20]

One can hardly imagine a more thorough restructuring of human relations than replacing violence with love, and one can hardly find a clearer expression of this than the Sermon on the Mount. The fact that the sermon is repeated, almost verbatim, by the resurrected Christ in the Book of Mormon means his words should be doubly significant to Latter-day Saints. These include what many have called the "hard sayings":

> You have heard that it was said, "An eye for an eye and a tooth for a tooth." But I say to you, Do not resist an evildoer. But if anyone strikes you on the right cheek, turn the other also; and if anyone wants to sue you and take your coat, give your cloak as well; and if anyone forces you to go one mile, go also the second mile. Give to everyone who begs from you, and do not refuse anyone who wants to borrow from you.
>
> You have heard that it was said, "You shall love your neighbor and hate your enemy." But I say to you, Love your enemies and pray for those who persecute you, so that you may be the children of your Father in heaven; for he makes his sun rise on the evil and on the good, and sends rain on the righteous and on the unrighteous. For if you love those who love you, what reward do you have? Do not even the tax collectors do the same? And if you greet only your brothers and sisters, what more are you doing than others? Do not even the Gentiles do the same? Be perfect, therefore, as your heavenly Father is perfect.[21]

Almost every one of these sayings is not only hard but seemingly impossible. As philosopher Robert Brimlow notes, by any earthly measure Jesus's advice, particularly asserting love in the face of unremitting evil, is "unrealistic, implausible, and absurd," and "it would be irresponsible, dangerous, and downright stupid to pursue it."[22] In a thuggish world, following Jesus's hard sayings—not to mention his broader message of indiscriminate love, universal forgiveness, selfless servanthood, undeserved suffering, and nonviolence—will get you hurt.[23]

True enough. But such hard and dangerous principles are also effective. In a later chapter we will have more to say about what nonviolent and assertive love actually looks like in practice and how it is geared toward strategic success. Here a single example, illuminated by biblical scholar Walter Wink, will suffice to illustrate that Jesus's hard sayings were not merely abstract expressions of idealized individual morality. Rather, they outlined a blueprint for a concrete social and political ethic—an ethic of nonviolent resistance to worldly dominion that gave his followers a faithful alternative between resigned passivity on the one hand and violent resistance on the other.[24]

Consider Jesus's famous injunction to "turn the other cheek." This catchphrase has far too often been used to justify violent oppression—keeping slaves subservient to their masters or keeping battered women in abusive relationships. But when we understand its historical-cultural context, we recover the teaching's remarkable yet surprisingly practical message of resistance based in both the assertion of the victim's dignity and love for the oppressor. Jesus's specific injunction was "if anyone strikes you on the *right* cheek, turn the other also." Visualize it—a blow to the victim's right cheek would necessarily come from the perpetrator's left fist. But in the Jewish culture of Jesus's day, the left hand was used only for unclean tasks. A left-fisted blow to the right cheek would be inherently unclean. Thus, if an observant Jew (presumably the only kind) were to strike you on the right cheek, it would necessarily come from a right-handed *backhand*. As Wink noted, "The backhand was not a blow to injure, but to insult, humiliate, degrade. It was not administered to an equal, but to an inferior. Masters backhanded slaves; husbands, wives; parents, children; Romans, Jews."[25]

Jesus's audience consisted of Jewish peasants—people who were used to being degraded by landlords or Roman soldiers. His advice was for them to refuse this kind of treatment. Turning the other cheek after a backhand to the right cheek would make another backhand impossible without the nose getting in the way (again, visualize it, or act it out with a friend). The left cheek would now be available for a straight jab with a right fist or open palm, but in Jesus's culture people only used fists or palms to strike equals. Let that sink in. Turning the other cheek didn't mean cowardly submission. It meant standing up to the abuse and inviting the aggressor either to stop striking (thus frustrating an attempt to dominate) or to strike in a way that recognized the intended victim as an equal (in another way, frustrating an attempt to dominate). As Wink observed, the recipient of the blow says in effect, "I'm a human being, just like you. I refuse to be humiliated any longer. I am your equal. I am a child of God." In making that statement with unwavering love, the person turning the other cheek has affirmed his or her full dignity, regardless of whatever power imbalance may remain in the relationship.[26]

What would happen to a culture of hierarchical violence if all oppressed people acted this way? Widely applied, this tactic would constitute a social and political revolution of human equality, with "superiors" gently but firmly denied their domination and "inferiors" nonviolently empowered. If this sounds familiar, it is because it is precisely the principle on which many social justice movements are organized. This is how Mohandas Gandhi led a noncooperation movement to overturn British colonial rule in India, Danes resisted Nazi occupation and saved thousands of Jews, civil rights activists overturned segregation in the American South, and Cesar Chavez and Dolores Huerta led farmworkers in California to secure fairer wages and better working conditions. "Turn the other cheek" was never meant to be a slogan for slave masters and domestic abusers to keep their victims in check. Rather, it was part of Jesus's absolute rejection of any violent culture of domination and the subordination it creates. His message, as Wink summarized, is "Stand up for yourselves, defy your masters, assert your humanity; but don't answer the oppressor in kind. Find a new, third way that is neither cowardly submission nor violent reprisal."[27]

Jesus consistently modeled this new way, even as his disciples remained trapped in their old cultural paradigms. When the armed squad came to seize Jesus in the Garden of Gethsemane, for example, an impetuous Peter drew his sword and sliced off the right ear of the high priest's servant. Jesus immediately yet gently rebuked his disciple, telling him to put away his sword, and prophetically pronounced that "all they that take the sword shall perish with the sword." Mass violence was a real option in that tense moment; Jesus announced that he could, if he wished, bring down "more than twelve legions of angels" to utterly destroy the puny arresting force—and perhaps all of Rome's occupying army. But violent resistance was not the path to the enduring influence and redemption Jesus was pursuing. Not only did Jesus fail to indulge the cycle of violence that began with Judas's betrayal and continued with Peter's martial defense, but he immediately stopped the escalating conflict by reaching out and healing the servant's ear. His actions represented a powerful alternative—neither cowardly submission nor violent reprisal, but rather assertive love. What's more, this alternative, expressed in quiet dignity and unfailing compassion, had such moral force that Jesus's attackers initially "went backward, and fell to the ground."[28]

The life and ministry of Jesus thus reveals a kingdom where worldly notions of power are turned upside down, even enemies are loved and prayed for, the meek inherit the earth, and the oppressed masses lovingly turn the tables on their oppressors. The centerpiece of that kingdom, its very essence and practical embodiment, was and is the suffering and death of Jesus

29

Christ—the moment in which his transforming atonement for both individuals and societies was fully expressed and actualized.

THE NONVIOLENT ATONEMENT OF JESUS CHRIST

All Christians recognize the centrality of Christ's sacrifice on the cross of Calvary. Latter-day Saints are distinctive in the prominence we also give to Christ's suffering in the Garden of Gethsemane. In his influential book *Jesus the Christ*, early twentieth-century apostle James E. Talmage suggested that Jesus's atoning work may have been accomplished principally in the Garden of Gethsemane.[29] As Luke reports, it was in the garden that "being in an agony he prayed more earnestly: and his sweat was as it were great drops of blood falling down to the ground."[30] This view was supported by another apostle, Bruce R. McConkie, when he noted in 1985 that Gethsemane was "holy ground" where "the Sinless Son of the Everlasting Father took upon himself the sins of all men."[31] Similar sentiments have been expressed by a multitude of modern Restoration thinkers and leaders, allowing apostle Jeffrey R. Holland to state with confidence that the "spiritual anguish of plumbing the depths of human suffering and sorrow was experienced primarily in the Garden of Gethsemane."[32] Thus, while latter-day prophets and apostles mention the cross more often than the garden, over the last century Gethsemane has received more and more attention.[33]

To be clear, Latter-day Saints have never ignored the cross of Calvary. Both sites of Jesus's atoning work are utterly essential. Yet the Restoration's emphasis on the salvific effects of Gethsemane opens up an intriguing theological question—namely, if Christ's shouldering of sin and entering into "the depths of human suffering and sorrow" was "experienced primarily" in the garden, as Elder Holland taught, then what purpose did Christ's death *on the cross* play? Of course, Jesus had to die as a precondition for his resurrection, and the cross certainly accomplished that purpose.[34] Yet did the precise mechanism of his death really matter? Did he necessarily have to die *on a cross* for his resurrection to occur? His agony in Gethsemane was excruciating enough, so why not die there, his racked body giving out after bleeding from every pore? Given what he had already accomplished in the garden, why bear the additional torture that culminated on Golgotha? Thinking theologically, we suggest that the Crucifixion must serve a deeper purpose, beyond simply being the means by which Jesus's body died.[35]

We might approach a richer understanding of why Jesus bore the sins of humankind (and experienced their suffering) in the garden and then *also* chose to die on the cross if we consider that Jesus may have been emphasizing and bringing about different elements of salvation at Gethsemane and Golgotha, respectively. One possible reading of events suggests that Jesus's atoning work in the garden may have targeted our individual sins and woundedness, while his intentional choice of dying on a violent cross may have focused primarily on our collective sins and the wounds we inflict on others.

The cross was neither accidental nor incidental for Jesus. The Savior not only prophetically foretold that crucifixion would be the means of his death, but also seemed to consciously and deliberately orient his ministry so the cross would be its inevitable culmination.[36] At multiple junctures, Jesus purposely confronted the ruling religious and political authorities, knowing he would pay for it with the ultimate penalty they could administer. He fully understood that his public displays of power, along with the messianic qualities of his ministry, would be perceived as a threat—both religiously and politically. As late as Gethsemane, he might have chosen the path of the sword assisted by angelic legions. But just as he had rejected the worldly kingship that the crowds tried to foist on him after he fed them in the wilderness, in the garden he opted for the cup of suffering as the path to victory.[37] He voluntarily proceeded from the garden, where the universal weight of individual sin and sorrow had descended on him, to follow a path of humiliation, torture, and finally crucifixion. We must conclude, therefore, that for Jesus the public spectacle of the cross was a deliberate destination. And when we recognize this purposefulness, the cross becomes even more meaningful— as not only the site where Jesus continued his work of saving our souls, but also the chosen method by which he redeemed our collective human society. How so? Because crucifixion's brutality and injustice revealed the violence of this world's kingdoms while simultaneously proclaiming the nonviolent and loving character of Christ's kingdom.

Before the cross and throughout his ministry, Jesus had tried to prepare his disciples to understand this distinction, perhaps best encapsulated in his well-known proclamation "the last shall be first, and the first last."[38] For many of his disciples, this seemed to promise a *reversal* of the social order, in which all the political, military, economic, and religious elites would get their comeuppance, while those who were poor and oppressed took their rightful places. The structures of domination and hierarchy would essentially remain the same, just with the bottom now on top. What the disciples had not fully appreciated was that the kingdom of God is not simply a matter of status inversion, but rather a *reconceptualization* of the very nature of society and politics. As he patiently explained: "Ye know that the princes of the Gentiles exercise dominion over them, and they that are great exercise authority upon them. But it shall not be so among you."[39] His kingdom was organized and governed by a different dynamic.

Jesus reiterated this distinction when he proclaimed before Pilate, "My kingdom is not *of*"—or even *like*—"this world: if my kingdom were of this world, then would my servants fight, that

I should not be delivered to the Jews: but now is my kingdom not from hence."[40] This was a bold proclamation, even a political manifesto. Jesus unblinkingly declared to Pilate—the highest earthly political authority in that land—not that Caesar could have his worldly kingdom and Jesus would later have his better version of the same, but rather that Caesar's very definition of politics, predicated as it was on dominion, lordship, and violence, was fundamentally perverted.[41] "If I ruled my kingdom the way you rule yours," Jesus was essentially telling Pilate, "you would have a violent revolt on your hands simply for detaining me. But my kingdom doesn't work like yours, or any other here in this world. I'm king of a new kind of kingdom, and my followers and my influence operate according to a different moral logic." Jesus was posting notice that his disciples would reside in this world but live in a different kingdom, with loyalty to a different king and under a different power dynamic.

With these few devastating words, Jesus gently but firmly undermined the ultimate authority of Caesar's empire, along with all empires whose power is based on violent coercion and domination. His proclamation to Pilate echoed his public pronouncement only days earlier when he had advised the Herodians to "render therefore unto Caesar the things which are Caesar's; and unto God the things that are God's."[42] At first, it might seem that Jesus was here bestowing divine legitimacy and even license to the secular empire. It was, after all, the emperor's visage etched on the coin. But a closer reading suggests that Jesus was actually challenging the emperor's claim to sovereignty. As he would later state in revelations to Joseph Smith, "all things [in the world] are mine," including "the destinies of all the armies of the nations of the earth."[43] With "all things" in Jesus's domain, that leaves precious little room for Caesar to exercise any kind of absolute claim on God's children. This reduces the Roman emperor—indeed, all earthly rulers—to their proper roles as temporary stewards of things that are rightfully and eternally God's.

Whether or not they fully comprehended Jesus's message, the "powers that be" recognized a threat when they saw one. None of his enemies ever claimed that Jesus was organizing an armed revolt—a telling fact in itself, when they were busy making up all kinds of other false claims to convict him. Yet the fact that the authorities were willing to go to such irregular extremes in neutralizing this threat was a recognition of the potency of Jesus's peaceful tactics. They understood this Jesus of Nazareth was far more than just another popular rabbi or miracle worker. When Pilate sentenced Jesus to death by crucifixion, he was eliminating a political rival—hence the sign affixed to the cross, "This is the King of the Jews."[44] In Pilate's calculations, sending the radically nonviolent Jesus to the cross guaranteed the security of Caesar's kingdom even more than would the execution of the violent rebel Barabbas, whom he released to the crowd.[45] In effect, Barabbas and Pilate shared the same tactics of violence but were playing against one another on different teams. This nonviolent Messiah, however, completely changed the rules of the game. Preserving the existing rules required removing this interloper from the field.

The paradox, of course, is that Pilate's ploy backfired. By going nonviolently to the cross, Jesus emerged with even greater and enduring influence than he had before and further undermined the fleeting power of Rome. Every lash of the scourge against his back, every swing of the mallet that pounded the nails into the flesh of Jesus's hands and feet, did two things. First, they testified of the fundamental incongruity between the violent kingdom of this world and the nonviolent kingdom of Christ. Though intended as a deterrent to others who would challenge the sovereign power of Rome, the crucifixion of the sinless Son of God unmasked the moral bankruptcy of all political systems that exercise power through "control or dominion or compulsion." Second, Jesus's crucifixion demonstrated and implemented a radically different political calculus—one in which power is exercised "by persuasion, by long-suffering, by gentleness and meekness, and by love unfeigned." Generations of citizens in God's kingdom have since willingly thrown themselves at the foot of that cross and sworn fealty to its king in ways that the Caesars of this world could only dream about. In the ultimate reversal, the cross (followed by the Resurrection) became the means by which the influence of Jesus Christ became "an everlasting dominion." Exercised "without compulsory means," true power began to flow unto him "forever and ever" at the very moment the world considered him most powerless.[46]

The political dimension of Christ's crucifixion is highlighted in the Epistle to the Colossians: "having disarmed the powers and authorities, [Jesus] made a public spectacle of them, triumphing over them by the cross."[47] Christ's suffering in Gethsemane was an intimate, private, deeply personal event in which he connected, in ways that remain largely mysterious, with every child of God in their infirmities, their pains and sicknesses, their sins and sorrows.[48] Christ chose the cross as a means of making a "public spectacle" of what sin looked like on a social and political scale and then demonstrating the godly alternative. The Romans thought they were making a humiliating display of the "King of the Jews," but in fact it was the innocent victim that put the injustice and violence of the empire's "powers and authorities" on shameful display. In stripping Jesus naked, the empire supposed that it was rendering him impotent and powerless before the mighty dominion of Caesar. But in the end it was the disrobed Crucified One who both stripped bare the naked brutality of Caesar's dominion and showed a better way—an "everlasting dominion" built on love and trust.

Thus, Jesus was not a passive victim on the cross, any more than he wanted those who turned the other cheek to be passive victims. He deliberately used the cross as a literal platform from which he both unmasked the true nature of the kingdoms of this world and revealed the true nature of God and his kingdom. To the Nephites, the resurrected Christ later declared, "My Father sent me that I might be lifted up upon the cross; and after that I had been lifted up upon the cross, that I might draw all men unto me."[49] In his public crucifixion, Jesus provided a revelation to the whole world—the Son of God lifted up for all to see, for all time.

When we "survey the wondrous cross," in the words of the old gospel hymn, we see a God who is suffering and vulnerable, a God who at once chastens those who have lost affection for their own kind but who is ultimately merciful and forgiving, indiscriminate in his love. In his vulnerability, mercy, and love, Christ draws all humanity to him. Shaken to the core by his unmerited suffering, the human heart swells with anguish and culpability for his torment. His unspeakable love for corrupted humanity and a fallen world becomes the means of our individual and collective transformation. We are drawn in by the power of his meek love and realize that the fruit of our violence is a crucified God. In this respect Isaiah's messianic prophecy proves more literal than poetic: "he was bruised for our iniquities: the chastisement of our peace was upon him; and with his stripes we are healed."[50] The fundamental and incontrovertible truth of the good news of Jesus Christ is that in his nonviolent vulnerability the crucified Christ exercises a power over the hearts of women and men that has been and will be maintained far longer than the violent, coercive dominion of Caesar.

TAKING UP THE CROSS

The cross of Christ simultaneously offers prophetic judgment and transformative compassion. We see this most poignantly in the crucified Jesus's words regarding the soldiers at his mangled feet. Jesus acknowledged, even in his anguish, that his crucifiers were only doing their jobs. Taking orders from their superiors, no doubt they were confident they were guaranteeing the safety of the Roman empire that they believed was the great arbiter of peace and prosperity in the world. Looking at his torturers, Christ implored our Father to "forgive them; for they know not what they do."[51] Note that Jesus did *not* declare the soldiers' actions to be morally neutral. By extending forgiveness to them, Jesus was explicitly declaring that their violence was offensive—in short, that they had sinned, even in the performance of their duty as agents of the state. Though they acted largely out of ignorance (regarding Christ's true identity), nevertheless the soldiers' violence was a moral wrong that required pardon. "Father, forgive them; for they know not what they do" is thus Jesus's dual message of condemnation and reconciliation extended to all those responsible for his death, including members of the crowd who called for his murder or looked on in passive complicity. His words from the cross suggest that ignorance and distance do not excuse us from at least partial moral accountability for acts of violence committed in our name and supposedly for our sake.

If Christ prevailed over individual sin and suffering in the garden, and proclaimed victory over death in his resurrection, the cross represents the moment in which the nonviolent God triumphed over the violence of fallen humanity. Since Cain slew Abel, violence has been a persistent feature of human life on earth. With seemingly no respect to time, place, or culture, we humans have traditionally used violence to get what we want, cover our sins, or exact vengeance. We typically escalate conflict rather than be the last one wronged. Golgotha exposes humanity's seemingly insatiable appetite for blood, which culminates only when we "crucify [our] God."[52]

Virtually every culture has perpetuated a "myth of redemptive violence," in which violence saves, might makes right, and war brings peace.[53] The crucified Christ gives lie to this myth. If there was ever an innocent victim that had the right to fight back, to call on heaven to stop the injustice, to use violence to save himself and bring about a higher and holier cause, it was Jesus. What he did instead is simply astounding. If Homer or Hollywood had written the story, we would expect that at the moment of extreme crisis the innocent victim would show a mighty display of power, escape from his bonds, and avenge himself against his enemies. Instead, Jesus goes way off script. He does not retaliate against the evildoers. He literally gives them the cloak off his back. He offers forgiveness to the bandit who begs it of him and to all those who "know not what they do." He prays for his enemies while they persecute him. In other words, he literally gives flesh and blood to his hard sayings.

But above all, he dies.

We cannot forget that on the afternoon of Good Friday, anyone "keeping score" would have concluded that Jesus had "lost." With the benefit of hindsight and faith, Christians know there will be a Sunday morning resurrection, but let us keep our gaze for a moment on Jesus hanging limply on Caesar's tree. It was one thing for Jesus to announce the coming of his nonviolent kingdom to Pilate on Friday morning. But here we are, only a few hours later, and the Messiah is dead, seemingly nothing more than another victim of the state security apparatus.

But something has happened. This victim is different. This victim has controlled the fury of nature, exorcised demons, and even raised the dead. Where others had been powerless in the face of Caesar's might, this victim had in fact created the very world that Caesar strode across. And yet the God of heaven and earth, uttering no complaint and only a few words of mercy and compassion, chose the cross, and chose to die. Philosopher John Caputo aptly captures the scene:

> What rises up in majesty from the cross is not a show of might but rather forgiveness, not power but a protest against the unjust execution of a just man, a great prophetic "no" to injustice and persecution. . . . Jesus displays the stunning power of powerlessness—of nonviolence, nonresistance, forgiveness, mercy, compassion, generosity. The divinity that shows through Jesus consists not in a demonstration of might but in a complete reversal of our expectations culminating in the most stunning reversal of all. It is the centerpiece of all this madness, the one that makes as little sense as possible from the point of view of worldly common sense, the most divine madness of all: love your enemies. The key to the kingdom is to love those who do not love you, who hate you, and whom you, by worldly standards, should also hate.[54]

In the cross, therefore, we find the absolute fulfillment of the nonviolent political ethic of Jesus. The myth of redemptive violence is revealed to be just that—a story that cannot save, an idol that distracts us from the true source and nature of our redemption. On the cross we see Jesus fulfilling the ethic of turning the other cheek, refusing to strike back because that only feeds the cycle of violence, all while finding a new way to be liberated—and liberate all humanity—from the degradation of Caesar's domination and coercion. Jesus took the very worst that Caesar could do to him, absorbed it, and reversed its energy, in jujitsu-like fashion, performing a destabilizing move on the very violence that assaulted him. In so doing he provided a radically new ethic, fundamentally the opposite of Caesar's, in which he countered evil but refused to imitate the behavior of his persecutors.

Rather than responding in kind and thus becoming trapped by a cycle of retribution, Christ chose to end violence and transform the conflict. Perhaps the most astonishing thing is that he invites us to do the same.

It cannot be emphasized strongly enough that in revealing this political ethic, Jesus was not guaranteeing immediate, demonstrable success. His crucifixion suggests just the opposite, in fact. He had already made it clear that to follow him meant a willingness to take up the cross—which in the mind of any subject of the Roman empire could only mean suffering and death. (If Jesus meant this *only* as a metaphor for self-denial, he might have invoked a less extreme image than the cross, such as fasting.) When Peter began to rebuke Jesus for his plain explanation that "the Son of Man must suffer . . . and be rejected . . . and be killed," Jesus immediately cut him off: "Get behind me, Satan! For you are setting your mind not on divine things but on human things." He then made perfectly clear the price that anyone must pay to walk with him: "If any of you want to become my followers, let them deny themselves and take up their cross and follow me. For those who want to save their life will lose it, and those who lose their life for my sake, and for the sake of the gospel, will save it."[55]

Peter wasn't actually Satan—but he was parroting him. In Peter's words we hear an echo of Satan's second temptation in the wilderness. The Great Deceiver failed then, as in the Council in Heaven, to overcome Jesus. But his enticing message continues to echo throughout the world—promising power and glory and authority in exchange for embracing the politics of violence and domination. As Peter demonstrated, even Jesus's closest followers were shocked by his ethic of loving nonviolence. Many of his disciples—then as well as now—have consistently sought to find "some other way" to qualify the "must" of suffering, rejection, and death that Christ himself declared to be his path.[56] According to the wisdom of the world, suffering is the antithesis of success, and death is the ultimate loss. To the contrary, Jesus's voluntary suffering in the garden and on the cross paved the way to victory.

Christ's victory is made all the more sure in light of his resurrection. This fundamental Christian proclamation—that "the grave hath no victory"—is the ultimate reality.[57] It reaffirms the indestructability and immortality of each human soul and becomes the foundation for social and political ethics rooted in human dignity. For if death is indeed the end, then the argument that humans should use all available means—even violence—to preserve their own life and well-being might seem reasonable, even compelling.[58] Resurrection extends the timeline for the achievement of God's peaceful kingdom, promising the fulfillment of Martin Luther King Jr.'s frequent assertion that "the arc of the moral universe is long but it bends toward justice."[59]

Faith in the Resurrection should not, however, diminish our commitment to working for justpeace here and now. As King also observed, "justice too long delayed is justice denied."[60] According to the Revelation of John, the glorified Christ proclaims victory not only over death but also over every other form of evil, including conquest, war, famine, and pestilence.[61] With our faith grounded in Christ's atonement and resurrection, Christians reject not only the violence of utilitarianism but also the moral passivity that defers all resolution of injustice to the next world. The vulnerable love of Christ displayed on the cross, compounded by the everlasting victory of Christ achieved in the Resurrection, solidifies a different calculation of cause and effect predicated on an eternal standard of power and influence that is "maintained . . . only by persuasion, by long-suffering, by gentleness and meekness, and by love unfeigned."[62]

To "preach Christ crucified," as Paul would have all followers of Christ do, is to proclaim the triumph of Golgotha as well as the victory over sin secured in Gethsemane.[63] What does it mean—not just theologically but also ethically—for us to witness that Jesus Christ's atonement really was the "great and last sacrifice"?[64] If we were to believe that Christ's bloody sacrifice was both *great* and intended to be *last*, then as followers of Jesus we would do all in our power to prevent others from becoming sacrificial victims of violence. We would perhaps be especially sensitive to those victims whose suffering has come, and continues to come, at the hands of all the Caesars of the ages.

Although on this side of Eden we are each implicated in the fallen structures of worldly violence, the good news is that Christ offers redemption for our societies as well as our souls. The Restoration provides ordinances whereby we are made ritually "clean from the blood of this wicked generation" of which we are a part.[65] But that ritual purification is only one step on the path of taking on the divine nature. The atoning power of Gethsemane and the victory of the cross and the Resurrection are designed not only to purify us but perhaps even more importantly to empower us, individually and collectively, to build God's kingdom of love, justice, and peace.

In the end, then, perhaps there is not so much distance between Gethsemane and Golgotha. What happened on the cross was brutal shorthand for what Christ suffered for in the garden. A countless multitude of personal sins and woundedness, hopelessly threaded into one another and then braided into the actions of our society and the state, results in untold suffering for the children of God. In taking on flesh, and then subjecting that flesh to the caprice of jealous rulers, a violent state, a fickle mob, and a host of gawking bystanders, Jesus allowed himself to be "judged of the world . . . [and] lifted up upon the cross and slain for the sins of the world."[66] He did so precisely to show us that this world—a world predicated on violence that kills its own God—is not the world we want. And that we can transform the world with love.

CHAPTER THREE

The Word and the Sword

I did exhort them with all the energies of my soul,
and with all the faculty which I possessed,
that they would give heed to the word of God.
—1 Nephi 15:25

And I, Nephi, did take the sword of Laban,
and after the manner of it did make many swords.
—2 Nephi 5:14

The Book of Mormon functions as something of a first among equals within the Restoration's scriptural canon. Mixed in amid its sublime and oft-quoted spiritual passages are frequent descriptions of bloodshed. Filled with flashing swords, massive armies led by prophet-generals, and epic battles between good guys and bad guys, the Book of Mormon can thus appear to be a quintessential primer on religious violence. Of course, the Book of Mormon hardly stands alone as a sacred text that features considerable violence—much of the Hebrew Bible, book of Revelation, and Bhagavad Gita is the same—but it is certainly a notable entry in the genre.

Yet readers of these scriptures have always found counternarratives and discerned deeper threads of nonviolent power and influence that complicate any notion that these are straightforwardly violent texts. Gandhi, for example, perceived a message of selfless, nonviolent sacrifice at the center of his beloved Bhagavad Gita. Likewise, numerous Jewish and Christian interpreters have reread the Bible in often-surprising but still faithful ways that reveal its violent passages to be not quite what they first seem and highlight the underlying message of *shalom* that God offers his people from Genesis to Revelation.

So it is with the Book of Mormon. Read with the Restoration's revealed principles of power and influence in mind, it emerges as a complex story evincing subtle but significant lessons about the limits of violence and the efficacy of nonviolence. Although violence permeates the Book of Mormon from beginning to end, the prophetic narrators' intentional construction of the text offers an invitation to consider the quandaries posed by that same violence. In other words, approaching the book from a slightly different angle—namely, the principles of nonviolent power and influence presented earlier—allows us to see ways in which the book's violence is "undone by the very text in which it is articulated."[1] The Book of Mormon simultaneously functions as another testament of Jesus Christ *and* a primer on peace precisely because it insists that those "beautiful" souls who "publish peace" are preaching the gospel of Christ, "the founder of peace . . . who has redeemed his people."[2]

Yet for a text that aspires to "publish peace," the Book of Mormon is undeniably saturated with violence. The narrative opens with the attempted murder of a prophet, moves quickly toward a nighttime killing and multiple near misses at fratricide, then exhaustively chronicles wars and assassinations that eventually culminate, after a relatively brief (but notable) respite, in the complete annihilation of not one but two civilizations. The final voices in the Book of Mormon are the prophets Ether and Moroni, each of whom is literally the last man standing at the twilight of their respective peoples. Both of them survey the carnage and ask, in so many words, "What went wrong?"

The Book of Mormon answers this question by going back to the beginning of the two civilizations that will eventually self-destruct, the Nephites and Jaredites. How could these two covenant peoples each meet such tragic ends? The seeds of both promise and peril were planted from the outset. The Book of Mormon is a witness that humans have two fundamental options—the Word or the sword. Read as a whole, this "voice from the dust" testifies to modern readers that Jesus is the way to life and salvation.[3] While an individual or community that opts for the sword may exert genuine authority in the short term, doing so will initiate a destructive cycle of violence that—left unchecked—has the capacity to consume entire societies in the long run.

Space does not permit a full examination of the entire Book of Mormon, so here we offer a close reading of a key section in order to model a method for understanding the text's persuasive and pervasive nonviolent patterns. In short, here we offer a nonviolent scriptural hermeneutic, or method of interpretation, based on the principles outlined in the previous two chapters. We will focus on the book's first, and perhaps most iconic, prophet-narrator—Nephi. His account, divided into two books, opens the Book of Mormon and enjoys significant popularity thanks both to its privilege of place at the beginning of the narrative as well as its captivating characters and compelling storyline. A nonviolent reading of 1 and 2 Nephi will be counterintuitive to most readers.[4] After all, Nephi's life is in many ways infused with violence—with him on both the giving and receiving ends—and at no juncture does he explicitly disclaim violence. All the more reason to begin here. If a nonviolent hermeneutic can be applied effectively to Nephi's writings, it has potential to interpret the remainder of the Book of Mormon.

It is important to remember that Nephi's record is a backward-looking account. Written probably sometime in his forties and fifties, Nephi's personal history is primarily a testimony of God's promises and mercy. But it also represents a poignant attempt to order and make sense of his remarkable but conflict-laden life. Nephi's retrospective record captures an inherent tension between godly and worldly power that will play out through subsequent authors, prophets, and societies long after Nephi has passed on. Consequently, his account both typifies and initiates a consistent Book of Mormon narrative pattern, offering a master class on the contrasts between enduring power built on persuasion, love, and truth and temporary influence predicated on coercion. His writings thus represent an expansive rumination on the nature of power—God's power, Nephi's authority, the influence of his father, and a long power struggle with his older brothers—with meaningful applications for both interpersonal relationships and broad societal dynamics.

BRASS PLATES AND STEEL SWORD

Nephi introduces the themes of power and influence in the very first sentence of his record. Raised by "goodly parents" who taught him well, the Jerusalem native recalls that from an early age he developed "a great knowledge of the goodness and the mysteries of God." As he remembers and relates, Nephi freely chose to be guided and governed by his parents and God, not because of any force or coercion on their part, but because he recognized their inherent goodness.[5]

The rest of Jerusalem didn't have the same reaction. After offering some scant autobiographical detail, Nephi quickly moves on to tell us that his father Lehi received a series of remarkable visions in which he was called to prophesy the ruin of the holy city because of its many "abominations."[6] The city's citizens mock Lehi as yet another doomsayer, but their derision takes a turn toward anger and even attempted murder. God commands Lehi and his family to flee into the wilderness, leaving behind their home and considerable fortune. The family has scarcely left Jerusalem, however, when God gives Lehi a new commandment. His four sons—Laman, Lemuel, Sam, and Nephi—are to return to the city to obtain a record inscribed on plates of brass that contain both the Hebrew scriptures and the family's genealogy. This is not an easy thing to ask. The family did not leave the city on good terms. Lehi had fled from people who "sought his life," so sending his sons back carries significant risk.[7] Furthermore, the brass plates are held by Laban, a local oligarch who enjoys leverage with the city's religio-political leadership and commands a militia, making him the personification of worldly, coercive power. Still, Lehi's sons accept their mission.

The brothers' first two meetings with Laban go poorly. He labels them thieves, steals their family riches, then orders his servants to kill them. By the time the four brothers reach safety outside the city walls, Laman and Lemuel have had enough of what they perceive as a fool's errand. Having been duly intimidated by Laban, and absorbing the lesson that violence "works," they take out their frustrations on Sam and Nephi, beating their younger brothers with a rod.

Laman and Lemuel's violent assault is curbed only when an angel appears on the scene and commands them to stop. The appearance of an angel sounds dramatic, but Nephi's narration of the incident is straightforward, even nonchalant. The angel "came and stood before them." No bright light. No thunderclap. No heavenly chorus. The angel rhetorically asks Laman and Lemuel why they are beating their younger brothers, reiterates God's earlier promise to Nephi that he would be their ruler, and admonishes them to trust in God to complete their mission in securing the plates. After that, "he departed," again with no fanfare.[8]

Placed in such close narrative proximity, the angel and Laban appear as contrasting characters. As opposed to Laban's intimidation, greed, and violence, the angel uses forceful rhetoric but not physical coercion. Acting as a third-party mediator, he asks a series of penetrating questions that cause Laman and Lemuel to consider the logic of their violence. Their fear, anger, and resentment do not magically disappear, but they do stop their attack. Alas, they also miss the deeper lesson. Laman and Lemuel remain more impressed with Laban's violent power than with the angel's persuasive power. "How is it possible that the Lord will deliver Laban into our hands?" they grumble. "Behold, he is a mighty man, and he can command fifty, yea, even he can slay fifty; then why not us?" Nephi counters by calling his brothers to remember God's power as displayed in his drowning of Pharaoh's army in the Red Sea, suggesting that the younger brother has also failed to fully grasp the meaning of the angel's appearance and message.[9] Yes, God can at times use spectacular and violent force, but that is not the only or even principal way divine power is manifest.

Bolstered by the angel's visit, Nephi persuades his brothers to make one more attempt for the plates. This time he volunteers to take the lead. Laman and Lemuel are still "wroth" and "continue to murmur," but they follow their younger brother—just as the earlier prophecy about his rulership had anticipated.[10] It is true that Laman and Lemuel's acquiescence to Nephi is reluctant and mercurial, but the key point is that they stop their assault and assent to his leadership. As night falls, Nephi's brothers hide outside the city walls as he ventures alone into Jerusalem's dark streets. Approaching Laban's compound, he discovers the powerful warlord alone on the street, collapsed on the ground in a drunken heap. So far Nephi's influence has steadily increased through the practice of persuasion. Suddenly his enemy, the man who literally tried to kill him and his brothers, lies fully incapacitated at his feet. Now what?

At that moment, Nephi is drawn to Laban's sword. Even decades after the event, the aging author easily recalls the wonder, even yearning, that his younger self experienced at the sight of this expertly crafted weapon: "I drew it forth from the sheath thereof; and the hilt thereof was of pure gold, and the workmanship thereof was exceedingly fine; and I saw that the blade thereof was of the most precious steel." With Laban at his mercy, the boy takes the man's token of violent power in his hands. According to his own account, it was only *after* Nephi had already unsheathed and gazed longingly at the sword that he felt or heard something that he describes as the Spirit "constrain[ing]" him to kill Laban.[11] Nephi's mission is to obtain the brass plates, which contain the word and law of God. Now the Spirit impels him to use Laban's own violent power against him and in so doing to break one of God's most serious prohibitions—"Thou shalt not kill"—in order to obtain plates containing that very law.

Nephi demurs. "Never at any time have I shed the blood of man," he protests in his heart.[12] He questions his capacity for violence. But looking back, Nephi does not describe his younger self as questioning the Spirit's command itself. Schooled in the Hebrew scriptures, the mature narrator probably knew there were ample precedents of righteous humans negotiating with God. He might have recalled the example of Abraham, who questioned God's announced destruction of the people of Sodom and successfully negotiated for God to apply a lower threshold of guilt against the city (though admittedly the final fiery outcome for most of the cities' residents remained the same). Or he might have thought about Jacob, who wrestled with the angel until he received his desired blessing. Or Moses, who successfully parleyed with God to preserve the lives of the Israelites in the wilderness. Or the servant in Zenos's parable, who repeatedly convinced the master to forbear and to spare the unruly trees in his vineyard.[13]

Given this tradition, then, it was therefore not out of the realm of moral possibility for Nephi to humbly challenge the Spirit's directive. Perhaps he could have negotiated a lesser, bloodless consequence for Laban—a long deep sleep or extended paralysis, for example—that might have allowed him to more cleanly accomplish his goal of retrieving the plates.[14] Indeed, readers of the Book of Mormon who continue beyond Nephi's account will learn of two later occasions in which God's followers would creatively take advantage of their armed enemies' drunkenness to secure a nonviolent deliverance.[15] Not here. Whether the young Nephi did not feel confident enough in his relationship with God to challenge the Spirit's instruction, or was convinced by the Spirit's utilitarian argument that "it is better that one man should perish than that a nation should dwindle and perish in unbelief," or could not imagine a nonlethal solution, or was unable to summon sufficient love for an enemy who had threatened his life, or simply was not inclined to question, in the moment the obedient Nephi felt compelled toward violence.[16] "Therefore I did obey the voice of the Spirit, and took Laban by the hair of the head, and I smote off his head with his own sword."[17] Nephi's clinical account obscures what must have been a truly gory affair.

Nephi's violence was performed with dread and reluctance, and—as he insists—in harmony with the voice of the Spirit. He did not go to Jerusalem, or even leave the cave, thirsting for blood. Nevertheless, Nephi's choice to kill Laban was just that—a choice. This is emphasized in another Restoration text, the August 1833 revelation to Joseph Smith in which the Lord commanded the

Saints to "renounce war and proclaim peace." We will discuss the full revelation at length in a later chapter, but for our purposes here it is sufficient to note that it lays out detailed guidelines for when it is justifiable for followers of Jesus to resort to force— after repeated attacks, after multiple attempts to settle the matter without violence, and when lives are endangered. All these factors were at play in Nephi's encounter with Laban. But the 1833 revelation also notes that even when violence is justified, there is always the option to "spare" the aggressor. In one of the most subtle and intriguing cross-textual commentaries in Restoration scripture, the revelation notes that God gave this law of forbearance to "my servant Nephi."[18]

Neither the 1833 revelation nor the Book of Mormon record makes clear exactly when Nephi would have become fully aware of these principles of justified violence and preferred forbearance. We might conjecture that as a young man confronting Laban he may not have known the law's intricacies, but that as an older prophet recounting his life and legacy he did. Thus the chronicler Nephi, many decades removed from the traumatic event he is recounting, may have understood in a way that his younger self did not that his action that dark night in Jerusalem was a choice. This would help explain why he goes to such great lengths in his narration to explore his interior psychology in that fateful moment—an interiority we rarely get from him or other Book of Mormon authors. Nephi writes the story in such a way as to convince the reader (and perhaps himself) that he *had* to act the way he did.

Still, all choices have consequences. The decision to kill Laban had serious repercussions for Nephi and his family (not to mention Laban), both in the immediately ensuing years and for the generations that followed. Violence has an imitative quality to it, with antagonists often mirroring those who have done violence to them.[19] Nephi's narrative captures this dynamic. Having wielded Laban's sword, Nephi now claims it as his own. In a richly symbolic move, he also clothes himself with Laban's garments and armor, enshrouding his body—"yea, even every whit"—with the very tokens of power that Laban had used when commanding violence against the brothers. Arrayed in the warlord's raiment, Nephi now assumes his identity. Adopting "the voice of Laban," Nephi tricks an unwitting servant, Zoram, to retrieve the brass plates from where they are secured. Nephi bids and Zoram follows. At this point Nephi has fully inhabited his role: "I spake unto him as if it had been Laban." He misleads Zoram to think that the pair are delivering the plates to his "brethren of the church" outside the city walls. Readers can hardly fail to recognize that Nephi succeeds in his mission to obtain the brass plates—the words of the "God of truth" that testify of the "Prince of Peace"—through violence and deception.[20]

Nephi seems to understand the nature of the power that he is yielding. He knows his influence over Zoram is built entirely on an artifice and that such influence would be transient. Once Zoram detects Nephi's fraud, he attempts to flee the scene and is stopped only when Nephi forcibly restrains him. But this too is a form of influence that cannot be maintained. No matter how strong he is, Nephi cannot hold Laban's servant forever. Once Nephi lets go, Zoram will bolt again and raise an alarm.

Whether coolly or frantically, Nephi realizes that the logic of violence has played out. He recognizes that brute force cannot accomplish his ends. So he turns from the power of coercion, abandons the power of deception, and returns to the power of truth and persuasion. Symbolically disrobing the tokens of Laban's power, Nephi speaks to Zoram with earnest honesty. He comes clean about his true identity, appeals to Zoram's compassion, and promises the freedom that any servant would desire. Despite Nephi's initial duplicity, Zoram seems to sense the integrity of Nephi's offer. Perhaps he senses a qualitative difference between his former master's model of power and the one in Nephi's heart. Or perhaps he feels he has no choice and cannot return to the scene of the crime. Regardless, it is through the power of Nephi's words, not his physical strength, that Zoram trusts him and makes an oath to join the family. By the power of the word Nephi has secured the company's safe passage out of the city—and, not incidentally, gained a lifelong friend and ally in Zoram.[21]

As Nephi and his brothers return to the family's camp, he is now custodian of two very different tokens of power—God's word and Laban's sword. The record provides no evidence that Lehi took any notice of the sword or approved of Nephi's possession (let alone prior use) of it. In fact, the opposite might be inferred by the fact that Lehi and his wife Sariah offered burnt offerings upon their sons' safe return, which according to scholar of ancient scripture Kent Brown may have been an attempt to purify the family from the stain of Laban's blood.[22] By contrast, Lehi is thrilled with the brass plates and the words they contain. As Nephi explores the records alongside his father, the words begin to sink into his heart and he exults in their "great worth."[23]

Throughout the family's subsequent journey in the wilderness and across the ocean to the promised land, the brass plates loom large in Nephi's account, and he quotes liberally from their pages. They, along with his father's and his own visions, clearly become the biggest influence in his life. Yet Nephi never divests himself of Laban's sword. It will assume no formal role in his life until after the family ruptures in the wake of his parents' deaths. He never wields it in self-defense, even during the several occasions when his brothers assault him in the wilderness and on the open sea. But through it all he always retains the sword—an alternative path to power and influence, and therefore an "exceedingly fine" and "most precious" temptation that he can never quite bring himself to jettison.

O WRETCHED MAN!

As Nephi's second book begins, Lehi and Sariah's family is leaning toward its ultimate conflict and eventual breakup. When the family patriarch and matriarch die, there is little that still binds the brothers to each other, and the fissures that have been evident since the beginning of Nephi's record now grow into a chasm. As his narrative approaches this climax, Nephi interrupts his story to indulge in a remarkable, and rare, moment of self-reflection. In anguish of soul reminiscent of David's psalms, he cries out, "O wretched man that I am! Yea, my heart sorroweth because of my flesh; my soul grieveth because of mine iniquities. I am encompassed about, because of the temptations and the sins which do so easily beset me." This all seems rather abstract and almost precious—after all, to this point Nephi's narrative has consistently contrasted his own faithfulness with his brothers' inconstancy. But in the middle of Nephi's psalm, he shifts to particulars and finally reveals the fundamental nature of his internal struggle: "Why am I angry because of mine enemy?"[24]

Nephi's brothers and their families are likely the only "enemies" he has, so this is clearly an expression of regret and longing for family harmony that might have been. At this moment Nephi does not express regret for his brothers' choices—their faithlessness and violence have already been detailed—but rather remorse for his own role in the strife. Maturity has brought greater self-awareness, and the seasoned prophet can now acknowledge that his own anger has also contributed to the family rift.[25]

A closer examination of Nephi's preceding record bears this out. Throughout the record of his family's troubled history, Nephi records his varying strategies to respond to his brothers' stubbornness. Sometimes he is gentle, loving, and long-suffering. At other times he is quick-tempered, harsh, even coercive. In some cases he takes both approaches in the same episode. For instance, during a second trip back to Jerusalem to recruit the family of Ishmael to join them in their wilderness journey, another brotherly quarrel breaks out, this time about whether to return permanently to the city or return to their parents in the desert. Exasperated with his brothers' "rebellion," Nephi speaks harshly to them. He accuses them of being "hard in your hearts" and "blind in your minds." Then, in what surely must have been felt by Laman and Lemuel as an intentional jab, he calls attention to the fact that he, the youngest brother, has to "set an example for you." Finally, Nephi caps his censure with a prophetic threat— that if his brothers return permanently to Jerusalem they will die alongside the city's inhabitants.[26]

Predictably, Laman and Lemuel become "angry," even "exceedingly wroth." Seizing their pious younger brother, they tie him up and leave him to be killed by wild beasts. Calling upon God, Nephi miraculously escapes and proceeds to reprimand them some more. When after this second lecture the older brothers are ready to tie him up again, other members of the group (including, notably, some of the women) intervene, saving Nephi with their powers of persuasion. This peaceful intervention is so efficacious that Laman and Lemuel plead for Nephi's forgiveness, and even bow down before him. To his credit, Nephi responds with love and forgiveness.[27] Significantly, however, it is the older brothers' hearts that seem to soften first in this standoff. While Nephi's sermons may have been theologically accurate, his brothers' willingness to listen to and be led by him was actually achieved through the words of interested and compassionate third parties. Nephi proves adept at reproving his brothers "with sharpness," but on its own such sharpness does not really increase his power or influence over them. He eventually shows them "an increase of love," but only after the crisis has been averted by others.

Laman and Lemuel remain stubborn enough to resist various forms of entreaties and repeatedly lapse into hostility toward their younger brother after temporary periods of calm. But Nephi's record does indicate occasional favorable responses to his softer appeals, suggesting that even their "hard hearts" were susceptible to persuasion, long-suffering, gentleness, meekness, kindness, knowledge, and "love unfeigned."[28] We see this, for instance, after Lehi and Nephi receive their respective visions of the tree of life, which represents "the love of God"—the most powerful redeeming force in the universe, incarnated in Jesus Christ.[29] Immediately after Lehi has his vision, he reaches out to his wayward sons with pure love, teaching them "with all the feeling of a tender parent."[30] Similarly, after Nephi's vision, when his brothers ask about its meaning, he gives them another sermon, but this one is different. Rather than castigating them, he encourages them to approach God in faith, promising that they too can receive divine revelation as did their father and brother. This time Laman and Lemuel are listening because Nephi is speaking out of love, and he reports that "they were pacified and did humble themselves before the Lord."[31] Even when Nephi feels compelled to say "hard things" to them, the general tenor of this conversation and the deeper trust it enables mean that Laman and Lemuel take this correction remarkably well, to the point that Nephi remembers having "joy and great hopes" for them.[32] In this instance, without compulsory means and with loving patience, Nephi genuinely and fully inhabits his prophesied role as their "ruler and teacher."[33] For at least this moment, his older brothers have willingly given their assent to allow him influence in their lives.

Over the next eight years the family will stagger through the wilderness and eventually settle for a time in a land they call Bountiful. The journey is arduous, and Nephi recounts a number of incidents when the family is thrown into crisis and the brothers' bonds are once again strained. The most dramatic confrontation occurs in Bountiful after God commands Nephi to build a ship that will carry the growing family (now with children in tow) across the sea. The incident begins again as a war of words between the brothers, with Laman and Lemuel taunting Nephi about his ability to build a seaworthy vessel. In a well-established pattern, Nephi responds with a long sermon on the merits of divine power. Beginning gently, the lecture gradually crescendos into a climactic explosion of accusations, with Nephi trotting out not only the well-worn complaints about his older brothers' faithlessness but now adding an explosive charge that "ye are murderers in your hearts." Nephi's discourse is not without compassion (or merit), but his love is often obscured by the stream of frustrated recriminations. All his brothers seem to hear is a torrent of blame. So the characters assume their normal roles in the plot—Laman and Lemuel respond with violence, attempting to seize Nephi and throw him into the sea.[34]

This time Nephi meets their violence with his most forceful language yet: "In the name of the Almighty God, I command you that ye touch me not, for I am filled with the power of God, even unto the consuming of my flesh; and whoso shall lay his hands upon me shall wither even as a dried reed." This statement can be read either as a violent threat or a protective warning. Either way, Laman and Lemuel are sufficiently intimidated that they back off. But this time Nephi does not settle for simply preventing their violence. With the Lord's encouragement he reaches out to "shake" his brothers with the power of God. On the face of it, this incident seems to be an example of divinely ordained and assisted violence—nonlethal violence, but violence nonetheless. However, the divine shock may also be read as God mitigating Nephi's rising anger, for he tells Nephi, "Stretch forth thine hand again unto thy brethren, and they will not wither before *thee*, but *I* will shock them."[35] Here God reminds Nephi who truly holds the power over life and death. By enabling Nephi to shake his brothers but not kill them, God protects Nephi from letting

57

his justified indignation—the anger that Nephi later confesses to in his psalm—spiral into a more violent act of retribution he will later regret. Read in this way, the episode can be understood as God both empowering Nephi and protecting him from potentially extreme consequences of his anger that he did not truly desire.

The divine "shake" works, but only to a point. Nephi secures his brothers' acquiescence, but his influence cannot be maintained because it was achieved through their cowed submission rather than freely given assent. Laman and Lemuel do help build the ship, but the incident seems to have extracted a cost. From this point on Nephi's influence over his brothers goes into sharp decline. Once the family embarks across the sea—and in response to another of their younger brother's lectures—Laman and Lemuel tie Nephi to the mast and are now impervious to any pleas in his behalf from people they see as his allies, such as their aged parents and Nephi's wife and children. Nephi's brothers release him only when they fear being swallowed in the depths of the sea during a sudden storm. Once in the new world, their increasing hostility toward Nephi is kept in check only by the continued presence of their father, Lehi, who to the very end seems to command their respect and assent, even if only grudgingly.[36]

This deterioration in fraternal relations is due in large part to Laman and Lamuel's stubbornness and repeated aggression, but Nephi is not merely an innocent and hapless victim of their violence. We can see this when we contrast Nephi's attitudes toward Laman and Lemuel with those of his father. Nephi gradually seems to give up on his brothers, although Lehi never does. Nephi evidently resigns himself to the notion that his brothers are "past feeling" and will always be hard-hearted, whereas Lehi continues to hold out at least some hope in their capacity to reform.[37] Perhaps this is simply the difference between parental love and sibling rivalry. But by the time they reach the promised land, the sons of Lehi and Sariah, led by Laman on the one hand and Nephi on the other, are irreconcilable. Neither will follow the other. The narrative moves toward the final traumatic family rupture with a certain sense of inevitability. This may of course be due to Nephi's hindsight as narrator. But at the cusp of the familial breakup—after the death of Lehi and following yet another sermon by Nephi—the narration abruptly stops and morphs into Nephi's soul-anguished psalm. It is as if Nephi, in the course of recounting this final lecture to his brothers, at last recognizes his own culpability in the tortured family dynamic and cries out in grief at missed opportunities for reconciliation: "O wretched man that I am!"[38]

By now it is too late to stop. Now that the family's patriarch and matriarch are dead and the leadership of the family is truly at stake, the older brothers, imbued with a persistent sense of entitlement and resentment, cannot get past their years of well-nurtured grievances. In the end, the divine promise that Nephi would be "a ruler and a teacher over [his] brethren" goes only partially fulfilled. A dividing line is drawn between Nephi's older brothers and their followers (who "will not have him to be [their] ruler" so that they "may not be afflicted more because of his words") and the remainder of the colony (who Nephi says "believed in the warnings and the revelations of God; wherefore, they did hearken unto my words").[39] Nephi's uneven attempts to apply the power of the word have persuaded some while alienating others. For their part, Laman and Lemuel ultimately determine to remain unpersuadable. By the time Nephi seems to fully recognize and repent of his anger, it is too late—his older brothers are too far down the path of nursing theirs. Festering, unreconciled grievance becomes the wedge that splits the family apart. Deep-seated hostility becomes the defining feature in the ensuing decades and centuries of conflict between erstwhile kin who now call themselves "Nephites" and "Lamanites."

EMPHASIZING THE WORD

When the colony formally splits into rival factions, Nephi takes with him the family heirlooms, including the sword of Laban. Such a decision makes sense, given the physical threat that he and his people now face from the Lamanites. But it also means that the Nephites' inheritance includes not only Nephi's visions and prophecies but also his old attraction to and new reliance on the sword. As their prophet, Nephi will teach his people the power of God's promises of deliverance; as their king, he will teach them to protect themselves with military might. Tellingly, one of the first things Nephi does in his new community is to unsheathe Laban's sword—and make copies of it.[40]

Having armed his people with swords, Nephi then builds a temple as the focal point for worship and instruction. With the separation of the Nephites from the Lamanites and the construction of the temple, we see a shift in Nephi's narrative. No longer capable of influencing his older brothers and saving them from their spiritual recalcitrance, Nephi now turns to the future of a group he tenderly refers to as "my people" and begins anew to emphasize the power of the word.[41] For the remainder of his account Nephi increasingly focuses on using loving persuasion to invite people to connect to God and one another. Shadows of the sword continue to linger—he refers vaguely to "wars and contentions with our brethren," and his younger brother Jacob informs us that Nephi "wielded the sword of Laban" in his people's defense—but they remain largely obscure.[42] The narrative of family strife disappears; indeed, almost all narrative disappears. The remainder of Nephi's record is saturated with the word of God—sermons, prophecies, interpretations, testimonies, and pleas, all imbued with love, faith, hope, and promised redemption. Having related his family's tortured past, Nephi turns now to the expectant future. He may have lost Laman and Lemuel and their followers and must now regretfully lead bloody battles with brothers and cousins fighting to kill one another, but he doesn't want to talk about any of that. Instead, Nephi seems determined to chart a different path for his descendants through the power of the word.

It is at this point that Nephi fully inhabits his role as a prophet. He becomes a gentle and patient but also forceful and earnest persuader. He quotes at length the words of Isaiah, selecting passages emphasizing the foolishness of trusting in earthly power dynamics such as military confederacies. His lengthiest quotation of Isaiah begins with the earlier prophet's vision of a future age when the people "shall beat their swords into plowshares, and their spears into pruning-hooks—nation shall not lift up sword against nation, neither shall they learn war any more."[43] Having seen in vision that a resurrected Christ will appear to his and his brothers' war-consumed descendants, Nephi prophesies that "he shall heal them, and they shall have peace with him."[44] He insists on the universality of God's love—"all are alike unto God," and "he inviteth them all to come unto him and partake of his goodness."[45] Nephi clearly longs to model this inclusive love—"I have charity for my people. . . . I have charity for the Jew. . . . I also have charity for the Gentiles."[46]

But notice who is missing from this list. Nephi is curiously silent on the question of whether his love extends so far as to include the Lamanites. Perhaps the inclusion of his estranged extended family members is implied by the expansive theology Nephi has laid out, including his hope that "many of us, if not all, may be saved."[47] But while he talks about the redemption of future generations of Lamanites, Nephi does not include their parents in the circle of his love. Perhaps the wounds of the family's violent rupture were still too raw, or perhaps the anguish of knowing his descendants would eventually be destroyed by the Lamanites was too exquisite. Whatever the reason, Nephi never utters the words, "I also have charity for the Lamanite." Though Nephi gestures in that direction and focuses his people on the transformative gospel of Jesus Christ, that level of Christian enemy-love would remain a project left to later generations to fully realize.[48]

AN AMBIVALENT LEGACY

The sword cast a long shadow, not only over the history of Lehi's family but also over the Nephites' prophetic imagination. Despite Nephi's efforts to focus his people on the persuasive power of the word, many of his descendants gravitated to the temptation of the sword. Over time, what began as a sibling rivalry is transformed into a deep-seated identity conflict characterized with scapegoating, stereotyping, dehumanization, and recriminations. As literary scholar Regina Schwartz has noted, the foundation of such conflict is an "act of distinguishing and separating from others, of boundary marking and line drawing." Once a different group has been demarcated as the "other"—a process that culminated when the two branches of Lehi's family separated and took on distinguishing names and identities—then whatever rhetorical or symbolic violence was used to separate "them" from "us" can be "literalized" into physical violence.[49] At that point, as author Amin Maalouf writes, "whatever happens 'the others' will have deserved it. 'We' can remember quite literally 'all they have made us suffer' since time immemorial: all the crimes, all the extortion, all the humiliations and fears, complete with names and dates and statistics."[50] Indeed, the often astounding and exact casualty numbers that Nephite record keepers include in their accounts of their battles can be understood as not only a testament to the human cost of the "continual round of murder and bloodshed" that characterizes Lehite history, but also a way of keeping score for their posterity—and modern readers—to help them remember the Lamanites' violent depravity.[51]

Those who inherit and extend Nephi's record—referred to as the "small plates"—seem to struggle between their longing for the word and the seductive power of the sword. When Nephi's younger brother Jacob assumes the spiritual leadership of the fledgling community, he recognizes that the Nephites, only one generation separated from the Lamanites, have already been infected with a spiritually dangerous attitude of moral and racial superiority, which he tries valiantly to address and correct. However, even Jacob cannot fully escape the divisive dynamic. While consciously referring to the Lamanites as "brethren," he also reinforces his people's emergent stereotypes of the "filthy" and "cursed" Lamanites and later records that all attempts to "reclaim and restore the Lamanites" were "vain" because "they delighted in wars and bloodshed, and they had an eternal hatred against us, their brethren. And they sought by the power of their arms to destroy us continually."[52] Jacob's description of his cousins is not entirely wrong, but he simultaneously obscures the larger dynamic. It is true that the Lamanites relied heavily on violence in their multigenerational conflict with the Nephites—yet it is equally true that the Nephites responded largely in kind. Jacob and other Nephite authors impute evil intent to the Lamanites' violence, portraying their own people's warfare as essentially reluctant and defensive and therefore defensible. The Nephites' moral imagination consistently stops short of considering their own culpability in the conflict.

The small plates of Nephi do end with a degree of hope as a new visionary leader, Mosiah I, heads another migration, this time from the ancestral land of Nephi to a new land called Zarahemla.[53] His rule, and especially the reigns of his son Benjamin and grandson Mosiah II, will constitute a spiritual restoration for the Nephites, reintroducing the primacy of the word and establishing at least the possibility of deemphasizing the sword.[54] The seemingly intractable conflict between Nephites and Lamanites would be transformed at least in part when the four sons of Mosiah II courageously and lovingly carry the word rather than the sword to the Lamanites. These missionaries' refusal to accept hardened stereotypes about their enemies, along with the generous response of the Lamanites who received them, produces not only widespread religious conversions but also personal and political reconciliation between former enemies.[55] We explore that remarkable story at greater length in the following chapter.

In their entirety, Nephi's small plates can be read only as a tragedy. The man who first made and etched the plates would have been dismayed by both the way his posterity ultimately treated his record and the cycles of violence that continued after his death. Nephi had moved in a trajectory toward greater reliance on the power of the word to save his people. His descendants, on the other hand, increasingly placed their trust in the sword and experienced a resultant dearth of prophetic vision.[56] Each succeeding author records fewer and fewer revelations (while chronicling frequent wars and conflicts) until the record finally peters out and the plates are placed in the Nephite royal archives, where they appear to do little but gather dust.[57] Mormon says that he discovered the small plates somewhat late in his editorial project but was so taken by the record that he inserted it in a way that it eventually superseded his own edited account.[58] This was a smart editorial decision. Why? Because read carefully, Nephi's account reveals attitudes, behaviors, and patterns that ultimately contributed to the cataclysmic destruction of Mormon's entire civilization—and Nephi's posterity.

Nephi's struggle, and the struggle of his descendants, is one to which any reader can relate. Faced with conflict, do we turn to loving persuasion or angry coercion to resolve our differences? Like Nephi it can be easy to despair of our personal and cultural affinities for anger and violence, to be discouraged with our "wretched" patterns of conflict. But the Book of Mormon testifies that there is another, better way available to us. Despite his repeated bouts of anger toward his recalcitrant brothers, Nephi testified, "I know in whom I have trusted."[59] Nephi's model derived not only from the words of scripture he treasured, but even more so from the incarnate Word himself, the Messiah in whom Nephi so earnestly proclaimed his trust.[60] Nephi's hope, in the end, resided not in the sword he copied but in the words he preached about the Word he emulated.

The sword of Laban is always there, always available. Like the young Nephi, we are easily drawn to its illusory power. But there are real, predictable, and tragic consequences for entering into or otherwise participating in destructive cycles of conflict. As Nephi learned the hard way, power and influence can be *ob*tained in multiple ways, but they can be *main*tained only according to principles that engender mutual trust, assent, and ultimately love. Conflict is inevitable in this life, as Nephi knew all too well. How we respond to that conflict will impact not only our own lives but potentially generations to come.

CHAPTER FOUR

A Theology of Conflict

And I, God, divided the light from the darkness. . . .
And I, God, made the firmament and divided the waters. . . .
And I, God, saw everything that I had made,
and, behold, all things which I had made were very good.
—Moses 2:4, 7, 31

For it must needs be, that there is an opposition in all things.
If not so, . . . righteousness could not be brought to pass.
—2 Nephi 2:11

A theology of peace that endorses the enduring and transformative power of love cannot pretend that conflict and violence are not real. Significantly, Restoration theology does not equate *conflict* with *violence*. Violence is a destructive form of conflict, but not all conflict is destructive. Rather, many if not most forms of conflict are potentially creative, even beautiful and necessary, because conflict is divinely ordained. Conflict is essential to the well-being of the universe in both its physical and moral sense. The better we understand the dynamics of conflict, the better we might shape it toward creative rather than destructive ends.

A positive assessment of conflict may at first seem counterintuitive from a Restoration perspective. After all, Restoration scriptures—like the scriptures of all the monotheistic traditions—are replete with good-evil dualities that shape our human perceptions of conflict, with the assumption that in any conflict one side has to be right and the other wrong. Furthermore, in the Book of Mormon the resurrected Christ specifically taught that "the spirit of contention is not of me, but is of the devil, who is the father of contention."[1] On the other side of the coin, we often assume that peace means unity, or the elimination of difference. Indeed, God admonished the early Latter-day Saint community to "be one; and if ye are not one ye are not mine."[2] Seen through the lens of conflict-as-contention, this would discourage any kind of disagreement and encourage conflict avoidance at all costs. This type of conflict avoidance often leads to passive aggressive attitudes and behaviors.

But Jesus didn't say that all conflict was wrong—only the destructive forms he labeled "contention." As our Creator, he knows better than anyone that the cosmos is full of tensions that are not divided along a good/bad axis. Many essential divisions—day and night, earth and water, male and female, justice and mercy, to name only a few—represent dualities in which *both* entities are inherently good (or at worst neutral). While often complementary, these entities are also mutually exclusive, so that when they engage with each other they can produce tension, even conflict. At the places or moments at which such good or neutral forces meet and clash, new entities or relationships often emerge that are greater or more powerful than the component parts. The conception of biological life, for example, usually requires the meeting of female and male, and the resultant creation is greater than the sum of the constituent parts. Restoration theology not only recognizes oppositional dualities but affirms that the space between or produced by them can be a place of creativity. "By proving contraries," Joseph Smith once observed, "truth is made manifest."[3]

Many conflicts are therefore neither regrettable nor unfortunate. They will not and should not be fully resolved, with the victory of one side over its opposite, or with some form of permanent compromise or synthesis. As the Book of Mormon prophet Lehi proclaimed, some tensions "must needs be"—implying unresolved permanence—or certain desirable things such as goodness, and even life itself, "could not be brought to pass."[4] In this sense, conflict is a necessary aspect of our existence to be embraced and harnessed for its creative capacities rather than avoided or vilified. It is a natural outgrowth of a world that God "divided" and "beautified" for the benefit of his children and then proclaimed to be "very good."[5] Rightly understood and engaged, conflict is one of God's great gifts to humanity.

Unfortunately, the limits of language hamper us. The English language does not have a good word to express positive types of conflict—though it has many synonyms for negative types of conflict—so we will use *creative* and *destructive* as qualifiers. To view all conflict only through the lens of its destructive aspects is to fail to appreciate its creative and regenerative capacities, on both the micro and macro scales. Consequently, one of the tasks of would-be peacebuilders is to learn to harness conflict's creative capacities while also transforming its more destructive forms into conditions in which humans can live together in peace and justice.

IN THE BEGINNING

Division and conflict are inherent in the four Restoration accounts of the Creation, narrated in the books of Genesis,

Moses, and Abraham, as well as in Latter-day Saint temples.[6] All four accounts characterize the initial acts of creation as divisive processes, establishing tension and conflict that perpetuate further creation. Light and darkness, for example, are divided from each other and named "day" and "night." Both are divinely proclaimed to be "good."[7] While complementary (it is impossible to define one without the other), light and darkness are also mutually incompatible (it is impossible to have both simultaneously) and thus exist in perpetual tension. The conflict at the moment when day and night meet creates something else—brilliant displays of color that grace the dawn and evening skies. Likewise, during the Creation, another set of mutually complementary but incompatible elements—water and dry land—are also separated from one another and placed in a relationship of enduring tension. The conflict between these elements becomes the mechanism by which God creates "the mountains, the valleys, the lakes, the rivers, the seas," accomplishing this "in such a way as to give variety" to the earth and "to beautify it and make it suitable for the abode of man."[8] Plants and animals, in their turn, are similarly divided into particular spheres and species. Creation is only completed once the human species is divided into male and female parts. While Adam and Eve are commanded to become "one flesh," thus implying an impulse toward unity, they also clearly represent differentiated beings with their own distinctive identities.[9]

Up to this point in all four narratives, the divisions and tensions produced through the creative process have been declared uniformly "good"—even "very good"—and have involved friction between two positive or neutral elements.[10] The arrival in the Garden of Eden of the great tempter, Satan, introduces a good-evil dynamic for the first time. While Adam initially rebuffs Satan's entreaties to eat the fruit of the tree of knowledge of good and evil, Eve chooses to partake, declaring that it is better for them to become acquainted with the full range of choices.[11] In traditional Christian interpretations, Eve's decision represents a cardinal sin, but in Restoration theology hers is a brave and wise choice to move the world forward through tension and conflict, without which there would be no capacity for the essential exercise of human agency.[12] As the story unfolds, both Adam and Eve articulate divergent "good" desires—he to remain true to God's original command to avoid the fruit, she to further God's plan by introducing fuller agency into the world—but their respective choices are mutually incompatible. If they each pursue their separate good interests, they can no longer remain together and fulfill the commandment to "be fruitful, and multiply, and replenish the earth."[13] Conflict has become crisis.

The way that Adam and Eve engage this first and foundational moment of human conflict is exemplary. Rather than entering a spiral of mutual blame and recrimination, they transform the conflict with love. Motivated by his deep affection for Eve and his desire to continue to pursue a united life with her, Adam joins his wife in partaking of the fruit. She in turn honors his desire for obedience by joining him in offering penitential sacrifices to God.[14] Together they enter a fallen world that remains perpetually divided in both good-good and good-evil tensions. Now realizing the productive capacity of divided identities, rather than naively assuming they are created identically, Eve and Adam have children. What has historically been lamented as the downfall of humans from their idyllic state of nature is reframed in the Restoration as a fortunate fall, even a fall forward, toward the realization of full human potential.[15] Together Eve and Adam model how difference poses real challenges but, engaged constructively and in love for the other, such conflict becomes a source of endless and life-giving creativity.

CREATIVE AND DESTRUCTIVE CONFLICT

Not all approaches to conflict are creative. When conflict is engaged with anger or out of fear or greed or by employing intimidation or violence, it will usually be destructive. When conflict is engaged with love and by employing principles of faith, trust, and compassion, it is more likely (though not certain) to be creative. Of course, even destructive conflicts can lead to positive outcomes, and creative tension can have negative, unanticipated consequences. Nevertheless, when we engage conflict lovingly it is more likely to be creative, and when we engage conflict selfishly or fearfully it is more likely to be destructive. One of the key lessons to learn in mortality is how to engage conflict creatively.

When the resurrected Christ warned his disciples in the Book of Mormon against "anger" and instructed that "there shall be no disputations among you, as there have hitherto been," he seemed particularly concerned about the *nature* of their conflict. Before his appearance, the disciples, or perhaps the people more generally, had apparently been engaged in vigorous disputes about the rite of baptism. Rather than issuing a general prohibition against all forms of disagreement, Jesus chided them for manufacturing points of division when none need exist. Counseling them to seek unity in doctrinal essentials, and laying out a remarkably sparse list of those essentials—love, faith, repentance, and baptism—Jesus seemed most concerned that they had engaged their disagreements with anger: "Behold, this is not my doctrine, to stir up the hearts of men with anger, one against another; but this is my doctrine, that such things should be done away."[16]

Contention, then, is not simply holding different opinions or seeing the world in different ways, but rather engaging that difference in a spirit of anger. At their best, religious and political leaders have urged their listeners to learn how to disagree without being disagreeable.[17] Unfortunately, our modern world, with its brash popular entertainment and estranging political cultures, neither provides many healthy role models nor highlights the ones that do exist. Television, talk radio, and social media constantly reinforce anger in our conflicts rather than engaging them with sanity and reason, let alone with love and forgiveness. Consequently, it is easy for many people to equate disagreement and conflict with anger and contention. A conflict engaged in a spirit of love, however, fosters dynamic creativity. Note this description of righteous unity among the Nephites after Christ's visit and instruction: "And it came to pass that there was no contention in the land, *because of the love of God* which did dwell in the hearts of the people."[18] The presence of love, rather than an absence of difference, was the key.

Scripture includes many illustrations of creative conflict. One prominent example comes from the first generation of Christians. Peter had received a revelation instructing him to welcome Gentiles into the church on equal terms with Jewish converts. For a variety of reasons, however, he continued to marginalize and avoid association with these Gentile converts, especially when he was in Jerusalem. Upon seeing this incongruence, Paul sharply reproved Peter for his "hypocrisy." Though unyielding in his commitment to truth, Paul also maintained love and respect for the "pillars" (or leaders) of the church in Jerusalem, even—or especially—when he knew they were wrong.[19] Christianity would emerge out of this tension between law and grace, God's ancient covenant and the adoption of new Israel, as articulated by strong and diverse personalities. The conflict between Paul and Peter teaches that inevitable and necessary tensions that exist even among the followers of God should be engaged with love, trust, and forgiveness—an ideal toward which we often strive but too rarely achieve.

CYCLES OF CONFLICT

All forms of conflict—from the most creative to the most destructive—occur in predictable cycles.[20] At the heart of each cycle is the establishment and maintenance of boundaries. Conflict is engaged when individuals or entire groups cross those boundaries, evoking some form of resistance to the encroachment. A subcycle of responses and counterresponses often emerges, usually with an element of escalation as each side seeks to strengthen its position. This subcycle may continue indefinitely, or it may eventually lead to some degree of surrender by one or both sides, at which point either the old boundary is reinforced or a new boundary is established, and the cycle begins anew.

CYCLES OF CONFLICT

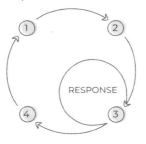

1. DEMARCATION
   drawing boundaries

2. ENCROACHMENT
   crossing boundaries

3. RESISTANCE
   pushing back

4. SURRENDER
   giving in

Words such as *encroachment* and *resistance* often carry negative connotations, and the notion of *surrender* can be particularly galling to some people, from libertarians to feminists, because of the myriad ways it has been used as an excuse for abuse. But similar to creative and destructive forms of conflict in general, each of the individual steps of the cycle can be implemented in both positive and negative ways. For example, the principle of spiritual surrender—the total submission of one's heart and soul to God—is the lofty goal of many religious traditions, including Islam (which is the Arabic word for "submission" or "surrender") and Christianity, as modeled by Jesus's prayer in the Garden of Gethsemane: "Father, if thou be willing, remove this cup from me: nevertheless not my will, but thine, be done."[21] The nature of conflict, with its attendant subelements, is often thus more a matter of *how* it is engaged, which we have at least some control over, rather than *whether* it occurs, which we often do not have control over.

Conflict is inevitable in human relationships because we live in a crowded, diverse world where our own personal and group boundaries cannot be maintained without encroachment by others. The moment of encroachment raises a series of questions that are simultaneously moral and strategic: How will I (or you or we or them) demarcate this boundary? How will I respond to the boundary you are drawing for me? Will I cross it? What will I do if you encroach? Will I resist or surrender? Most importantly, *how* will I approach each step? With love, trust, forgiveness, and selflessness? Or with fear, deceit, anger, and selfishness? Our choices will often (though not always) determine whether the conflict will tend toward a creative or destructive dynamic. Even inaction is a decision with consequences; as the band Rush sings, "If you choose not to decide, you still have made a choice."[22] And every choice regarding how we engage conflict has moral dimensions. This principle was eloquently expressed by John Paul Lederach, a prominent peacebuilder and originator of the conflict transformation paradigm:

> It is useful to ask what exactly is meant by the phrase *constructive social change*. . . . It might best be understood with the metaphor of a continental divide. Such a divide defines how water

flows: On one side, the water flows toward a shore on the far reaches of the continent; on the other side of the divide, it flows toward the opposite shore. In social conflict these two distant shores are fear and love. . . . The question at each moment of violent conflict and its sustained cycle is this: Which way will the water flow that defines our relationship, toward the shore of fear or that of love?

When the water flows toward fear, the relationship is defined by recrimination and blame, self-justification and protection, violence and the desire for victory over the other. When the water flows toward love, it is defined by openness and accountability, self-reflection and vulnerability, mutual respect, dignity, and the proactive engagement of the other.[23]

Lederach's image of the continental watershed is a useful tool in understanding the range of moral options open to us in our conflicts. Our responses are rarely pure, but they do tend to pull us more to one slope than the other.

CHOICE CONTINUUM

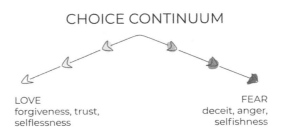

LOVE	FEAR
forgiveness, trust, selflessness	deceit, anger, selfishness

When our decisions in conflict tend toward love, forgiveness, and selflessness, the cycle is more likely to move in the direction of the creative conflict Martin Luther King Jr. described as the "constructive, nonviolent tension which is necessary for growth."[24] But when we are primarily motivated by fear, anger, or selfishness, the conflict is more likely to move in destructive directions. Spurred by such negative emotions, demarcation becomes a form of disconnection, segregation, and marginalization; encroachment is more likely than not to be an act of violation; resistance almost always becomes some form of violence, whether physical or emotional; and surrender usually represents defeat and subjugation.

When trapped in a destructive spiral, we use the negative choices of our opponents, whether real or perceived, to justify our own behavior. Philosopher Terry Warner has referred to this phenomenon as "mutually provocative collusion," in which both parties to a conflict engage in processes of self-deception that permit us to believe that our violent actions are warranted, even necessary, to "fix" or "solve" a destructive cycle.[25] Blind to our own contributions to the conflict, we characterize the other side as unjust aggressors and ourselves as just defenders. *Their* violence is unnecessary and evil, while *ours* is requisite and righteous.[26] In the process of our destructive choices we often entertain a fantasy of absolute victory—a triumph so total in its scope that our opponents are swept from the field of battle,

DESTRUCTIVE CHOICES

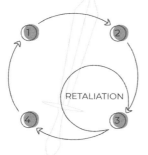

1. DEMARCATION
   unilaterally or deceptively

2. ENCROACHMENT
   ignorantly or greedily

3. RESISTANCE
   coercively or violently

4. SURRENDER
   fearfully or angrily

permanently subdued, or eliminated altogether. This represents a linear perception of conflict in which all tensions have a beginning (an original act of unjust aggression) and a potentially glorious conclusion (when just defenders prevail and vanquish evil). But such two-dimensional, linear perceptions are usually just that—myths and illusions that fail to recognize the complexities of conflict and our own complicity, let alone the humanity of the other party or parties.

CASE STUDY: LAMANITES AND NEPHITES

Destructive cycles of conflict are on full display in the Book of Mormon. We have already seen how the tragic family schism between the Nephites and Lamanites sparked generations of bloodshed. At the center of the tension were different levels of faithfulness to God's commandments and competing perspectives regarding the proper establishment and maintenance of family boundaries, particularly distinctions regarding who had rights to leadership and property. On the one hand we have what historian Richard Bushman has labeled "the Lamanite view of Book of Mormon history," which was predicated on the idea that Laman and Lemuel were "robbed" of their natural rights by Nephi.[27] As the eldest son of the family patriarch Lehi, Laman claimed a right to rule, and he expected deference from his younger brothers. Consequently, Laman interpreted Nephi's visions not as a divine gift but rather as a threatening encroachment to his birthright.[28]

Nephi, on the other hand, believed he had been granted a divine right to lead based on his greater faithfulness to God's commandments—not to mention his successful leadership in securing the brass plates, obtaining food in the wilderness, and building the ship that carried the group to the promised land. Since the account we have was written many years after the events it narrates, how much Nephi publicly asserted his claim to rule while his father was still alive is difficult to tell. But there is some indication that the threat to Laman's birthright was more perceived than real. Lehi certainly downplayed the encroachment, telling his oldest sons, "Ye have accused him that he sought power and authority over you; but I know that he hath not sought for power nor authority over you, but he hath sought the glory of God, and your own eternal welfare." Lehi's words conveyed a mixed message, paradoxically declaring that if the older brothers would follow Nephi they would keep Lehi's "first blessing" of family leadership. "But if ye will not hearken unto him," he warned, "I take away my first blessing, yea, even my blessing, and it shall rest upon him."[29] For his part, Nephi clearly came to believe that the mantle of leadership had bypassed his older brothers and rested on him.

The strength of Lehi and Sariah's parental influence, in addition to some timely divine interventions, kept the conflict cycle from becoming lethal during their lifetimes. But after the parents' deaths, the older brothers plotted murder to thwart Nephi's encroachment on the right "to rule over this people," which they believed "belongs unto us."[30] Laman and Lemuel were indulging the fantasy of absolute victory, consoling themselves with the thought that if they could simply eliminate their upstart brother, the family conflict would be resolved. (This has echoes, of course, of numerous conflicts between brothers in the Bible, including Cain and Abel, Jacob and Esau, and the sons of Jacob.) The larger Book of Mormon narrative presents this line of reasoning as suspect for many reasons, not least because rather than solving the problem, targeted killing and assassinations generally plunge a conflict into deeper and more entrenched cycles of retributive violence. The book of Ether, for instance, demonstrates how such tactics sent the Jaredite civilization reeling into genocidal warfare and subsequent oblivion.

Nephi's response to his brothers' aggression was to flee with his immediate family and followers. Even this act of surrendering the family's "land of inheritance" to his brothers, however, did not solve the conflict. Instead, the removal of Nephi and his followers to another location, while forestalling immediate violence, simply established new physical and psychological boundaries. The two groups began to distinguish themselves by ethnic titles and by religion. Nephi's departure represented a surrender to Laman and Lemuel's aggression and a demarcation of new boundaries, but it was perceived by Laman and Lemuel as a further encroachment. By taking the brass plates, the sword of Laban, and the Liahona—items he believed he had earned through his obedience—Nephi only provoked greater resentment from his elder brothers, who clearly interpreted his actions as a theft of their inheritance.[31]

Over time, what started as personal conflict between brothers became a deeply embedded societal antagonism that would stretch over centuries. The personal perceptions of the two brothers became entrenched as social stereotypes for their descendants. Even centuries later, Lamanites perceived Nephites as "sons of a liar," a people constantly trying to "rob us of our property."[32] Any disenchanted or manipulative person who wanted to "stir up the Lamanites to anger against the Nephites" simply had to dust off these familiar tropes and rehearse the ancient history of Nephi's supposed theft and deception.[33] This logic often led to fantasies of absolute victory in which the Nephites would admit that Nephi and all his descendants had been completely wrong all along and would then make restitution by subjecting themselves "to be governed by those to whom the government doth rightly belong." Failing that, they would be completely annihilated. This destructive cycle of conflict was aptly dubbed by one of its chief proponents "a war which shall be eternal."[34]

However, it takes two to tango. In order for the destructive cycle to be indefinitely perpetuated, the Lamanites needed willing dance partners. Too often they found eager participants among the Nephites, who frequently trafficked in similar forms of stereotyping. Laman and Lemuel's inclination to be stiff-necked and lazy, even would-be "murderers," was legendary in Nephite culture and came to be considered the defining characteristic of all their descendants.[35] Nephites could be harsh toward the Lamanites, whom they considered to be "wild" and "ferocious," a "blood-thirsty people, full of idolatry and filthiness," and having an inherently "evil nature."[36] As with the Lamanites, such Nephite attitudes could lead to fantasies of absolute victory, whereby the Lamanite threat would be permanently eliminated. "Let us take up arms against them," some Nephites preemptively proposed, "that we destroy them and their iniquity out of the land, lest they overrun us and destroy us."[37]

The Book of Mormon provides ample testimony that violence provides the seeds for its own perpetuation, even if the conflict cycle takes years to play out. One of the primary heroes of the narrative is the Nephite military captain Moroni. At one point he makes a tactical decision to drive out a group of Lamanites who were living in the wilderness east of Nephite land but who appear not to have provided any particular provocation for this ethnic cleansing. From a narrow military perspective, the decision has a compelling logic—"cut[ting] off all the strongholds of the Lamanites in the east wilderness" and "fortifying the line between the Nephites and the Lamanites." Moroni then establishes new Nephite communities in the formerly occupied Lamanite lands and names those settlements after Nephite political leaders and military commanders, thus producing new facts on the ground. However, this strategy of displacement and settler colonialism soon provides a pretext for the Lamanites' (admittedly depraved) leader, Amalickiah, to rile his subjects to go again to war against the Nephites. The Lamanites direct their first attacks toward the new Nephite settlements, presumably in what they consider a justified act of reconquest to drive out the invaders and occupiers of their native land.[38] Violence can—and often does—rebound on itself.

Destructive cycles of conflict are all around us, from the personal to the geopolitical. The divide in Islam between Shia and Sunni has simmered (and occasionally exploded) for nearly fourteen centuries and, similar to the Nephite-Lamanite divide, originated in a dispute over rights of succession. Palestinians and Israelis have formally struggled over the Holy Land for a century or centuries, depending on who tells the story. Some trace the dispute back millennia to the time of Abraham and the question of whether Ishmael or Isaac was the birthright son. The war and genocide in the Balkans was fueled by grievances that people said they felt even hundreds of years after the initial conflict.[39] Nor is this dynamic characteristic of only large-scale armed conflicts. Family feuds, workplace tensions, domestic abuse—all exhibit the same cyclical elements of demarcation, encroachment, resistance, and surrender, engaged in fear or anger or selfishness. As with the Nephites and Lamanites, in most of our destructive conflicts we use the "facts" of history—whether broadcasting them over the airwaves or speaking them across the dinner table—as bludgeons to air our grievances, assert our dominance, and justify our violent resistance to the "aggression" (real or perceived) of our opponents.

CREATIVE CONFLICT

When we are caught in cycles of destructive conflict—whether as societies or as individuals—we can often feel constrained, as if we have no other options than to either surrender in defeat or resist our opponents with mutual or greater aggression.

However, there are always other choices. If Restoration theology stresses anything, it is the ability of a person to make meaningful choices in virtually any context. Responding to the call of Christ, we can move to the other side of the great continental watershed of motivations. Rather than letting our choices flow into oceans of fear and anger, Jesus invites us to embark on the waters of love and trust. "God hath not given us the spirit of fear," the New Testament affirms, "but of power, and of love, and of a sound mind."[40]

Creative options are always open to us, regardless of the choices others are making. Just because our opponents may be choosing a path that leads to destructive engagement does not mean we are constrained to respond in kind. Although our range of choices may be limited by a variety of circumstances, we can seek forms of creative rather than destructive engagement. And we can make more creative choices at any point in a cycle of conflict. We can choose to create boundaries through mutual decisions and with honesty and clarity. We can choose to encroach, when encroachment is necessary, with faith, trust, and forgiveness. When we need to resist, we can do it with charity and compassion and try to engage cycles of creative reciprocation, whereby we show respect even as we push against one another. When surrender is required, we can submit out of a sense of love, trust, or forgiveness—seeking to transform enemies into friends, aiming for conversion rather than merely admitting defeat. Achieving fully pure motives is perhaps beyond our mortal capacity, but it is territory toward which Christ invites us to continually strive. When we act creatively, however haltingly or imperfectly or mixed with other motives, we open the possibility that our conflict might ultimately become constructive. We can change the nature of conflict, or at least nudge it in more creative directions.[41]

CREATIVE CHOICES

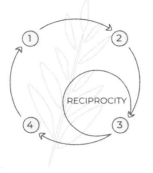

1. DEMARCATION
   mutually and honestly

2. ENCROACHMENT
   with trust and forgiveness

3. RESISTANCE
   with love and compassion

4. SURRENDER
   with charity and faith

At its core, creative conflict is about a recognition of the full humanity of others and a love born out of the realization that we are all children of God. This love is a gift from God, available for the asking, "bestowed upon all who are true followers of his Son, Jesus Christ."[42] This love is transforming—an act of grace, a natural outgrowth of trust in Christ's atonement. It liberates and empowers people, not to "repay anyone evil for evil," but rather to "bless those who persecute you . . . and do not curse them," to "live peaceably with all," and ultimately to "overcome evil with good."[43]

CASE STUDY: THE SONS OF MOSIAH AND LAMANITE CONVERTS

A dynamic of creative conflict can be clearly seen in the Book of Mormon story of the sons of King Mosiah II—Ammon, Aaron, Omner, and Himni. Characterized early in their lives as "the very vilest of sinners," the sons of Mosiah initially engaged in destructive conflict with their father and their God—"seeking to destroy the church," "stealing away the hearts of the people," and "causing much dissension."[44] Their destructive conflict was transformed by a dramatic act of loving encroachment (or resistance) in the form of an angelic reprimand. With a voice that shook the earth, the angel brought Mosiah's four sons a message of stern but redemptive love.[45] Shaken from their destructive behavior by this encounter, the sons of Mosiah opened their hearts to a new dynamic. "Who could have supposed," they later recalled, "that our God would have been so merciful as to have snatched us from our awful, sinful, and polluted state?"[46] Filled with gratitude for God's mercy to them, they worked to repair the damage they had inflicted among their fellow Nephites. Their repentance entailed a literal reversal of the destructive cycle of conflict they had so zealously pursued up to the moment of the angel's appearance.

Having engaged in reconciliation among their own people, the sons of Mosiah then turned their energies toward transforming the long-standing conflict with their enemies. Centuries of destructive conflict had entrenched the Nephites' boundaries with the Lamanites, with any violation constituting a potential act of war. The young princes' decision to "impart the word of God to their brethren, the Lamanites" therefore constituted a deliberate act of physical and political encroachment. Moreover, they also encroached on cultural and religious territory by promoting a historical and spiritual narrative about Nephite stewardship of true religion that challenged Lamanite perceptions of history and the cosmos. The sons of Mosiah thus crossed multiple boundaries, but with extraordinary faith, courage, and love. They hoped that "perhaps they might cure [the Lamanites] of their hatred towards the Nephites, . . . that they might become friendly to one another, and that there should be no more contentions."[47]

Their encroachment into Lamanite territory was immediately met with suspicion, resistance, imprisonment, and even the threat of death. This was especially true when their encroachment was characterized by argument and debate. Aaron and his companion Muloki, for example, initially "contend[ed] with many about the word," but their Lamanite audience predictably "harden[ed] their hearts," and the missionaries subsequently found themselves languishing in a Lamanite prison.[48]

By way of contrast, Ammon, either by accident or profound spiritual insight, engaged the conflict according to divine principles of power and influence—offering not verbal contention but rather surrender and selfless service to his traditional enemies. The Lamanites he engaged, most notably King Lamoni, were intrigued by this young Nephite who acted in such unpredictable ways. Here was the son of a king, who disavowed political power and privilege in exchange for a life of menial service among his enemies—a prince *choosing* to be a stable hand. His encroachment was of an entirely different order than the type the Lamanites had come to expect from Nephites. Of course, Ammon was not entirely immune to the allure of the sword (and the sling), which he wielded dramatically in defending the king's flocks from marauding bandits, killing seven and literally dis-arming many more. But his resort to violence, while expedient and immediately successful, also nearly undid whatever gains it had apparently achieved. The brother of one of the robbers Ammon killed would have slain the missionary in retribution were it not for divine intervention. Readers often remember Ammon's dramatic display of violence, but the account emphasizes that it was primarily his *service* and *love*, not his acumen with the weapons of war, that opened King Lamoni's door—and heart—for an even more audacious encroachment of the Nephites' religion and history, which Lamoni and many others eventually surrendered to.[49]

This dynamic of creative conflict played out with even greater clarity in the story of Lamoni's father, the king of all the Lamanites. When Lamoni and Ammon met the old king on the road, Lamoni's father responded to the audacity of Ammon's encroachment and Lamoni's surrender with predictably destructive behavior, attempting to play out the conflict according to the centuries-old patterns to which he was accustomed. "Whither art thou going," he demanded of his son, "with this Nephite, who is one of the children of a liar?" When Lamoni responded that he not only felt affection for Ammon but also intended to help free his Nephite brethren from prison, the old king responded violently, commanding his son to slay Ammon and drawing his own sword when his son refused. The rationale by which Lamoni's father justified this violence was the ancient complaint that Nephi "robbed our fathers; and now his children are also come amongst us that they may, by their cunning and their lyings, deceive us, that they again may rob us of our property." The king drew his sword, and Ammon drew his. When in the ensuing struggle he was disarmed by the Nephite prince, the old king knew exactly how events would play out. He would surrender and be killed or perhaps held hostage. Ammon, as the descendant of a liar and a robber, would seize his property and right to rule. That the old king anticipated this turn of the cycle was clear in his offer to Ammon: "If thou wilt spare me I will grant unto thee whatsoever thou wilt ask, even to half of the kingdom."[50]

Ammon's failure to play by the standard rules of destructive conflict tilted the dynamic in a different direction. Rather than accepting the king's offer of territorial concessions, he instead presented him with more surprising terms of surrender—that the king free his brethren from prison and allow Lamoni to retain his kingdom and "be not displeased with him." This unanticipated turn of events, and especially the love that Ammon had for his son, left the king "exceedingly astonished."[51] Later when Aaron, now adopting his brother's approach of loving encroachment, offered to be the king's servant, the old man refused the offer and instead invited Aaron to make further encroachments into his cultural and religious beliefs. Why? Because, as the king explained, "I have been somewhat troubled in mind because of the generosity and the greatness of the words of thy brother Ammon."[52] The transformation of an enemy into a friend was underway, thanks to the power of generosity and persuasion. In response to Aaron's teaching, the king confessed that he was willing to "forsake [his] kingdom" and "give away all [his] sins" to obtain the same spiritual knowledge as these missionaries he quite recently considered to be "children of a liar."[53] Both kings' remarkable spiritual surrender was effected by loving, forgiving, creative engagement *in the midst of* a bloody, multigenerational, and seemingly intractable conflict. Ammon and Aaron did not let the destructive choices of either their enemies or their own people determine their choices. They acted out of different motivations, responded in lovingly creative (and surprising) ways, and thereby brought about a seismic transformation of this conflict.

In a fairy-tale ending, all boundaries between the Nephites and Lamanites would subsequently evaporate, and they would all live happily ever after. But the Book of Mormon, with its finger on the pulse of real-world conflict, shows otherwise. The distinctions—and conflict—between the Nephites and the Lamanite converts continued, although the conflict now took on creative rather than destructive dimensions. New boundaries were drawn, but this time through a process of mutual negotiation. Rather than simply merging into Nephite identity and claiming the Nephite name, the Lamanite converts retained their distinctive identity, albeit with a curious new name as the "Anti-Nephi-Lehies."[54] While the Anti-Nephi-Lehies became "friendly with the Nephites" and "open[ed] a correspondence" and even eventually lived among them, they always maintained a level of geographic and cultural distinction. Because of these boundaries, the Anti-Nephi-Lehies existed in perpetual tension—albeit a creative one—with the Nephites.[55] Whereas the Nephites embodied a certain interpretation of righteous living, the Anti-Nephi-Lehies pursued an even more rigorous model of Christian discipleship. Mormon explicitly notes that the Anti-Nephi-Lehies were "distinguished" from other groups, including Nephites, by "their zeal towards God, and also towards men; for they were perfectly honest and upright in all things; and they were firm in the faith of Christ, even unto the end."[56]

Interestingly, Mormon bestows the honorific "firm in the faith of Christ" on only one other person, Captain Moroni. As we will explore in a later chapter, Captain Moroni and most Nephites followed an ethic of justified violence in self-defense. The Anti-Nephi-Lehies, on the other hand, embraced an ethic of sanctifying nonviolent resistance, which we will also explore in some detail in the next chapter. For now, we simply note that by honoring them equally, with what seems to be the greatest praise he can lavish, Mormon promotes both Moroni and the Anti-Nephi-Lehies as exemplars, thus setting up a creative tension in the text regarding how individuals and societies ought to respond to violence and evil in the world. Both approaches can be commendable, even as they are specifically contrasted against each other. The missionary Ammon observes, for example, that the Anti-Nephi-Lehies would "rather sacrifice their lives than even to take the life of their enemy . . . because of their love towards their brethren" and contrasts this with the Nephites who "would take up arms against their brethren" and "would not suffer themselves to be slain." Ammon's celebration of Anti-Nephi-Lehi nonviolence—"has there been so great love in all the land?"—does not necessarily represent a categorical condemnation of Nephite culture.[57] After all, he eventually led his converts to dwell in Nephite land and encouraged them to provide material support for Nephite armies. But it does draw a clear contrast between the two groups, who will not truly become united until after the visit of Jesus Christ more than a century later.

These two approaches—justified self-defense and nonviolence—persisted throughout the ensuing years of Nephite-Lamanite war and led to innovative arrangements. For instance, the Nephites' defensive campaign inspired the Anti-Nephi-Lehies to send their sons into a protracted war with their former Lamanite compatriots. Likewise, the Anti-Nephi-Lehies' deep pacifism and godly love for both friend and foe allowed Captain Moroni to send his Lamanite prisoners of war to live among the Anti-Nephi-Lehies (now called the people of Ammon). There the prisoners joined themselves to this post-Lamanite community and embraced its nonviolent ethic, thus relieving Moroni's armies of the burden of incarcerating large numbers of enemy combatants.[58]

It is tempting to resolve the tension between these two ethics by dismissing Anti-Nephi-Lehite nonviolence as anomalous, unique to their particular circumstances, and thus irrelevant to modern life.[59] However, this is not how the Book of Mormon itself handles the tension. The text extols *both* nonviolence and just warfare, without explicitly resolving any apparent contradictions, and holds them in perpetual tension. If anything, as we shall see, the weight of the endorsement leans toward love and voluntary suffering rather than justified self-defense. But the text itself seems either unconcerned with the contradiction or comfortable embracing the creative tension between the two divergent ethics.

WHICH TYPE OF CONFLICT?

The Book of Mormon thus traces three types of conflict in the dynamic between Nephites, Lamanites, and Anti-Nephi-Lehies. Initially the conflict between Nephites and Lamanites was almost universally negative, pairing destructive choices. For centuries each side used the supposed crimes and violence of the other to justify its own hatred and violence. Both sides engaged in cyclical patterns of self-justified warfare that left thousands of individuals, families, and whole societies shattered. The second type of conflict was between those who made creative choices and those who held to destructive patterns. The sons of Mosiah, and later the Anti-Nephi-Lehies, chose to engage the conflict creatively with unconverted and even violent Lamanites. In the process of responding to anger and hate with confrontational love and forgiveness, they began to nudge the destructive cycle in more constructive directions, resulting in thousands of conversions and intercultural reconciliation with some, while others chose to further entrench their hostility. Finally, the narrative describes a dynamic in which both sides chose creative engagement. When the Anti-Nephi-Lehies moved to Nephite territory and accepted that protection, a spirit of mutual love and acceptance informed a much more healthy and creative tension between the distinct groups.

These patterns of conflict find parallels in our modern world. Over the past century, nonviolent movements around the world—in places as diverse as India, South Africa, Denmark, Poland, Chile, East Germany, and the United States—successfully mobilized the power of creative conflict in order to combat and transform various forms of direct, structural, and cultural violence.[60] Racial segregation in the United States, for example, represented a destructive cycle, with white citizens unilaterally imposing boundaries on African Americans, then brutally enforcing those boundaries with periodic lynchings to remind African Americans not to cross those cultural, political, or geographic lines. (Similar forms of violence were employed against other racial, ethnic, and religious minorities as well.) Some Blacks fought back with violence. Many surrendered in resignation. Both choices, however understandable, perpetuated the destructive conflict. In contrast, the civil rights activists of the 1950s and 1960s, many of whom were motivated by their Christian faith, realized that the way to transform the cycle was through more creative choices. As Martin Luther King Jr. noted:

The ultimate weakness of violence is that it is a descending spiral, begetting the very thing it seeks to destroy. Instead of diminishing evil, it multiplies it. . . . Through violence you may murder the hater, but you do not murder hate. In fact, violence merely increases hate. So it goes. Returning violence for violence multiplies violence, adding deeper darkness to a night already devoid of stars. Darkness cannot drive out darkness; only light can do that. Hate cannot drive out hate; only love can do that.[61]

The moral genius and tactical success of the American civil rights movement came when African Americans began to confront the segregationist system with loving resistance—deliberately crossing unjust boundaries but refusing to strike back against the inevitable violence, to be beaten back into submission, or to hate their oppressors. They endeavored, in King's words, to "create such a crisis and establish such a creative tension" that it would compel the entire community, both Black and White, to confront its destructive tendencies and to repent and make necessary changes.[62] Ultimately King envisioned a "beloved community"—not one where cultural differences were erased or one that was "devoid of interpersonal, group or international conflict," but rather one where such conflicts were engaged with "adversaries cooperating together in a spirit of friendship and goodwill."[63] This is also precisely the dynamic at play when John Paul Lederach and other contemporary peacebuilders speak of "conflict transformation" rather than the more linear notion of "conflict resolution."[64]

King's philosophy corresponds well to the message of the Book of Mormon. Violence never fully overcomes violence. Only decisions to love—as expressed by persons such as the sons of Mosiah and the Anti-Nephi-Lehies, and ultimately by Jesus Christ himself—manage to transform the destructive cycles of conflict that plagued the descendants of Lehi. The message to readers seems clear. Conflict is inevitable, but destructive conflict is a choice. Will we continue to engage our conflicts, both as individuals and as societies, with destructive choices, or will we seek creative alternatives? At times we might actually be justified in responding to violence with violence, but such responses will ultimately never heal or transform our conflicts into opportunities for creative growth. Only love can do that.

CHAPTER FIVE

The Power of Assertive Love

Be not overcome of evil, but overcome evil with good.
—Romans 12:21

*Now when the people saw that [their enemies] were coming
against them they went out to meet them.*
—Alma 24:21

Among the most difficult, if not *the* most difficult, of Jesus's teachings is his injunction to "love your enemies."[1] No command goes against the grain of the "natural man" or our modern social training more sharply, making it both counterintuitive and countercultural.[2] Yet it was considered by the earliest Christians as one of the most defining characteristics of their community. No other commandment of Jesus was repeated more often in the writings of early Christian leaders, leading one New Testament scholar to observe, "Loving one's enemies was the ethical heartbeat of early Christianity."[3]

One reason why loving one's enemies seems so counterintuitive is that it appears "weak"—a call to *passive* suffering and self-sacrifice while letting the evil forces of the world have their way. Yet the exact opposite is true. While loving one's enemies does constitute a willingness to suffer and sacrifice oneself, this Christlike standard actually marshals suffering in the defeat of evil. Enemy-love represents a dynamic and underappreciated form of *active* resistance to anger, hatred, aggression, and violence. The Apostle Paul hinted at this active dynamic when he repeated Jesus's injunction to "bless them which persecute you." He counseled the early saints to "recompense to no man evil for evil" and "avenge not yourselves," but rather "if thine enemy hunger, feed him; if he thirst, give him drink." The overall effect of such enemy-love, Paul promised, is not as the world might predict—to be "overcome of evil"—but rather, unexpectedly, to "overcome evil with good."[4] Paul spoke not of some distant or otherworldly victory. Rather, he attested that good can literally overcome, overwhelm, subdue, neutralize, and defeat the evils of this world—including all forms of violence—here and now.

Assertive love is *both* a spiritual ideal *and* a stronger and more effective method for waging the struggle against injustice. It is principled *and* pragmatic. Nonviolence works because it is right and because it is based on the principles of enduring power established from the foundations of the world. As we will explore in the next chapter, meeting aggressive violence with defensive violence can under certain strict conditions be justified, especially when it is followed by "an increase of love."[5] But the higher, better, and "more excellent way" of Jesus reverses that order—increasing our love *first* instead of last.[6] In fact, increased love suffuses the entire dynamic of Christian nonviolent resistance from first to last. As exemplified consistently by Jesus from the Council in Heaven to the garden and the cross, love is the essential tool in overcoming evil. And, as with any tool, nonviolent love becomes more effective the better we understand how it works and the more we practice its application.

THE "GODLIKE" ANTI-NEPHI-LEHIES

Perhaps the best way to understand the principles by which nonviolent love works is to observe it in action. The Book of Mormon contains some remarkable examples of overcoming evil with good, but one in particular stands out. As one Latter-day Saint commentator observed, the story of the Anti-Nephi-Lehies demonstrates that "the doctrine of non-resistance [or nonviolent resistance], which our Lord and his apostles proclaimed, when carried out in practice, even in the face of death, is a conquering, regenerating, irresistible force."[7]

The story begins with events we have already explored—the decision of the sons of Mosiah to engage a violent cycle of conflict with active and assertive love, which transforms the centuries-old conflict between Nephites and Lamanites into a new dynamic that is holy, healing, and creative. As some Lamanites willingly surrender to the influence of these young men's love, they experience a fundamental conversion in their attitude toward God and the Nephite people. Then the students become the masters, embracing enemy-love to such a degree that it surpasses even the love of their teachers. As Ammon observes of the converted Lamanites, "Has there been so great love in all the land? . . . Nay, there has not."[8]

The story of the Anti-Nephi-Lehies, perhaps better than any example in sacred scripture save the atonement of Christ, captures the inherent power of nonviolently loving our enemies. Conflict arises when the unconverted Lamanites sense that the converts represent a fundamental threat to their identity and culture—a threat that is not imaginary since the Anti-Nephi-Lehies have abandoned the "traditions of their fathers" along with other cultural markers, including the very name "Lamanite." The Lamanites marshal their military forces to eliminate this threat and secure an absolute victory over the converts, whom the Lamanites consider to be traitors. But the Anti-Nephi-Lehies refuse to meet violence with violence. In one of the Book of Mormon's most memorable scenes, they bury their weapons of war deep in the earth, "as a testimony to our God . . . that we have not stained our swords in the blood of our brethren since he imparted his word unto us and has made us clean."[9]

To be sure, one of the motivations for this unusual voluntary disarmament was a desire to renounce a violent past—to offer permanent contrition for "many sins and murders" out of a "fear to sin" again.[10] But this was not the only motivation for the Anti-Nephi-Lehies' behavior. When he reflects on the converts' action, Ammon doesn't mention any violent past or fear of sin, but rather attributes their decision only to love for their attackers: "For behold, they had rather sacrifice their lives than even to take the life of their enemy; and they have buried their weapons of war deep in the earth, because of their love towards their brethren."[11] Ammon uses two terms—*enemies* and *brethren*—to refer to the unconverted Lamanites. But the Anti-Nephi-Lehies always refer to their attackers as "brethren"—the same term they apply to each other and to the sons of Mosiah.[12] They steadfastly refuse to be alienated even from their aggressors. They have wholeheartedly accepted the Christian gospel preached to them by the Nephites, but they reject the cultural violence of Nephite stereotypes regarding Lamanite depravity; in this regard they have come to understand Christianity even better than the Nephites themselves. At the heart of Jesus's ethic is the affirmation that we are all sisters and brothers, children of God, so the designation "enemy" may be temporarily useful to describe a pattern of behavior but is never fundamentally correct in referring to a person's core identity.

What happens next is easy to overlook. When the Lamanite army attacks, the Anti-Nephi-Lehies, rather than sitting passively and waiting to be slaughtered, go "out to meet them." This is assertive love—proactive, even confrontational, and anything but passive or weak. Similar to the Chinese man who stood in front of the tanks approaching Tiananmen Square in 1989, the Anti-Nephi-Lehies place their bodies between their attackers and their kin. Similar to the nonviolent Egyptian revolutionaries facing police in Tahrir Square in 2011, they prostrate themselves to pray in front of those who wielded violent weapons. Similar to Gandhi's activists, who nonviolently stormed the Dharasana Salt Works in 1930, they gladly and willingly receive the brutal blows of their "brethren" without raising a hand.[13] As Mormon puts it, "rather than shed the blood of their brethren they would give up their own lives."[14] Latter-day Saint painter Minerva Teichert captured the moment when they courageously prepared to absorb

Minerva Teichert (1888–1976), *Christian Converts*, 1949–1951, oil on board, 36 x 48 inches. Brigham Young University Museum of Art, 1969.

the oncoming violence. In a telling detail, Teichert painted the palm of an expectant martyr with a spot of red. This mark subtly yet vividly connects the Anti-Nephi-Lehies' willingness to endure their brethren's violence with Christ's similar nonviolent self-sacrifice. In so doing, these "Christian converts," as Teichert aptly labels them, anticipated in a real sense Jesus's invitation to follow him to the cross.[15]

The Lamanite attackers descend with ferocious violence, slaughtering more than a thousand of the Anti-Nephi-Lehies. But here the story takes its most extraordinary and yet, as we shall later see, predictable turn. When the attackers realize "that their brethren would not flee from the sword, neither would they turn aside to the right hand or to the left"—in other words, when they realize that their violence is neither intimidating nor returned in kind—they are stunned. With their brutality stripped bare, these Lamanites do something that at first seems to make no sense— they stop the killing. Left exposed in their unjust aggression, and touched by their brethren who "praised God even in the very act of perishing under the sword," many of the attackers feel "stung for the murders which they had committed." Throwing their weapons to the ground, they also prostrate themselves, "even as their brethren, relying upon the mercies of those whose arms were lifted to slay them." In his prophetic narration, Mormon reports that the slain martyrs were obviously saved in heaven. Furthermore, "the people of God" were joined in salvation by a thousand-plus attacking Lamanites who were convicted of their own sins and converted by the Anti-Nephi-Lehies' assertive and nonviolent enemy-love.[16]

However impressive, the numbers are less important than the principles revealed in this remarkable story. Crucially, the Anti-Nephi-Lehies' "love your enemies" method proved to be an effective form of self-defense. *It worked.* The attackers stopped. The majority of the people—the women, the children, the old and infirm—were shielded from the impending violence. The Anti-Nephi-Lehies did not receive another attack for at least four years—only one year less than the longest peace interval that Captain Moroni was able to secure through his military campaigns (and most of the time, his intervals were much smaller). Furthermore, the Anti-Nephi-Lehies' tactic, if we can call it that, depleted the opposing forces by more than a thousand men—not through death, wounding, capture, or desertion, but rather through conversion. Finally, although 1,005 deaths sounds (and is) horrific, by Book of Mormon battle standards this loss of life is relatively low. Captain Moroni typically lost thousands of men in his violent battles, and the death tolls escalated over prolonged years of war.[17] Furthermore, if the Anti-Nephi-Lehies had resorted to the sword, the total number of deaths (their own plus their attackers) would likely have been much higher and the resultant state of affairs far more grim.

Of course, effectiveness is not the only or even the most important metric by which the nonviolent ethic of Jesus should be judged. The Anti-Nephi-Lehies probably did not choose the path of nonviolent enemy-love for strategic reasons. Rather, their choice to love in the face of violence flowed naturally from their converted hearts—they *actually* loved those who hated and abused them. It was the right thing to do, especially for a people who had so completely turned their lives over to God. Yet we shouldn't overlook the fact that their genuine love was both ethical and effective. What's more, the Anti-Nephi-Lehies pursued this course not simply as a matter of personal morality, but also as a public and societal ethic. As such, their story offers both spiritual lessons *and* a very real socio-political alternative. For example, as the hounds of war began to howl in Europe in 1939, the official Church Sunday School manual encouraged readers to follow the Anti-Nephi-Lehies'—and Jesus's—example:

If one should question the wisdom of the decision of the people of Anti-Nephi-Lehi made on the occasion of this lesson, let him remember that they did as a nation what Jesus did as an individual when he gave his life for mankind. . . . It would have been "human" for him to have saved his life and for the [Anti-Nephi-Lehies] to have resisted the attempts of their brethren to destroy them, but there was something "godlike" in the decision of both Jesus and the [Anti-Nephi-Lehies] to sacrifice their mortal existence that the standards of righteousness might be preserved.[18]

Following the Second World War, with the destructiveness of war in plain hindsight, another Church manual reiterated a similar point: "Many have said [this nonviolent ethic of Jesus] cannot be lived, but here in the Book of Mormon it is put into life by a large mass of people. . . . Truly these people are an inspiration to us today, who are brought up on revenge and retaliation."[19]

THE FIRE OF VIOLENCE

History, especially in the past century, has demonstrated that the story of the Anti-Nephi-Lehies is incredible but not singular. Indeed, rather than being exceptional, the operative dynamics are both understandable and predictable. Love, like any force in the universe, operates according to certain principles. Similar to the forces of gravity or electricity, the dynamics of love can at first seem mysterious, even magical or supernatural, until we can name and describe them. Once we articulate the principles by which any force operates, we can begin to predict its results and, more importantly, begin to harness its energies. French philosopher and Catholic theologian Pierre Teilhard de Chardin predicted this would eventually happen with love: "Some day, after we have mastered space, the winds, the waves, the tides, and gravity, we will harness for God the energies of love. And then, for the second time in the history of the world, man will have discovered fire."[20]

Chardin's image of fire is an apt metaphor insofar as love—like fire—can warm, protect, enliven, and give light. Yet fire can also be a terribly destructive force. Before fire's power can be channeled for positive ends, its negative potential needs to be neutralized and transformed. In this respect fire is also an apt metaphor for violence. Although our ultimate goal is positive peace—a systematic social organization built on love's warming, protecting, enlivening fire—to get there we have to first understand the principles that contribute to negative peace, or the cessation of violence and its fiery destructive capacity.

Fire needs three elements to survive—heat, fuel, and oxygen. Fighting a destructive fire involves trying to cool the heat, starve the fuel, or smother the oxygen. Achieve any one of these things and the fire will be extinguished. It is technically possible to achieve some of these aims with a second fire—to fight fire with fire, as the saying goes—using another, controlled blaze to consume a fuel source or suck oxygen so it isn't available to the original flames. But such techniques are extremely dangerous and carry the potential of either feeding the original fire or spiraling out of control and creating another crisis, thus multiplying rather than reducing the devastation. Other agents are both more effective and less risky. Water, for example, is especially effective in fighting many types of fires because if it is applied well and in the right quantity it can simultaneously achieve all three goals—reducing heat, separating flames from their fuel source, and smothering their oxygen supply.

Similar to fire, violence needs three elements to survive: distance, a rationale, and a predictable response. Eliminating any or all of these elements will extinguish violence and help create the conditions of negative peace that can then allow for the cultivation of positive peace.

DISTANCE

Violence needs distance, meaning a disconnection between those who use violence and the people who are their targets. The distance might be physical, but more crucially it entails a psychological or emotional dissociation that overcomes humans' hardwired connection with each other—what the scriptures refer to as "natural affection."[21] As both Paul and Joseph Smith emphasized in their writings, we need each other; we are part of one another.[22] Given this inherent impulse to see ourselves in relationship to other human beings, most of us find it hard to harm others to whom we feel a strong emotional connection. We realize that on some deep level, hurting them is akin to hurting ourselves.

In addition to being designed to connect, however, humans are also hardwired to compete—to vie for some sort of advantage over others. Ironically, our impulse to compete can feed our impulse to connect because our conflict with "enemies" will often compel us to seek allies.[23] Yet even as the conflict draws us closer to our "allies" it simultaneously pulls us further from our "enemies." Violence draws strength from this interplay, as fire draws strength from oxygen, with the key ingredient in this case being a sense of physical, psychological, and emotional distance from the people we seek to harm.

Geographic distance is frequently an ingredient in perpetuating violence. Of course, for victims of abuse, creating physical distance between themselves and their attackers is often an effective and necessary strategy to protect themselves. But in many other cases, the farther someone is from us, the easier it is to inflict violence because we may not have to directly confront the immediate results of our violence. It is also easier to create or maintain emotional distance from people when we cannot look them in the face. Militaries have long sought to create war technologies that operate from a distance (such as artillery, missiles, or remote-controlled drones). These technologies provide a physical and emotional buffer between the people inflicting the violence and their victims. Furthermore, war propaganda often works to make the enemy seem as far away—emotionally, culturally, religiously, geographically, even physiologically—as possible. The more distance and disconnection war can create, the less "like us" the enemy can be made to seem and the easier it is to inflict violence.[24]

Creating and maintaining distance is also a core element of structural and cultural violence. Racial segregation, for instance, is predicated on the cultural logic that "inferior" people must be kept separate from those who are "superior," so as to avoid "pollution" or inappropriate mixing. Political, economic, and social structures of violence are then created to reinforce such cultural notions. This is why oppressors commonly dehumanize their victims by labeling them "animals," "cockroaches," and "devils."

Emotional distancing can even happen between people who might otherwise be quite closely connected. In families and among neighbors, anger can almost instantly create emotional distance. This distancing can lead to direct violence, or it can insidiously fuel resentment that drives wedges between people for generations. The perpetuation of emotional distance between Muslims and Hindus, Israelis and Palestinians, native-born citizens and immigrants, even Democrats and Republicans, allows various forms of direct, structural, and cultural violence to survive and thrive. These constructed but nevertheless powerfully real divisions within the human family were precisely what God decried during the time of Noah, another age in which "the earth was filled with violence." "Behold," the Father sorrowfully observed, "they are without affection, and they hate their own blood."[25] Surely this is why Jesus so vigorously condemned not only violence itself but also the anger we often feel toward our brothers and sisters.[26]

RATIONALE

Besides distance, violence also needs a rationale or logic for inflicting harm. Because of our natural impulse to connect, most people aren't naturally sadistic. They don't inflict harm on others simply for sport. Most people who engage in violence—as individuals or as entire societies—are not psychopaths. They use violence because they believe that there is a good reason, even a necessity, to do so. Hatred or violence typically has a logic that makes sense to the perpetrators, no matter how obscure, vague, or tenuous it might appear to others.[27]

While such reasons come in all shapes and sizes, they can be generally categorized into two broad categories—threats and grievances. Threats are destructive forms of encroachments (from our cycle of conflict nomenclature). They may be real, perceived, or exaggerated. Regardless of their actuality or severity, threats *feel* real and immediate, encouraging an existential logic—we must use violence or be destroyed, we must kill or be killed, we must strike back or be defeated. Grievances, on the other hand, do not constitute immediate or existential threats, but rather are memories of prior defeats (or unwilling surrenders) experienced either by ourselves or by those with whom we feel some connection. They are wrongs that need to be righted, humiliations that need to be compensated for, devastations that need to be redressed. Grievances encourage a retributive logic: past violence must be punished with present violence; territory (whether geographical or relational) must be reclaimed. An eye for an eye, a tooth for a tooth.

Both types of rationales—threats and grievances—are "fuel" that feeds the fire of violence and perpetuates cycles of destructive conflict. It's not just the "bad guys" who do this. In virtually every conflict both sides will see themselves as responding to a threat or grievance rather than initiating violence for no reason. Everyone tends to see themselves as the "just defenders" and the people with whom they are engaged in violent conflict as the "unjust aggressors." Even if "we" were the first to use violence, it's only because "they" gave us no other option.

As long as such rationales can be maintained, no matter how tenuously or disingenuously, the fires of violence can rage on, or at least periodically flare up, for hundreds of years. This is why the stories we tell, both about ourselves and about others, are so important. Rationales for violence both sustain and are sustained by the emotional distance between warring parties. The Nephites' desire to "take up arms" against the Lamanites, "that we destroy them and their iniquity out of the land," was directly related to the longstanding cultural perception that Lamanites were so "stiffnecked" and "bloodthirsty" that they were beyond human connection and divine redemption.[28] Why do "we" resort to violence? Because "they" won't respond to anything less.

PREDICTABLE RESPONSE

Finally, violence requires a predictable response to sustain itself. We often speak of the available responses to aggression as "fight, flight, or freeze." Paradoxically, all three tactics are forms of "heat" that encourage more violence. Take the "fight" response, for example. When someone fights back, or responds violently to our violence, we feel our aggression is doubly justified, with our original rationale now accentuated by the harm they are currently inflicting on us. A violent response justifies the rationale that we always knew they were violent at heart, hence the need to eliminate their violence to protect ourselves.

It's fairly easy to understand how the fight response might beget more violence. But surrendering—by fleeing or freezing—also sustains future violence. Both options appear to the attackers to validate their violent acts—see, it worked!—which only encourages more violence in the future. Surrender, while sometimes the only immediate option, reinforces the aggressor's sense of superiority, righteousness, and emotional distance because in their mind only inferior, guilty, or "not-like-us" beings would refuse to fight back. Running away may be preferable to getting dominated or slaughtered and is certainly advisable for many victims. Yet rather than ending the conflict, fleeing often provides only a temporary reprieve and does little to alter the fundamental dynamics of conflict.

Fundamentally, "fight, flight, and freeze" all tacitly allow aggressors to control the conflict, stoking their illusions that violence is an effective form of perpetual power and making it more likely that they will continue to use violence in the future. But if these three choices are insufficient (if sometimes expedient), what other options are available to actually dowse the flames of anger, aggression, and domination?

EXTINGUISHING THE FLAMES

Rather than feeding the fire of violence, we need to extinguish it. In the midst of active violence, we need to find ways to secure a negative peace, so that we can work toward positive peace. How do we counter the distance, rationale, and predictable response that fuel violence? What is the corollary for water's ability to smother the heat, fuel, and oxygen that fuel fires?

Love. Active, assertive, even confrontational love.

Love is the powerful agent that extinguishes rather than fans the flames of human violence. Love is the unpredictable response, flummoxing would-be attackers and opening space for emotional temperatures to drop. Because it is difficult to experience genuine love as a threat or a force that rekindles past grievances, love deprives violence of its rationale. Finally, love stubbornly refuses to perpetuate or expand emotional distance, stretching across the chasm of alienation to either establish or hold firm to human connection. Like water on fire, love simultaneously neutralizes all three of the elements that sustain violence.

When their enraged Lamanite brethren attacked the Anti-Nephi-Lehies, the aggressors' brutality was predicated on distance, rationale, and predictable response. They felt emotionally alienated from the Anti-Nephi-Lehies, whose new faith and disavowal of Lamanite traditions posed an existential threat to Lamanite culture and identity, providing a potent rationale. And as they attacked, they predicted how the scenario would play out—the Anti-Nephi-Lehies would respond with violence, surrender, or flee the territory. Any of these responses would both justify and stoke the attackers' own violence. But the Anti-Nephi-Lehies refused to participate in this destructive pattern, responding with assertive love that was both unanticipated and forceful. They refused to accept any emotional alienation from their "enemies," going out to meet, confront, and connect with their "brethren." Their attackers were confounded. Without a predictable response that would allow them to maintain their tenuous rationale for violence, they were left naked in their unjust aggression, stripped of any sense of existential threat by these loving brothers (and perhaps sisters) who insisted on embracing their attackers in their hearts and absorbing their violence rather than returning it. The Anti-Nephi-Lehies' love stung the aggressors more deeply than any sword could have. The living water of love doused the deadly flames of violence.

Consider a more modern, personal example. Dallin H. Oaks, who would go on to become an apostle and then a member of the First Presidency of The Church of Jesus Christ of Latter-day Saints, was a law professor at the University of Chicago in 1970 when he deflected potentially lethal violence with love. His wife, June, attended a meeting at the church one night when he came to drive her home. Another woman needed a ride to her apartment, which was located in a neighborhood with a reputation for violence. Having lived several years in the area, Dallin and June Oaks had developed certain precautions for instances like this. She remained in the car, with the keys in the ignition and doors locked, while he walked the other woman to her door. After seeing the woman safely into her apartment, he surveyed the street from the lobby and observed that it was empty except for three young men. He waited until they were out of sight before stepping out of the building and into the street. But as he reached the car, and just as June was reaching across to unlock the door, one of the young men came running back, brandishing a gun. There was no time to get in the car. June saw the approaching threat and wisely left the door locked. Then, as she watched in horror, the young man thrust the barrel of the gun into her husband's stomach and said, "Give me your money."

The professor took his wallet out of his pocket and showed the young robber that it was empty. "Give me your car keys," the young man demanded. When he was told they were in the car, the young man demanded that June open the door. When this request was denied, the young man became furious, pushing the gun into the stomach and saying, "Do it, or I'll kill you." When his intended victim again refused, the young robber repeated his demands with an even angrier tone and greater gesticulations with his gun. As President Oaks later recalled, "I remember thinking that he probably wouldn't shoot me on purpose, but if he wasn't careful in the way he kept jabbing that gun into my stomach, he might shoot me by mistake. His gun looked like a cheap one, and I was nervous about its firing mechanism."

The stalemate continued for what felt like an eternity. Finally, a city bus approached. It stopped close to the two men, and a passenger got off. But even though the driver looked directly at them, he was not inclined to intervene and began driving on. This happened behind the young robber, out of his view, and the unseen activity made him anxious and distracted, so that he lowered his gun a little. The professor saw an opportunity. If he acted quickly, he could grab the gun. He was bigger than the young man and was convinced he could overpower him in a one-on-one struggle.

Up to this point, the possible responses that this younger Dallin H. Oaks considered were the predictable ones—either give in (by unlocking the door and endangering his wife) or violently strike back (by seizing the gun). But then came a flash of insight that completely transformed the dynamic: "Just as I was about to make my move, I had a unique experience. I did not see anything or hear anything, but I *knew* something. I knew what would happen if I grabbed that gun. We would struggle, and I would turn the gun into that young man's chest. It would fire, and he would die. I also understood that I must not have the blood of that young man on my conscience for the rest of my life."

In that moment, the intended victim realized his profound connection to his attacker. Their fates were linked. If he tried to seize the gun, *both* of them would be harmed. Rather than paralyzing him, this thought liberated him, opening up new avenues of possibility: "I relaxed, and as the bus pulled away I followed an impulse to put my right hand on his shoulder and give him a lecture. June and I had some teenage children at that time, and giving lectures came naturally. 'Look here,' I said. 'This isn't right. What you're doing just isn't right. The next car might be a policeman, and you could get killed or sent to jail for this.'"

The touch of his hand, along with the surprise of his stern but kind fatherly concern, threw off the whole dynamic. Having opened himself to the humanity of this young man, and having established both an emotional and physical connection, he was subtly inviting his assailant to recognize their connection and consider a different course of action. This father's genuine love for another young man emotionally disarmed him. The young robber responded by repeating his demands, but this time his voice was quieter, less agitated. Finally, he put the gun in his pocket and ran off. A violent and potentially lethal conflict was transformed. The would-be assailant could have chosen to hurt this man who had expressed genuine concern for him but now had very little justification for such a cold-blooded act. So he left, and no one got hurt.[29]

It is tempting to think of this robber's reaction as an outlier. Surely, as our culture conditions us to suppose, most attackers would not have responded to love so meekly. But once we know what to look for, the more we begin to see similar patterns whenever people have the courage to confront violence with assertive love. One cold evening, for example, a young social worker was being mugged when he felt a genuine concern for his assailant and offered to give him the coat off his back and buy him a meal. By the end of the encounter, the mugger returned the money and surrendered his weapon.[30] On another occasion, a woman, who was about to be raped by a stranger who had broken into her bedroom, realized—as President Oaks had—that her fate and the fate of the stranger were connected. In a flash of genuine concern she surprised him by asking him what time it was, throwing him off and initiating a sympathetic conversation that diffused the situation and protected both of them from the harm he originally intended.[31] An elementary school employee stopped a mass murder and saved the life of a troubled young man simply by expressing sincere love and concern for the well-armed stranger who walked into her school hoping to kill children and die in an explosive shootout with police.[32] As the examples multiply we realize that the response of President Oaks's attacker to genuine assertive love was not an outlier. Through their wielding of love in the face of aggression, all of these intended victims prove that the divine command to love our enemies is possible and practicable. Furthermore, they reveal that assertive love is not an overly idealistic and impractical ethic, but rather "a conquering, regenerating, irresistible force."[33]

ASSERTIVE LOVE ON A LARGER SCALE

It is tempting to consider these principles as relevant only to interpersonal relationships, but both scripture and history affirm that many groups and even nations have transformed destructive conflict into positive relationships without resorting to violence. The sons of Mosiah used love as their primary weapon in transforming the generations-long conflict between Nephites and several Lamanite principalities.[34] An equally if not more astounding example came sixty years later, when the usual pattern of Nephite-Lamanite conflict was once again in full swing and the Nephite general Moronihah had just failed to militarily reclaim land taken by the Lamanites. Two unarmed Nephite brothers, named Nephi and Lehi (after their better-known ancestors), go on a preaching tour throughout Nephite territories and then take their message deep into Lamanite lands. They convert thousands, but others feel threatened by the Nephite encroachment and the brothers are thrown into prison. After a miraculous divine deliverance, in which the walls of the prison tumble and Nephi and Lehi appear to the several hundred Lamanite onlookers as if they are encircled in flames of heavenly fire, a "pleasant voice" from heaven proclaims peace and angels appear to the dumbfounded crowd. Hundreds of witnesses spread word of these remarkable events, resulting in the immediate convincing of "the more part of the Lamanites." The fruits of their conversion parallels that of the Anti-Nephi-Lehies several decades earlier: "as many as were convinced did lay down their weapons of war, and also their hatred." Not only that, but the converted Lamanites voluntarily relinquish *all* the land they had captured from the Nephites over the previous decades of warfare. In one fell swoop, the message of love embodied by Nephi and Lehi transforms generations of inter-civilizational warfare and leads to a remarkable process of reconciliation resulting in "peace in all the land."[35] Throughout the Book of Mormon, peace is always more effectively won through love and reconciliation efforts than by force of arms. As Mormon concludes, the power of "the word," lovingly delivered, has a "more powerful effect upon the minds of the people than the sword, or anything else."[36]

Along with these ancient scriptural examples, twentieth-century social movements also provide us with many examples of effective nonviolence.[37] In a completely unforeseen chain of events, communist governments throughout Eastern Europe fell in the autumn of 1989. Most of these political revolutions were brought about through internal pressure consistently applied by nonviolent movements. In East Germany, home to one of the Eastern Bloc's most notoriously repressive secret police appara-tuses, it was the Christian churches that provided a home base for nonviolent protest throughout the 1980s. Although the churches were relatively freer in East Germany than in many other com-munist countries, Christians still faced significant structural vio-lence, with young Christians barred from universities because they were "intellectually unsound" and adult Christians declared ineligible for promotions in the workplace. Nevertheless, the churches persisted as a site for an alternative moral and political vision. In the early 1980s, inspired by Old Testament imagery, a youth pastor printed a logo (borrowed from a Soviet artist) of a man beating a sword into a plowshare, and thousands of school-age children wore it on their sleeves in protest of the state's man-datory military education. At a regional church conference, a pastor melted down a sword in the courtyard of Martin Luther's home in Wittenberg with television cameras rolling. Christian women began to refuse their draft cards. Churches joined an international ecumenical movement calling for the abolition of nuclear weapons. People in the pews began to pray for political reform. By the late 1980s, churches were helping secure the release of prisoners charged with political crimes. And when the revolution culminated in 1989, churches became sites for peaceful dialogue between state representatives and protesters, helping defuse tension and avoid violence in many cities. Though a marginalized minority in an officially godless country, East German Christians—laity and clergy alike—played a crucial role in nonviolently overthrowing communism.[38]

A half century earlier, in his struggle to establish Indian independence from the British Empire, Mohandas Gandhi proposed a nonviolent national defense force called the *Shanti Sena*, or peace army. His idea was inspired by the example of the *Khudai Khidmatgars*, or Servants of God, founded in 1929 by Abdul Ghaffar Khan among the Pashtun tribal communities in Pakistan as the world's "first organized nonviolent army." Khan conceived of the *Khudai Khidmatgars* along military lines, with strict training and discipline but no weapons. As scholar David Cortright notes, "They were prepared to die for their cause but not to kill for it." They led demonstrations, boycotts, and other mass noncooperation campaigns in the struggle against British colonialism, which in turn inspired Gandhi to do the same. Gandhi was in fact a brilliant tactician and trainer. He drilled his nonviolent troops and they waged highly disciplined campaigns against the British army, which eventually withdrew voluntarily from Indian territory. The full notion of the *Shanti Sena* as a replacement for the Indian national army—now one of the world's most formidable—never came to fruition. Nevertheless, in the midst of the communal violence that wracked India in the aftermath of British India's 1947 partition into an independent India and Pakistan, the *Shanti Sena* would intervene in riot situations to de-escalate the conflict and provide mediation at the community level.[39]

While the idea of a nonviolent army at first glance seems incompatible with national defense, an audacious thought experiment based on the tactics of the Anti-Nephi-Lehies reveals some of the cultural biases and blinders that keep us from using greater moral imagination. Current military training, especially in the United States, focuses on overcoming the natural human impulse to avoid violence. In response to an internal study that discovered that less than 25 percent of soldiers in combat situations purposefully fired their guns at the enemy during the Second World War, the US military developed an exercise known as Reflexive Fire Training. Soldiers are placed on a firing range with moving targets and through unrelenting repetition are conditioned to develop a fire reflex that overrides their natural reluctance to shoot at a human target.[40] Firing rates have since increased to over 90 percent and have been further enhanced in recent decades by the development of new technologies such as first-person-shooter video games.

Imagine, if you will, similar commitment, energy, and resources being put into a different form of reflexive training— one that channels our desire to compete in constructive ways while also enhancing our impulse to connect. We might call it Reflexive Compassion Training, and prototypes of it already exist on a small scale. In the early 1960s James Lawson, for example, trained civil rights activists in the effective strategies of loving nonviolent resistance on a shoestring budget in the basement of a church. "We were warriors," one participant later observed. He described Lawson's rigorous evening workshops as "a nonviolent academy, equivalent to West Point."[41] Another of Lawson's young pupils, John Lewis (who passed in 2020 after serving as a long-time member of Congress), described how the training worked:

> Several of us would sit in a row of folding chairs, acting out a sit-in, while the others played waitresses or angry bystanders,

calling us niggers, cursing in our faces, pushing and shoving us to the floor. Always James Lawson would be there, hovering over the action, pushing, prodding, teaching, cajoling. It was not enough, he would say, simply to endure a beating. It was not enough to resist the urge to strike back at an assailant. "That urge can't *be* there," he would tell us. "You have to do more than just not hit back. You have to have no *desire* to hit back. You have to *love* that person who's hitting you. You're *going* to love him."[42]

Throughout the training, Lewis remembered that Lawson stressed that assertive love was "not simply a technique or a tactic or a strategy or a tool to be pulled out when needed"—it was a way of life. "It is not something you turn on and off like a faucet. This sense of love, this sense of peace, the capacity for compassion, is something you carry inside yourself every waking minute of the day." This is not romantic love. As Lewis said, it was "broader, deeper, more all-encompassing." This kind of love "recognizes the spark of the divine in each of us, even in those who would raise their hand against us, those we might call our enemy."[43] In other words, the type of love that Jesus exemplified and preached.

Similar to new soldiers in basic training, these nonviolent recruits were honing their reflexes, steeling themselves for battle, learning how to restrain their natural impulses to give in or strike back, and finding ways to establish a connection with their adversaries. Now imagine such training scaled up within our communities and even nations. Imagine dedicating even a fraction of police and military budgets for the type of nonviolence training Lawson conducted. Imagine the rigor and sophistication that would come if governments created a National Peace University to study and develop best practices and then a National Department or Ministry of Peace to convert principles into policy. Imagine police officers and other first responders—including social workers—who have been trained primarily in how to safely de-escalate high-conflict situations. Imagine entire armies—hundreds of thousands, even millions of recruits around the world—expertly trained in the capacity to connect and protect, willing to put their own bodies on the line to nonviolently shield people and communities from violence.[44]

We shouldn't be naive about the possible outcomes of nonviolence. Some of these nonviolent troops would be killed—just as happened with the Anti-Nephi-Lehies, *Khudai Khidmatgars*, and civil rights activists. But violence is hardly a guarantee of personal safety; how many millions of soldiers and police have died with a gun in their hands? Is it possible that many enemy soldiers—even fascists or terrorists—might be reluctant to kill an army of loving nonviolent "warriors" who pose no physical threat to them, insist on loving them, and act in such an unpredictable way that they strip them of all justification for their violence? Violence requires a violent response to sustain itself, but an army wielding only assertive love deprives their attackers of fuel, heat, and oxygen.

The notion of entire nations transitioning from violence to nonviolence is not purely theoretical. One of the best contemporary examples is Costa Rica, which abolished its national army in 1948. The Central American nation retains only a civil police force and dedicates what would otherwise be its defense budget instead to education, health care, infrastructure, economic development, and other forms of social welfare. In a region racked with poverty, corruption, and violence, Costa Rica stands alone as a beacon of relative prosperity and calm. Even without an army, Costa Rica has not been invaded, despite the fact that its neighboring countries have often been led by dictators otherwise unhesitant to wield violence in the pursuit of power. The army-less nation ranks near the top of most indices of human happiness, has successfully sheltered some of the planet's richest biodiversity, and is universally respected.[45] Costa Rica's leaders correctly discerned and courageously determined that the "power and influence" of this small nation would only increase with the moral authority and trust achieved through nonviolent leadership and a national policy informed "by persuasion, by long-suffering, by gentleness and meekness, and by love unfeigned."[46] If Costa Rica can do it, then perhaps other countries and communities can as well.

BUT IF NOT . . .

As we have seen, robust and confrontational love for our enemies can lead to stunningly effective results, overcoming evil with good. But the forces of loving nonviolence are not foolproof. In a universe populated by freewill beings who can still choose evil in the face of goodness, nothing is foolproof. There will be losses and failures. Even God's perfect application of love's power and influence has not led to universally positive outcomes. Our Father could not keep Lucifer and a third part of the host of heaven within the fold. Christ ended his mortal life tortured and crucified. Love is not guaranteed to work. Then again, neither is violence. Violence often fails to achieve its goals, and yet we keep coming back to it. Somehow we have convinced ourselves that despite thousands of years of practice we either have not mastered the technique or have not found the right combination of lethal force to always attain our objectives. Conversely, as soon as love—in the form of forbearance, forgiveness, reconciliation, persuasion, negotiation, mediation, diplomacy, and nonviolent resistance—doesn't produce immediately desirable outcomes, we tend to toss it aside for something "stronger." This is akin to firefighters turning off their hoses and employing flamethrowers instead because an initial burst of water doesn't immediately douse the flames. Because of deep biases regarding the so-called efficacy of violence, we constantly forgive its failings while holding nonviolent love to an unreasonable standard of performance.

The reality is that love and other nonviolent resistance tactics are not only morally superior to violence, but they are also more likely to succeed. God's ultimate loving victory over evil—the triumph of the crucified over the crucifiers—will one day demonstrate this once and for all. In the meantime, there is ample evidence that nonviolence really works. Political scientists Erica Chenoweth and Maria Stephan conducted a comprehensive study of every popular resistance campaign of the twentieth century and concluded convincingly that nonviolent movements are twice as likely as their violent counterparts to successfully achieve their goals.[47] Not only are nonviolent campaigns more likely to drive out foreign occupiers or overthrow brutal dictators, but their methods of engaging the struggle are also better at creating conditions for sustainable peace afterward. In short, nonviolence is better at pulling conflict out of destructive cycles and initiating more creative dynamics.[48] Love and nonviolence aren't perfect. Sometimes they fail. But they fail less often than violence.

Even when it appears to flounder, assertive love frees us from our enemies' ultimate control. They may harass us or imprison us or even destroy our bodies, but such "victories" are ultimately hollow because they can never capture or destroy our souls. They cannot maintain power over us in the long run unless we give it to them. Believers in an afterlife obviously bring an eternal perspective to this, but the same principle applies here and now. Victor Frankl affirmed this truth based on what he learned from his harrowing years in a Nazi concentration camp:

> The experiences of camp life show that man does have a choice of action. There were enough examples, often of a heroic nature, which proved that apathy could be overcome, irritability sup-

pressed. Man can preserve a vestige of spiritual freedom, of independence of mind, even in such terrible conditions of psychic and physical stress.

We who lived in concentration camps can remember the men who walked through the huts comforting others, giving away their last piece of bread. They may have been few in number, but they offer sufficient proof that everything can be taken from a man but one thing: the last of the human freedoms—to choose one's attitude in any given set of circumstances, to choose one's own way.[49]

We cannot ultimately control what others do, but apart from a few rare exceptions (such as the use of mind-altering drugs), the one thing other people can't take away from us is how we choose to respond to what they do. Gandhi understood this principle as he struggled to awaken his countrymen to the power within them to throw off British rule. "Even the most despotic government," he said, "cannot stand except for the consent of the governed." When "the subject ceases to fear the despotic force, [its] power is gone."[50] This refusal to surrender to the logic of violence may not immediately alter the proximate conditions of the victim, but it creates the conditions, even by way of simply maintaining hope, for eventual liberation. As the Apostle Peter observed, "If you do suffer for doing what is right, you are blessed," in part because you will "not [be] afraid of their terror" and are not "intimidated."[51] In spite of conditions not of one's own choosing, assertive love preserves the maintenance of personal agency.

One of the greatest advantages of assertive love, even when it appears to fail, is that it clears a redemptive path for others—including our aggressors—to follow. Short-term losses can be absorbed as part of a long-term strategy for the eventual transformation of conflictive relationships. This is the essence of Christ's message and mission that led to the cross—a willingness to absorb violence and even die on behalf of others, including those who intend us the greatest harm, with the goal of saving their souls and reconciling all people.[52] Martin Luther King recognized that part of "the power of nonviolence" is that "the nonviolent resister does not seek to humiliate or defeat the opponent but to win his friendship and understanding."[53] As Christ, the Anti-Nephi-Lehies, and King's associates in the civil rights movement demonstrated, assertive love—with its willingness to suffer nonviolently but creatively—sows the seeds of reconciliation. It may be years or even generations before that seed takes root, but the potential is there and we will have cleared any obstacles from the path of redemption that we have power to remove.

To be clear, assertive love does not celebrate victimhood or invite masochistic martyrdom. A willingness to suffer nonviolently is not the same thing as actively seeking it out. Nonviolent love is in the business of preserving life; cultivating an unselfish readiness to die rather than kill is fundamentally different from developing an unhealthy death wish. Furthermore, nonviolence cannot be imposed on an individual or group as a requirement— the way they *must* act. Each person has to come to his or her own conclusion; nonviolent love can only be freely chosen. Echoing Shadrach, Meshach, and Abednego, we believe that those who adopt and apply the principles of assertive love will more often than not be delivered. "But if not," as the young men bravely affirmed, we will still not "worship the golden image" of violence, confident that in the long run right prevails over might.[54]

Not all aggressors will respond to a sincere offer of love. Some people are "past feeling"—so far removed from human connection that their hearts cannot be reached, cannot be touched, at least in this life.[55] Modern psychiatry refers to such a condition as "antisocial personality disorder," characterized by the incapacity to feel empathy for other people. Such pyschopathologies are caused by a variety of factors—including genetic or environmental factors—beyond a person's choice or control. For the well-being of all, it is important that societies develop humane strategies and institutions to mitigate the destructive impact of these psychological conditions. But unreachable sociopaths are rare. The vast majority of people, including most of those who do horrific acts of violence, have hearts that are capable of being touched and transformed.

Unfortunately, this is not the message our culture teaches us. From an early age we are acculturated with the notion that those who engage in aggressive violence are "bad guys" who are irredeemable. This skepticism toward the transformative power of love and the corresponding trust in violence as the most (and indeed only) effective response reflects a heartbreaking lack of faith—in others, but also in God. When we instinctively assume that violence is the only way to respond to our enemies, we demonstrate disbelief that they are capable of change. We deny their basic humanity and deny the capacity of Christ to reach them with his atoning grace. We also demonstrate a lack of faith in God's promise of the Resurrection, which should overshadow "the sting of death" in the heart of the believer and render moot the grave's apparent finality.[56]

Love is both a new and old answer to the challenge of violence. Modern scientists are describing with greater and greater accuracy the essential physiological and psychological truths on which the forces of love operate.[57] Yet the essential dynamics of these truths have been hiding in plain sight for two millennia in the teachings of Jesus. His injunction to love our enemies is for the believer and nonbeliever, for individuals and nations. It is the way of holiness and human dignity. We hear echoes of Christ's teachings in Abraham Lincoln's reminder that even in the midst of deadly conflict, God's children "are not enemies, but friends." "Our bonds of affection" may be "strained," but we can choose "the better angels of our nature" as the path to peace, prosperity, and reconciliation.[58] Though not fail-proof, assertive love is stronger and more effectual than violence. Loving nonviolence is the better way, and loving nonviolence works.

CHAPTER SIX

Is Violence Ever Justified?

*We know that justification through the grace of
our Lord and Savior Jesus Christ is just and true; and we know
also, that sanctification through the grace of our Lord
and Savior Jesus Christ is just and true.*
—Doctrine and Covenants 20:30–31

*If thou wilt spare him, thou shalt be rewarded for thy
righteousness. . . . Nevertheless, thine enemy is in
thine hands; and if thou rewardest him according to
his works thou art justified.*
—Doctrine and Covenants 98:30–31

As part of their mortal probation and divine tutelage,
God's children are entrusted with limited but real portions of his two most consequential powers—creation
and destruction. Accompanying such awesome and fearful powers comes a strict set of rules regarding how to employ them.
As apostle Jeffrey R. Holland has noted: "Clearly God's greatest
concerns regarding mortality are how one gets into this world

and how one gets out of it. . . . These are the two matters that he has repeatedly told us he wants us never to take illegally, illicitly, unfaithfully, without sanction."[1]

In Restoration scripture, the misuse of divinely given procreative power is "second only to murder" in offensiveness to God. Given its moral seriousness, Latter-day Saints rightly spend a substantial amount of time and energy articulating and policing the boundaries of sexual activity. Far less effort, however, is dedicated to thinking and talking about "the shedding of innocent blood," which the Book of Mormon states is even more "abominable" than unchastity. Most Latter-day Saints could probably complete the sentence "God has commanded that the sacred powers of procreation are to be employed only _____."[2] Far fewer, however, could fill in the prompt "God has commanded that the tragic powers of destruction are to be employed only _____."

Tellingly, both powers—of creation and destruction—involve a wide spectrum of attitudes and behaviors. Jesus admonished his followers to patrol the parameters of our procreative impulses, even in their earliest forms.[3] Lust and sexualization, usually of women by men, is often a component and contributor to various forms of structural and cultural violence in which others are objectified and treated as less than whole human persons. Impure sexual desires can also lead to direct violence in the various forms of sexual assault. The urgency with which Christians raise a prophetic warning against the abuse of our God-given creative powers is therefore entirely appropriate. A robust sexual ethic is not separate from a commitment to peacebuilding but instead a necessary part thereof.[4]

Unlike the powers of creation—which can create greater unity, connection, and life itself—the powers of destruction are forces that typically alienate and damage both perpetrators and their targets. Consequently, when the powers of destruction are not controlled, they create a fire that consumes both bodies and souls, with the capacity of eliminating entire societies. These powers therefore have even stricter divine controls than those of sexuality. Jesus commanded his followers to guard the path of violence, even the earliest steps, with the utmost vigilance. Anyone who is merely angry with another human being "is in danger of hellfire"—in other words, in danger of alienation from the love that characterizes celestial glory.[5]

The casualness with which our contemporary culture promiscuously traffics in both sexuality and violence—especially as forms of entertainment—is an indictment against our collective attitudes toward the sacred powers to create and destroy life. "I have set before you life and death, blessing and cursing," Jehovah told the ancient Israelites. "Therefore choose life, that both thou and thy seed may live."[6] With life and death set before us, the tragedy is how quickly we criticize a thorough ethic of life and how easily and frequently we opt for a culture of death. Rather than fully affirming life, we too often search for ways to wriggle out of Jesus's hard sayings to accommodate our violent desires. From our entertainment to our political culture, violence is frequently celebrated and glamorized rather than mourned and renounced.

Because God desires to save rather than condemn us,[7] he often acknowledges our spiritual and moral incapacities by granting lesser laws that we can live in preparation for embracing higher laws. For instance, when the children of Israel "hardened their hearts," God took the higher priesthood from them but gave them the "lesser priesthood . . . and the preparatory gospel" that would, if they heeded it, purify their desires and allow them to eventually abide a more celestial law.[8] In modern times, God gave the Saints the law of tithing as a lesser manifestation of the law of consecration, therefore accommodating human weakness while still calling covenanted disciples of Christ to voluntarily subscribe to a higher, holier way.[9]

In the same fashion, to counteract and channel the destructive human impulse that is as old as Cain, God has made provisions for our mortal frailty by revealing an ethic to inform how, if ever, women and men can deploy their divinely allowed power to destroy. This strict ethic of justified violence is secondary and supplemental to God's clearly preferred ethic of peace, love, and forbearance. The injunction to emulate Jesus's total commitment to loving nonviolence has never been rescinded nor superseded. But God knows the human heart. While he repeatedly, even emphatically, discourages his children from illicitly employing the fearful powers of destruction, in his merciful accommodation of human weakness he has also provided a clear set of guidelines and commandments that allow for but also severely restrain the use of violence. This secondary ethic rests upon principles of lesser and higher moral laws, and they apply only to the question of whether *direct* violence is ever justified. The Restoration's remedy for structural and cultural violence will be explored later in our discussion of Zion. What follows here is an effort to describe and understand the Restoration's revealed guidelines for justified violence and then to consider the implications of these principles.

THE LESSER LAW OF JUSTIFIED RETRIBUTION

The Book of Mormon prophet Abinadi referred to the Mosaic law as a "very strict law," given to the children of Israel to circumscribe their behavior, "to keep them in remembrance of God and their duty towards him."[10] So also are the divinely ordained laws surrounding justified human violence. They exist to restrain our natural tendencies toward retaliation, vengeance, and hate—to keep the "dogs of war" as tightly leashed as possible.[11]

The place in which the Lord's lesser law of human violence is most explicitly and thoroughly laid out is in Doctrine and Covenants section 98, a revelation received by Joseph Smith in August 1833 as mob violence against Church members was escalating in western Missouri. Through the revelation, God encourages his "friends" to learn patience and cultivate a willingness to make the ultimate sacrifice if necessary: "I will try you and prove you herewith. And whoso layeth down his life in my cause, for my name's sake, shall find it again, even life eternal." With advice that is simultaneously comforting and discomforting, God tells his children to "be not afraid of your enemies"—not because he will protect his children from harm, but because "I have decreed in my heart . . . that I will prove you in all things, whether you will abide in my covenant, even unto death." The test of his disciples, it seems, is whether or not they are willing to suffer death for his sake—not inflict it. "For if ye will not abide in my covenant," the Lord warns, "ye are not worthy of me." Echoing the Sermon on the Mount, he commands his children not to strike back against their persecutors. Rather, God's people should "renounce war and proclaim peace."[12]

The patience with which God's children are to bear violent persecution is described in great detail in subsequent passages, first concerning violence against individuals and families and then concerning violence against communities and nations. The same principles apply in both cases, though the scale differs. On the individual and family level, the revelation states that "if men will smite you, or your families, once, and ye bear it patiently and revile not against them, neither seek revenge, ye shall be rewarded; but if ye bear it not patiently, it shall be accounted unto you as being meted out as a just measure unto you."[13] In other words, God expects his followers to exercise patience and respond nonviolently in the face of aggression. If we choose to strike back the first time we are attacked, then the original abuse to which we are responding is evened out by our retaliation. Each act of violence cancels out the other. This corresponds to the Old Testament's *lex talionis*, or an eye for an eye, tooth for a tooth.[14]

But the 1833 revelation does not settle on or for retributive violence. Rather, it suggests that as aggression against us increases, the rewards for bearing it with patience—and by implication, with genuine love for our attacker—will also increase, even exponentially: "And again, if your enemy shall smite you the second time, and you revile not against your enemy, and bear it patiently, your reward shall be an hundred-fold. And again, if he shall smite you the third time, and ye bear it patiently, your reward shall be doubled unto you four-fold."[15] Even assuming this quantification of blessings is more symbolic than literal, God's promises are overwhelmingly tilted in favor of nonviolence.

So far this sounds like the higher law delivered by Jesus in the Sermon on the Mount, which is the binding personal and social ethic for all Christians. But the 1833 revelation allows for human frailty by providing a lesser alternative to nonviolent love and forbearance. In the face of repeated attacks the Lord does *justify*, or excuse, a violent self-defensive response. Even then, the criteria for doing so are rather stringent. First, we must wait for God's justice to prevail. If the offender remains unpunished and undaunted, we are to issue a clear warning for that person to stop. After that warning, if our enemy attacks us yet again, then the Lord says, "I have delivered thine enemy into thine hands . . . and if thou rewardest him according to his works thou art justified."[16] In other words, the decision about what to do next is now squarely in our court. We are "justified" in our choice to use self-defensive violence, but only in the face of a recalcitrant and insistent aggressor.

The word *justified* is crucial to understanding this divine law, which was confirmed by the Church in 1835 when it resolved that people are "justified in defending themselves" from "unlaw-ful assaults and encroachments" when "immediate appeal cannot be made to the laws, and relief afforded."[17] There is an import-ant theological distinction between *justification* and its oft-paired term *sanctification*. In its theological sense, justification means to excuse, or make righteous or just, in the sight of God.[18] Sanctification is the process whereby God purifies our hearts and souls in order to make us holy—"saints," based on the Greek root—and presumes a starting point of moral innocence or cleanliness.[19] If an attitude or action is already just, righteous, or holy—for instance, pure love for others—then it does not need to be justified. Only actions or attitudes that fall short of a celestial standard require justification. Implicit in the Lord's promise to justify an action is therefore a recognition that the action itself is less than holy. Sin itself cannot be sanctified, but the sinner once justified can thereafter be sanctified. The good news of the gos-pel is that fallen humans can be justified (made right) and then sanctified (made holy) by the grace and power of Jesus Christ.[20]

Significantly, then, while justifying violent self-defense under certain highly constrained circumstances, the 1833 revelation makes clear that the Lord's preferred choice is that we love our enemy and bear even repeated attacks patiently and nonviolently: "And then if thou wilt spare him, thou shalt be rewarded for thy righteousness; and also thy children and thy children's children unto the third and fourth generation."[21] Rather than being a *jus-tified* response in which our less than celestial actions can be excused, nonviolent forbearance is a *sanctified* (and *sanctifying*) response that not only helps make us more holy but also blesses future generations.

To see the veracity of this promise, given to the Latter-day Saints but with broader application to all of God's children, we have only to think of the remarkable movements led by Mohandas Gandhi, Martin Luther King Jr., and Nelson Mandela, who transformed entire nations with their capacity to absorb blows without striking back. The movements led by these men were not passive in the face of injustice, but rather organized active resistance to various forms of violent oppression. There is nothing about Christian forbearance that precludes nonviolent resistance to evil or requires people to be passive punching bags. To the contrary, as we have seen, nonviolence is most powerful when it is not neutral in the face of evil but rather a form of "anxiously engag[ing] in a good cause."[22] Iron-willed love in the face of violence is a moral choice that unleashes an exponentially expansive morality, far beyond anything retribution can accomplish. Violence, on the other hand, no matter how justified, contributes to a destructive cycle that can unleash exponentially expansive retributions.

Still, the 1833 revelation suggests it is our God-given choice as to whether we wish to move the conflict cycle upward or downward. In short, is self-defensive human violence ever justified? Under very strict conditions, yes. Does it ever sanctify us? No.

The 1833 revelation dictates that a similar set of rules also applies to the violence of communities and nations, belying any proposition that Jesus's nonviolent ethic is a purely personal one. The Lord commands that groups—especially his covenanted disciples—should not inflict violence "against any nation, kindred, tongue, or people, save I, the Lord, commanded them." (The thorny subject of God's commanding violence is taken up in the next chapter.) But what should a community or nation do if attacked? The revelation's instructions to groups are parallel to its directives to individuals. If an assault is imminent, communities must "first lift a standard of peace unto that people" who are attacking. If aggressors reject the offer of peace—not once, but three times—then when the beleaguered victims bring their testimonies of innocent suffering before the Lord, he will "give unto them a commandment, and justify them in going out to battle."[23] Note that even when God gives an explicit command to go to battle, the resultant violence is only justified, not sanctified; God's people still and always have the preferred option to respond nonviolently. So it is essential to emphasize that at no point, in this revelation or any other, does Restoration scripture contain the possibility of a holy war.

Granted, the Lord promises his people that he will "fight their battles, and their children's battles, and their children's children's, until they [have] avenged themselves on all their enemies, to the third and fourth generation."[24] But what is commonly read as an assuring promise of divine assistance in human retribution may actually be a profound note of warning. God may strengthen his people if they choose to fight, and he may even assist them against unrepentant and abusive enemies, but the resultant cycle of destruction will likely last for generations. A decision to pursue violence, even if justified, may drag our children and our children's children into a multigenerational cycle of retribution and destruction. By the time the conflict ends, there may be little left beyond a legacy of carnage. Jesus's warning to Peter—"all they that take the sword shall perish with the sword"[25]—thus plays out on a macro stage. If multigenerational devastation is the result, what real use is it to say you were legally justified in your cause?

Importantly, God's promised assistance in justified human violence is not a blank check. The promise applies only as long as our aggressors are unrepentant repeat offenders. If someone attacks us but then repents and sincerely seeks our forgiveness, God insists that "thou shalt forgive him, and shalt hold it no more as a testimony against thine enemy." This injunction to forgive applies "as oft as thine enemy repenteth." Likewise, in a multigenerational conflict, the moment any generation asks for forgiveness, God promises to embrace them and commands us to do the same, saying "thine indignation shall be turned away."[26] God's preference is always that we exercise love and mercy, because those are the only qualities that can make us like him. Just as the negative consequences of destructive violence have an impact on future generations, so do the positive consequences of forbearance, forgiveness, and reconciliation.

The Lord's command to forgive is a hard saying for victims who have suffered real harm and continue to experience the long-lasting effects of trauma. Crucially, the divine injunction to repeatedly forgive does not give license to serial abusers. For one, their repentance must be genuine and lasting. God does not dispense "cheap grace," as Dietrich Bonhoeffer memorably put it, and neither must we.[27] The Lord's preference for love and mercy does not suggest that victims of violence should surrender in defeat, hesitate to report to the proper authorities, and passively await the next assault.[28] A divine command to forgive is not an excuse for bad behavior, nor a tool to keep victims subservient. For any abuser who twists God's teachings of forbearance and forgiveness to suit his or her own destructive purposes, Jesus's ancient warning holds—"it is better for him that a millstone were hanged about his neck, and he were cast into the sea."[29]

RESTORATION PRINCIPLES OF JUSTIFIED VIOLENCE

The Restoration's principles of justified violence offer an important update to an ethical tradition known as "just war."[30] The Christian just war tradition, or just war theory, is built on a presumption that war is always a tragedy but in dire circumstances may be necessary to protect innocent lives and correct injustice. The tradition's most important contribution has been to put tight parameters around excusable reasons for violence, known as *jus ad bellum* ("right to war") standards. These criteria include having a just cause (such as protecting innocent life), using it with competent authority (instead of acting extralegally), and employing force as a last resort (after all peaceful alternatives have been exhausted). But simply fulfilling these benchmarks for going to war is not enough. According to the just war tradition, the manner in which the war is conducted must also follow certain criteria, known as *jus in bello* ("right in war") standards. These include using force with appropriate discrimination (between combatants and innocents) and proportionality (only as much as necessary to secure the just cause and no more).[31]

From the perspective of lesser and higher laws, the just war tradition represents an important improvement on the continuum of human behavior. This venerable tradition is thus commendable for its efforts to constrain warfare, and humanity would have experienced far less suffering had nations and putatively Christian rulers heeded just war principles throughout the centuries. Still, the categories and criteria of just war are neither broad enough nor comprehensive enough to inform the wide scope of human violence. Just war theory concerns itself only with nations and armies. While the Book of Mormon does seem to confirm some just war principles, especially in the chapters describing Nephite wars in the century before the coming of Christ, on the whole Restoration scripture qualifies the just war tradition in several ways and provides even more rigorous standards for when violence may be justified. In particular, the Restoration offers standards that encompass (and constrain) all lethal forms of direct violence and destruction, for both individuals and communities.[32]

So with a nod to just war theory, we divide the Restoration's divinely revealed standards regarding justified human violence into two general categories: *choosing violence* and *engaging violence*. Since structural and cultural violence are never authorized by Restoration theology, note that these principles, like the just war tradition more broadly, focus on restraining direct violence.

CHOOSING VIOLENCE

Violence is always a choice. When we opt for a path other than the sanctifying power of loving nonviolence, Restoration scripture and prophetic teaching postulate that the following criteria must be met in order for our violence to be justified. Of course, humans are also free to choose the path of *unjustified* violence, but that choice would take a person or society beyond the scope of Latter-day Saint Christian ethics.

DISINCLINATION
Violence should be avoided, even at great cost, because it is always destructive and never sanctifying. This is the crucial attitudinal starting point. As the 1833 revelation emphasizes, violence should never be the first response—or even the second or third. It is something to which we should be thoroughly—not just nominally—disinclined, both individually and collectively. This principle is further articulated in a statement by the First Presidency of The Church of Jesus Christ of Latter-day Saints, delivered in 1942 as the United States entered World War II, declaring that "the Church is and must be against war." Since "war is of Satan,"[33] and "force always begets force," the Church of Jesus Christ "cannot regard war as a righteous means of settling international disputes."[34] Violence inherently alienates us from our fellow human beings and, by extension, from God. Because violence can never sanctify us, we should strive mightily to "touch not the evil gift, nor the unclean thing."[35]

FORBEARANCE
We should receive and endure violence ourselves before employing and inflicting it against others. This second criterion follows naturally from the first. In addition to being profoundly disinclined toward violence, Restoration scripture suggests God also wants

us to demonstrate—as Jesus did—remarkable, even heroic, forbearance in the face of aggression, patiently enduring repeated attacks before resorting to violence that might be considered justified. We are to "turn the other cheek"—not as passive submission to aggression but as an active and loving nonviolent response to it. This is a revision of the just war theory's principle of "last resort," which implies that in exhausting other possibilities we can (and will) reach a point where we have "no other choice" but violence. The Restoration's deep commitment to human agency suggests that it is impossible for humans, while in possession of their conscious faculties, to have "no other choice." The 1942 First Presidency statement expresses this principle when it describes restored Christianity as being "a gospel of love and peace, of patience and longsuffering, of forbearance and forgiveness."[36] The 1833 revelation suggests that God's children should endure attacks, both individually and as societies, multiple times before any violent response might be divinely justified. While the use of justified violence is strictly regulated in Restoration theology, there is never a limit on when we can employ loving nonviolence to resist evil.[37]

DIVINE CONSENT

We should receive divine endorsement, even guidance, before resorting to violence. This standard is more rigorous than simply believing one has God on one's side. The 1833 revelation clearly suggests that violence can be engaged only after God has given his direct approval. As both individuals and societies, we should lay the evidence of our assailants' abuse—in addition to evidence of our disinclination and forbearance—before the Lord. In regard to *personal* violence, the standard for divine permission (which is not the same as endorsement) is implicitly fulfilled only after disinclination and forbearance have been sufficiently demonstrated, our enemy has escaped God's own punishment, we have warned our enemy against attacking us again, and the enemy ignores our warning. Only then, God says, has he "delivered thine enemy into thine hands . . . and if thou rewardest him according to his works thou are justified."[38]

This standard for divine consent might feel unnecessarily restrictive, especially in the face of immediate danger. As US Supreme Court Justice Oliver Wendell Holmes noted in upholding a right to lethal force in self-defense, "Detached reflection cannot be demanded in the presence of an uplifted knife."[39] Fair enough. But God's law of justified violence is not interested in meeting the minimum threshold of statutory law, or even terrestrial "common sense." God's law endeavors to make us not only Christians but eventually Christ*like*. Jesus did not ask for Peter's "detached reflection" in the face of their enemies' swords and staves; he simply commanded his disciple to put away his sword. For his part, Peter didn't respond with a rational defense of why his violence in that moment was justified; he simply obeyed.

The 1833 revelation's standard for *nations* to receive God's approval to go to war is even more stringent. Rather than allowing for an implicit endorsement if the necessary criteria are met, here God requires an explicit endorsement to engage in defensive warfare: "And again, this is the law that I gave unto mine ancients, that they should not go out unto battle against any nation, kindred, tongue, or people, save I, the Lord, commanded them." More specifically, after repeatedly raising banners of peace and being repeatedly rebuffed by the attackers, then the aggrieved nation "should bring these testimonies before the Lord; then I, the Lord, would give unto them a commandment, and justify them in going out to battle against that nation, tongue, or people."[40] The revelation does not specify, and thus leaves open for discussion and debate, precisely to whom the Lord's directive would come and how it would be communicated to the public and recognized as legitimate. The revelation originally came to the restored Church, which presumably would receive the Lord's command through the living prophet. But how does the principle apply in the modern secular realm, where ecclesiastical leaders have no formal authority and where political rulers might not even be people who pray? This question—which corresponds to the just war tradition's criterion of competent authority—admittedly requires further clarification (and potentially additional revelation).

The criterion of divine consent also applies to a person's response to his or her nation's call to arms, whether or not the nation has fulfilled the standards for its violence to be justified. Citing a passage in the 1833 revelation, the First Presidency's 1942 statement notes that it is "justifiable" for God's followers to "'befriend that law which is the constitutional law of the land.'" (We will reflect further on this principle in chapter 8.) Therefore, the statement argues, when members of the Church are called "into the armed service of any country to which they owe allegiance, their highest civic duty requires that they meet that call." This is not an enthusiastic directive for voluntary enlistment, but a resigned acknowledgment of the terrestrial duties of citizens. Since God has given his prior consent for his children to meet their civic obligations, the First Presidency affirmed that the violence they perpetrate in the course of fulfilling their lawful duty "will not be held against them."[41] This is precisely the moral calculus of *justified* but not *sanctified* violence.

At the same time, disciples of Jesus Christ should keep in mind that conscientious objection or requests for noncombatant duty are legal alternatives in most countries. Refusal to serve, based on a deeply principled Christian commitment to nonviolence, is also always an option. Those who choose nonviolent resistance of this sort should be aware that their actions may lead to imprisonment or other forms of retribution.[42] Choices have consequences, but the point is that fighting on the front lines is not a foregone conclusion for followers of Christ even in the context of national mandatory military service. Violence is always a choice, even when nonviolent alternatives are problematic.

No one can claim conscientious objector status simply by virtue of membership in The Church of Jesus Christ of Latter-day Saints. Throughout the twentieth century, the Church's leaders have generally justified military participation by Church members and have on multiple occasions actively discouraged conscientious objection. However, respecting personal agency, the Church also "recognizes the right of individual members to determine for themselves whether their deep, spiritual consciences will allow them to serve in combat."[43] As of 2020, the Church's handbook of instructions for leaders contained no language either supporting or prohibiting conscientious objection. But the historical pattern has been that the Church will countenance the decision of a conscientious objector after "he or she has consulted with the appropriate bishop and stake president and has spiritual confirmation that the way decided upon by the member concerned is acceptable to the Lord."[44]

ACCOUNTABILITY

Since there are always other options, we must accept responsibility for our decision to use violence. Restoration theology posits that blessings received from God typically come "by obedience to that law upon which it [the blessing] is predicated."[45] The August 1833 revelation predicates limited blessings to those who carefully follow the principles of justified violence, and exponentially greater blessings to those who pursue the path of sanctifying nonviolence. Even after divine consent has been received, therefore, justified violence remains a choice. Since there are always alternative paths, and since individuals and societies always have agency, if we do choose the violent option we must also assume responsibility for our actions and accept the consequences. We cannot blame others—even God—for our choices. The justified choice *is* justified, but it is still a decision with a holier alternative. As in all things, we must take accountability for our actions— whether they are unjustified, justified, or sanctified.

ENGAGING VIOLENCE

The four standards for *choosing violence*—disinclination, for- bearance, divine consent, and accountability—constitute a code by which we might evaluate a decision to use direct violence, whether in personal defense or when our society contemplates war. Once the choice has been made, however, Restoration scrip- ture stipulates that justified violence should also adhere to addi- tional criteria for actually *engaging violence*. These standards correspond roughly to the just war standards of *jus in bello* but include (again) significantly higher standards.

RESTRAINT
Justified violence must be measured and must cease at the earliest opportunity. This standard resembles the just war principle of pro- portionality, which requires that combatants use only the amount of force that is absolutely necessary (or proportionate) to the justi- fied end. This is a useful starting point. But restraint encompasses an even wider field of concern, with an eye for ending the violence at the earliest possible moment. This principle is frequently dis- played by Book of Mormon armies, which successfully reclaim ter- ritory with little or no bloodshed, cease to shed more blood after their enemies are surrounded, and refuse to engage in preemptive strikes even when a serious threat is clearly imminent.[46]

GRIEF
Justified violence must be mourned for the suffering it inflicts. Deep, heartfelt sorrow must accompany both the contemplation

and use of justified violence. It should evoke in us only deep anguish, not joy or delight; violence should never be glorified or celebrated. God told the prophet Ezekiel that he took "no pleasure in the death of the wicked."[47] At their best, the Nephites emulated God's example. As Mormon characterized the Nephite attitude during one of their prolonged wars, "they were sorry to take up arms against the Lamanites, because they did not delight in the shedding of blood; yea, and this was not all—they were sorry to be the means of sending so many of their brethren out of this world into an eternal world, unprepared to meet their God."[48] This standard of grief applies not only to warfare but also to interpersonal violence. If we ever choose to use force to defend ourselves or others, such an action ought to be accompanied with deep grieving for the soul we have chosen to injure or rend.

STEADFAST CONNECTION

We must remain emotionally and spiritually bound to those against whom we use justified violence. As we've seen, violence is based on emotional distance between perpetrator and victim. But the gospel of Jesus Christ works against that alienating dynamic. We must never lose sight of the fact that on the other side of violence—no matter how justified—is a spiritual sister or brother, a fellow child of God. We cannot objectify or dehumanize our enemies, near or far. In order for our violence—individually or societally—to be truly justified before God, and in order for us to fully grieve the violence we inflict, we must retain a lively sense of our profound interconnectedness, even in the midst of our destructive actions. Dead or broken bodies are tragedies, not trophies.

This principle of steadfast connection surpasses that of any other loyalty. Our identity as children of God transcends racial, ethnic, tribal, political, national, or religious boundaries. Disciples of Christ cannot and must not reduce any other person, even an aggressor, to the status of a mere "enemy" or "other," something less than a fellow child of God.[49] *Enemy* is best used to describe a person's actions, not his or her nature. In an official statement regarding war, The Church of Jesus Christ of Latter-day Saints pronounces, "If Latter-day Saints must go to war, . . . they should go with love in their hearts for all God's children, *including those on the opposing side.*"[50] Jesus's command to "love your enemies, bless them that curse you, do good to them that hate you, and pray for them which despitefully use you, and persecute you" must be part and parcel to the law of justified violence.[51] No justification of violence suspends or supersedes Christ's law of all-encompassing love.

INCREASED LOVE
Justified violence must always be followed by an increase of sanctifying love. Perhaps the most striking difference between the Restoration and the just war tradition involves what is called for in the aftermath of violence. According to Restoration theology, even justified force (which might be considered an extreme form of "reproving") should be followed by "an increase of love toward him whom thou hast reproved." This standard serves to maintain, or attempts to reestablish, the sacred connections between all of God's children that have been inevitably strained by violent conflict. While the standard of steadfast connection requires that we do not alienate ourselves from our opponents, they are nevertheless likely to have at least *felt* alienated from us. (Most people do not appreciate being on the receiving end of violence, no matter how "justified.") Thus, an increase of love toward any person or group we have injured is all the more important, "lest he esteem thee to be his enemy."[52]

As mortals, we cannot take back or reverse the effects of lethal violence. We do not have the power to reconcile with those whom we have sent to their graves. Only God can offer redemption to our enemies after they are dead. What *is* in our power is to offer forgiveness toward those who trespassed against us and demonstrate increased love toward those who remain alive. We have a special obligation to care for and seek reconciliation with the friends, relatives, and especially children of those whom we might kill. This is true on both the individual and societal levels. No justified war or act of personal self-defense should conclude without some version of a Marshall Plan to help our opponents get back on their feet. Indeed, this is the only moment in which *dis*-proportionality is appropriate, as our expressions and concrete manifestations of love should outweigh and overwhelm our previous violence. We should do everything in our power to restore that which we have caused to be lost, and then some. An "increase of love" goes beyond merely rebalancing the moral and material ledger.[53]

These eight criteria—disinclination, forbearance, divine consent, accountability, restraint, grief, steadfast connection, and increased love—may seem unreasonably constraining and all but impossible to meet in the world in which we live. It should not surprise or trouble us that God's standards for justified violence are far higher than anything we see in the fallen world, even in the Christian just war tradition. Christians are not called to be content with the world as it is, but rather to envision a better world conforming to the kingdom of God. We should expect the divine parameters placed around the tragic powers of destruction to be as stringent and countercultural as those principles that protect our powers of creation. The restored gospel of Jesus Christ's default orientation is toward peace and love. Hence, the bar for justifying direct violence is so high that it should only rarely be met. Instead of a dynamic in which violent responses are the norm, and those who wish to forbear and to love are required to explain or "justify" their nonviolence, these revealed standards flip the calculus. The Restoration privileges the use of loving nonviolence and places a heavy burden of proof on the use of retributive violence.

THE LIMITS OF MORAL IMAGINATION

If God wants his children to choose a higher way, why do so many sincere Christians opt for the use of force when dealing with their enemies? Why, for instance, did Nephite military leaders such as Moroni and Gidgiddoni, who had great faith and hope in Christ long before his birth, choose the lesser law of justified violence rather than the higher law of love and non-violence? They knew from the example of the Anti-Nephi-Lehies that it was possible to "renounce war and proclaim peace." Why then choose the sword?

The best answer may be the simplest—the higher law feels too costly, too difficult, maybe even impossible to achieve. Let's be honest. Nonviolent resistance rooted in love is extraordinarily hard. Not only is nonviolence hard to do, but in the face of violent threats to one's loved ones and community it is often hard to even imagine. Most people, even the best of us, are constrained by the limits of our cultural conditioning. Such cultural blinders mean that the only solution to violence we can often see is more or "better" violence. When the only tool in your hand is a hammer, then every problem looks like a nail.

Justified violence was the lens through which the Nephites typically viewed their conflict with the Lamanites. They had faith that if they kept God's commandments, he would instruct them how to respond to an attack—whether to "flee" or "prepare for war." Once they were engaged in battle, they believed that God "would make it known unto them whither they should go to defend themselves against their enemies."[54] Given the options of flight or fight, it is evident that the Nephites typically chose the latter. Perhaps surprisingly, then, a careful reading reveals that every time the Nephites seek God's aid *before* engaging in violent conflict, God commands them to flee (there are also a couple instances when the people choose to flee on their own).[55] Curiously, there are no recorded instances in which the Lord specifically warns the Nephites to prepare for a coming war, but there are at least two instances—both involving Alma the Younger—in which he tells them "whither they should go to defend themselves" after a conflict has already begun.[56] Most of the battle descriptions in the Book of Mormon don't necessarily imply divine assistance; to the contrary, many battles are characterized as just punishment for Nephite or Jaredite wickedness.[57] It is true that Mormon and other narrators clearly perceive God working with and strengthening the Nephite armies and commanders on several occasions.[58] But the overall pattern is striking. In short, while God seems to assist the Nephites on several occasions *after* they choose to engage in warfare, nowhere in the Book of Mormon does God directly tell the Nephites *beforehand* to engage in war. When the Nephites prepare for war, they appear to do so of their own accord.

The Lord's decision to help the Nephite armies after they opt for war may be an instance of how the Lord works within the limits of our moral imagination. One of the hardest things for any individual or community to do is to see beyond our own finite perspective, to imagine a path other than the one we are currently on. The scriptures record rare occasions in which God suddenly intervenes and explodes the boundaries of his people's understanding.[59] The vast majority of the time, however, God works within the limited bounds of what we are capable of considering.[60] When he does expand the boundaries of our vision, it is most often with a nudge rather than a shove—gently, slowly, "line upon line, line upon line; here a little, and there a little."[61]

This may explain the divine strength God lends to the Nephites in war. Having already, through their own reasoning, decided to go to battle against their enemies, they seek the Lord's assistance *in* the fight—not to ask *whether* they should fight or try some morally imaginative strategy of assertive love instead. God's preference for peace is clear. Yet it seems that he elects to support his children in their flawed condition rather than reserving his assistance only for occasions in which their desires perfectly align with his higher laws. Indeed, if God waited for our motivations and behaviors to be entirely pure before he assisted us, he would never have occasion to act in human history. It is important, however, not to confuse divine aid with divine approval. That we receive providential assistance from a loving Father who "maketh his sun to rise on the evil and on the good, and sendeth rain on the just and on the unjust" does not necessarily mean our actions have his full endorsement.[62]

A merciful God provides lesser laws to guide us in our individual and collective frailty. Even so, he is always poised to lead us to higher ground if we can manage to break our culturally conditioned blinders and lift up our eyes to imagine holier, stronger, more effective possibilities. The prophet Alma testified that God "granteth unto men according to their desire, whether it be unto death or unto life."[63] The question before us is whether we will be content to orient our desires around a lesser law of justified violence, or instead strive for a higher law of assertive love and nonviolence; whether we will settle for justification alone, or strive for the holier way of sanctification. God sets before us the ways of death and of life—which will we choose?

CHAPTER SEVEN

The Conundrum of Divine Violence

Man shall not smite, neither shall he judge;
for judgment is mine, saith the Lord, and vengeance
is mine also, and I will repay.
—Mormon 8:20

And the fire of mine indignation is kindled against them; . . .
but behold . . . misery shall be their doom; . . . wherefore
should not the heavens weep, seeing these shall suffer?
—Moses 7:34, 37

R estoration scriptures offer many descriptions of God's character, but perhaps the simplest and most elegant is provided by the First Epistle of John: "God is love."[1] There are no boundaries to his love. As the Book of Mormon testifies, God invites all of his children "to come unto him and partake of his goodness; and he denieth none that come unto him, black and white, bond and free, male and female; and he remembereth the heathen; and all are alike unto God, both Jew and Gentile."[2] This echoes Paul's teaching that "there is neither

Jew nor Greek, there is neither bond nor free, there is neither male nor female: for ye are all one in Christ Jesus."[3] God's love is indiscriminate and works to break down rather than reinforce human categories of difference that fuel structural and cultural violence.[4]

Indeed, if God does show any kind of preference, it is in favor of the poor, the vulnerable, and the marginalized, thereby enacting precisely the opposite dynamic as structural and cultural violence. In the kingdom of God, everyone is invited to feast at the same table. There are no second-class citizens. There is no back of the bus. Recall the lines from the prophet Isaiah that Jesus chose to open his public ministry with: "The Spirit of the Lord is upon me, because he has anointed me to bring good news to the poor. He has sent me to proclaim release to the captives and recovery of sight to the blind, to let the oppressed go free."[5] God is passionate for justice and sides with the oppressed. Thus, it is safe to say that God does not endorse nor perpetuate structural or cultural violence.

So then how do we make sense of all the scriptural accounts of God's *direct* violence?

There are many episodes in which God either apparently commands or conducts violence against his human children, any one of which could potentially pose a problem not only for a robust ethic of Christian nonviolence but indeed for faith in the Christian God.[6] Other scholars have grappled with the divine violence contained in the Bible and have come up with answers and interpretive strategies that are compelling from a purely biblical standpoint.[7] Latter-day Saints can learn much from these approaches, but we also have to contend with additional instances from Restoration scripture that pose a challenge for the conception of a loving God who is also completely nonviolent.

Perhaps the most vexing case comes from the Book of Mormon, immediately preceding the climactic moment in which the resurrected Jesus Christ personally visits and ministers to the descendants of Lehi. Christ's arrival is preceded by extraordinary destruction, beginning with a "great and terrible tempest" followed by "terrible thunder" and "exceedingly sharp lightnings." As the storm rages across the land, even more calamitous natural disasters strike many Nephite cities and their inhabitants. Severe earthquakes alter the very contours of the landscape, causing buildings to fall and many people to die. A tornado carries people away, their bodies never to be found again. Then, after the horror of all this loss and destruction, a "thick darkness" descends, enshrouding the entire land with a gloom so thick the survivors can "feel the vapor." For three days the surviving inhabitants see absolutely no light; there is no light from the sky, and for some reason they are unable to kindle any fire. In the utter darkness, the people are bereft, left with nothing other than their own "great mourning and howling and weeping."[8]

All of this destruction stems from the fact that on the other side of the world "the God of nature suffers."[9] Jesus, the Son of God and Creator of the world, has been crucified, an event so horrific that the earth itself is rent with grief. In the midst of the darkness and devastation, the surviving Nephites and Lamanites hear a voice from heaven that explains their plight. But rather than attributing the destruction to nature's response to the death of its creator, Jesus Christ takes full credit for the violence. It is one of the most chilling passages in all of scripture:

> Behold, that great city Zarahemla have I burned with fire, and the inhabitants thereof. And behold, that great city Moroni have I caused to be sunk in the depths of the sea, and the inhabitants thereof to be drowned. And behold, that great city Moronihah have I covered with earth, and the inhabitants thereof. . . . And behold, the city of Gilgal have I caused to be sunk, and the inhabitants thereof to be buried up in the depths of the earth; yea, and

the city of Onihah and the inhabitants thereof, and the city of Mocum and the inhabitants thereof, and the city of Jerusalem and the inhabitants thereof; and waters have I caused to come up in the stead thereof. . . . And behold, the city of Gadiandi, and the city of Gadiomnah, and the city of Jacob, and the city of Gimgimno, all these have I caused to be sunk, and made hills and valleys in the places thereof; and the inhabitants thereof have I buried up in the depths of the earth. . . . And behold, that great city Jacobugath, which was inhabited by the people of king Jacob, have I caused to be burned with fire. . . . And behold, the city of Laman, and the city of Josh, and the city of Gad, and the city of Kishkumen, have I caused to be burned with fire, and the inhabitants thereof. . . . I did send down fire and destroy them. . . . And many great destructions have I caused to come upon this land, and upon this people.[10]

Such divine violence provides one of the most significant challenges to both a theology of a compassionate and merciful God and a human ethic of nonviolence. The epic scope of the devastation raises epic questions. If "God is love," how can he be directly responsible for such cataclysmic—and targeted—destruction? Mass destruction may prove God's power and might—that he should be feared—but how is this a God whom we should love and trust? And what are the implications for us? Is retributive violence a sacred option for God's children? Such questions become all the more pressing when we consider not only scriptural moments when God inflicts violence directly but also times when he enlists his children to carry it out. Nephi is commanded to slay Laban. Israel is commanded to destroy the Amalekites. In light of the power of nonviolent love, what are we to make of these commands? In sum, what are we supposed to learn from scriptures that narrate a God of love doing (or directing) violence against his children?

Discerning answers to such questions is a delicate business, not least because we do not have direct access to the mind of God. Some people prefer to ignore or disregard the various scriptural accounts of divine violence. Through their own reasoning and experience, they have decided that because "God is love," he simply cannot and would not ever use violence of any kind, and therefore any account that says he does must be wrongly recorded, translated, or understood. While we appreciate the peace-loving impulse behind this perspective, we feel that the scriptural record of divine violence is too abundant to simply dismiss, even for reasons we may personally sympathize with. As believers it is important to us to preserve the integrity of scripture as a faithful, though not flawless, witness of God's character and his dealings with his children. We believe that while not all scriptural passages carry equal weight, a serious theological approach must elucidate a set of principles or standards by which readers can determine, based on more than personal preference, which passages are truly determinative for Christian theology and ethics.

Restoration theology and scriptures do offer potential answers to some of the most vexing questions about divine violence. As we shall see, the picture is more complex than first appears. Even if we are to grant that God does or can employ direct violence—an admittedly hard pill for many to swallow—then we propose that it still does not give humans license to do the same.

FOLLOWING THE CONDESCENDED GOD

Our theory of scriptural interpretation, or hermeneutic, rests on an assumption that the various scriptural accounts of divine violence are just as trustworthy on their face as the passages that reveal our Father to be a God of peace. In other words, if we are going to admit one set of texts into evidence, there is no compelling reason, from a purely textual standpoint, to dismiss the other out of hand. Two principal questions thus arise: What do the passages narrating divine violence mean for our understanding of God's character? And what do those passages mean for us? More pointedly, since one of the primary purposes of our mortal existence is to develop the attributes of God, should we use accounts of God's violent judgment and retribution to perform our own personal acts of violent judgment and retribution? We strongly assert that the answer is an emphatic "no." But why not?

The answer may lie in the distinction between the "condescended" Son of God and the "ascended" Godhead. *Condescension* is meant here not in the usual modern sense of an attitude of patronizing superiority or disdain, but rather in the more literal meaning of "to come down with."[11] As Immanuel, or "God with us," Jesus Christ came down from celestial realms not only to save fallen humanity but also to provide a perfect example for how we should live our lives.[12] In terms of our moral and ethical life, then, God's children are invited to follow the example of the "condescended" Jesus. The defining text here is Christ's teaching in the Book of Mormon: "What manner of men ought ye to be? Verily I say unto you, even as I am."[13] We suggest that our imitation of Christ must necessarily be limited to the perfect example he displayed during his mortal life and post-resurrection ministry on earth. It is true that Jesus commanded us to "be ye therefore perfect, even as your Father which is in heaven is perfect."[14] But as President Russell M. Nelson has taught, it is essential to distinguish between the "mortal perfection" that is attainable for us in this life and the "immortal or eternal perfection" that will be available to us only in the Resurrection, when through Christ's grace we can be empowered to fully live "the kind of life that God lives."[15]

Precisely because we are finite mortals, it is impossible for us to imitate the divine powers—including final judgment and destruction—that the perfected, or "ascended," Father and Son control from their glorious heavenly realm. In fact, quite the opposite. In the Book of Mormon, God plainly declares that "man shall not smite, neither shall he judge; for judgment is mine, saith the Lord, and vengeance is mine also, and I will repay."[16] It seems that we are to emulate those aspects of Christ's character that were part and parcel of his "condescended" state that we share, but not those aspects of godhood that are reserved for glorified and perfected beings. Therefore, since violent judgment and retribution are occasionally exercised by the "ascended" Godhead but not the "condescended" Son of God, the more violent aspects of the divine character are off the table for God's children here on earth.

As finite mortal beings, we are in a weak position to render fully righteous judgment or parcel out just retribution. Even within a Restoration theology affirming our divine potential as children of God, there lies an enormous gulf between imperfect mortals and a perfect God—a chasm in perspective, experience, knowledge, wisdom, character, and capacity for love. "For my thoughts are not your thoughts," God reminds his children, "neither are your ways my ways."[17] As the Book of Mormon notes, "man doth not comprehend all the things which the Lord can comprehend."[18] To worship a God who is beyond our understanding (even if we are his offspring) is to admit that he can and will act in ways we are not allowed to act, because he sees things we do not see. But we can see, and therefore emulate, the perfect example of the Son of God in his "condescended" state.

It may be helpful to bring this closer to home with an analogy. Think of a nuclear family in which the oldest sibling is a model child, exemplary in every way. Although the parents and children share the same genetic material and all the children are

155

destined to someday follow in their parents' footsteps, for now the parents have capacities, abilities, and rights that are not yet available to the children. In terms of right behavior, then, the younger children can learn more from modeling themselves after their exemplary oldest sibling than by immediately imitating their parents. The time will come, down the line, for the children to do all their parents do. But for now, their job is to learn to be the best children they can be, in gradual preparation for adulthood's many complexities and responsibilities that for now remain beyond their grasp.

The prescribed ethic for humanity, then, is the example of the condescended Christ, which is decidedly the opposite of retribution. Shortly before his death, Jesus gave his disciples a "new commandment" that would constitute the defining feature of their Christianity: "Just as I have loved you, you also should love one another."[19] By way of comparison, a revelation to Joseph Smith pointed to a crucial distinction between the ethic to which God is bound versus the one he insists on for his mortal children: "I, the Lord, will forgive whom I forgive, but of you it is required to forgive all men."[20] In short, one of the most important acts of discernment we learn in fallen mortality is knowing which aspects of divine behavior we can and should emulate and which ones we must simply leave to God.

UNDERSTANDING DIVINE JUDGMENT AND RETRIBUTION

Our incomprehension of God's eternal nature includes the rules and rationales by which on occasion he apparently uses violence against his own children. Like Nephi, we cannot claim to "know the meaning of all things," but we can affirm that God "loveth his children," even when in the short term he inflicts violence and death on them.[21] If we seek to "exercise faith in God unto life and salvation," then we have to try to develop "a correct idea" of how divine violence fits into his "character, perfections, and attributes."[22]

Scriptural examples of divine mass violence include the ancient deluge in the time of Noah, the fiery destruction of Sodom and Gomorrah, and the widespread destruction at the time of Christ's crucifixion.[23] There are also more targeted acts of violence against individuals such as Uzzah (who steadied the ark of the covenant), Ananias and Sapphira (who withheld their consecrated property), and Sherem (who preached against the coming of Christ), all of whom were struck down by God.[24] Taking these narratives at face value, we authors must admit some befuddlement at what constitutes a capital crime in God's eyes—many people throughout history have committed far greater evils without immediate divine punishment. The moral calculus by which God decides to strike one person or society and not another remains hidden to us. But when we consider the totality of the record of God's interactions with his children, we may be able to infer at least a few principles that inform his approach to violence.

As the supreme being in a universe predicated on "opposition in all things," God holds and exercises both the ultimate power to create and the ultimate power to destroy.[25] God's default and preferred orientation is clearly toward the creation and sustenance of life. As Latter-day Saint theologian Adam Miller writes, "By raising Jesus from the dead, God demonstrates his unwavering fidelity to life."[26] It is in this attitude that God most often reveals himself to us and admonishes us to do likewise.

When God engages in acts of destruction, he retains his perfect love for his children against whom he acts. Even in his righteous anger, he is never alienated from those he loves, though they may distance themselves from him. He never engages his violence from some safe emotional distance. He is perfectly present in the tragedy of those moments and feels deep sorrow for the destruction he inflicts. We see this in the inspired expansion of the biblical story of the prophet Enoch, the great-grandfather of Noah. Shown in vision the eventual coming flood, Enoch is surprised to find God weeping over the "residue of the people." "How is it that thou canst weep," the prophet asks, "seeing thou art holy, and from all eternity to all eternity?" God responds by noting that the people who will suffer are "the workmanship of mine own hands" and "thy brethren"—a categorical refusal to distance either himself or Enoch from the kinship and solidarity that all humanity shares with their Father and with each other. Filled with sorrow at the free choices made by his children, God recalls that he gave them a commandment "that they should love one another, and that they should choose me, their Father; but behold, they are without affection, and they hate their own blood." Although consumed with "hot displeasure" and "fierce anger" at a corrupt world, God still loves his wayward children. So he weeps. When Enoch asks why, God responds, "Wherefore should not the heavens weep, seeing these shall suffer?" And God doesn't stop at offering his tears, thoughts, and prayers for the victims. He goes to work redeeming them. Even in mass destruction lie the seeds of love and hope, for God announces to Enoch that Jesus Christ will atone not only for the sins of Noah's generation but for all of humanity.[27] A unique feature of Restoration theology is the belief that the spirits of those killed in the flood—and by extension all others who suffer from divine violence—are not only resurrected through the grace of Christ but also given opportunities for repentance and redemption after their mortal death.[28] God sometimes gives death, but beforehand and afterward he also—and always—gives life.

God's refusal to alienate himself or turn away from the tragedy of his violence, and his subsequent and simultaneous love for the subjects of his destruction, perfectly reflect the principles articulated in Joseph Smith's letter from Liberty Jail. The rare episodes of God's direct violence against his children can be understood as a form of "reproving betimes with sharpness," but his subsequent behavior also exemplifies the principle of "showing forth afterwards an increase of love toward him whom thou hast reproved, lest he esteem thee to be his enemy; that he may know that thy faithfulness is stronger than the cords of death."[29] We see this pattern on display in the cataclysmic divine violence recorded in the Book of Mormon. Before claiming credit for the devastation that has just occurred, the voice from heaven first exclaims poignant sorrow and then, immediately after a description of the violence, offers a message of compassion and an invitation to reconciliation: "O all ye that are spared . . . , will ye not now return unto me, and repent of your sins, and be converted, that I may heal you? . . . Behold, mine arm of mercy is extended towards you, and whosoever will come, him will I receive."[30] This notion of otherworldly compensation will admittedly be cold comfort to those who do not accept Restoration doctrines of a universal bodily resurrection and the redemption of postmortal spirits. However, a thoroughgoing secular critique must also acknowledge that it cannot be God inflicting violence on humans if there is no God. Therefore, to enter the logic of divine violence is also to engage the reality of divine compensation.

Theologically, God is ultimately responsible for both the cosmic mystery and miracle of life as well as the temporal tragedy of death that eventually visits all living things. One solution to the conundrum of divine violence is therefore to acknowledge God's exclusive right to destroy life as a form of judgment or retribution, precisely because God alone can also grant life everlasting. Violence remains a tool in God's toolbox in a way it is not for his mortal children because he can control his use of the tool and has the power to reconcile with the dead and make right whatever damage is done, while we do not. Still, even if we can accept it, there is nothing that says we have to be happy about God's occasional resort to violence. If we shrink from divine violence and are morally troubled by it, it means our sensitive souls are simply a reflection of God's own profound sorrow over the violence he sometimes deploys. We can rightly weep over the victims of divine violence because God wept first. God's promise to us, and to all those who taste death in whatever fashion, is that he will ultimately wipe away those real tears of sorrow and swallow up the sting of death in the resurrection and redemption of Jesus Christ.[31]

INTERPRETING THE DIVINE COMMAND

In addition to scriptural examples of violence perpetrated directly by God, there are also passages that portray him commanding or commending human violence. Most divine violence in the scriptures is of this second variety, namely, killing done by humans acting in the name of God or apparently at his behest. But what are the principles on which divinely commanded violence is initiated and the standards by which it should be carried out? Again, the mind of God is usually inscrutable. Given all the bloodshed recorded in the scriptures, it is notable that the instances where God specifically outlines any rules are very rare.[32]

Therefore, most of what we think we know about divine violence through human agents is actually inferred from observing the behavior of scriptural warriors. When the scriptures describe generally righteous persons engaging in violence, it is easy to assume all their actions are divinely approved or even commanded. But to describe an activity is not necessarily to condone it. An essential interpretive strategy, then, is to differentiate which instances of violence in the scriptures are meant to be *prescriptive* as compared to those that are merely *descriptive*. Prescriptive passages are those in which the Lord appears to specifically direct or endorse an action or attitude and intends it to be an ethical norm. Prescriptive passages feature behavior that righteous followers of God *should* or *should not* do—the most obvious example being the Ten Commandments. However, many if not most other passages are merely descriptive, meaning they describe human behavior without necessarily endorsing it or intending it as a pattern for imitation. There are many unrighteous actions and attitudes in scripture, for example, that are clearly intended for readers to learn from but not imitate.

As we've repeatedly emphasized, in Restoration theology the ideal model for all human behavior is Jesus Christ, the Son of God made flesh. Jesus is the gold standard. His consistent commitment to nonviolence throughout his life reveals the primary orientation of God's character and actions. Even the well-known story of Jesus cleansing the temple demonstrates rather than undermines his nonviolent character. In that instance, his righteous indignation at the desecration of his Father's house translated into forceful action against property (including animals) but not violence against persons.[33] For a disciple of Christ, it is theologically and ethically risky to turn away from the example of Jesus and extrapolate divine rules for violence from the lives of fallen human beings, no matter how admirable they might be.

With Jesus as our true model and standard, we can still learn valuable lessons from the prescriptive and descriptive texts narrating the behaviors and attitudes of our fellow imperfect humans. Consider the case of Captain Moroni, the most prominent military figure in the Book of Mormon. Moroni left such an impression on the prophet-editor Mormon (also a Nephite general) that he enthused, "If all men had been, and were, and ever would be, like unto Moroni, behold, the very powers of hell would have been shaken forever." There is indeed much about Captain Moroni that is highly commendable. His heart "[does] not delight in bloodshed." He clearly loves his people and is willing to sacrifice his life to protect them. He seems quick to take the first possible opportunity to cease hostilities and can be generous toward prisoners of war. But the prophet Mormon's own portrayal of this powerful military leader reveals a human being whose character is far from perfect, especially when compared to the example of Jesus. Moroni can be rash and quick to anger. He is not a particularly diplomatic negotiator, and he summarily executes large numbers of Nephite dissenters. Furthermore, in his anger he falsely accuses the government of malfeasance, citing an obviously incorrect (or incorrectly understood) personal revelation. Book of Mormon scholar Grant Hardy suggests that Mormon's ringing endorsement of Moroni, calling him "a man of perfect understanding," may be better understood as an attempt to assure readers that this man was an instrument of God's will and can be considered an exemplar in spite of some of his questionable actions.[34]

Hence, while there is much to recommend Captain Moroni as a role model, we should be careful not to read Mormon's account of the Nephite wars as the equivalent of a divine endorsement of everything Moroni is and does. The same principle holds true for any of the other necessarily flawed characters in scripture. Readers have to assess the various descriptive accounts in scripture and then make judgments about their moral applicability. The prescriptive value of descriptive accounts should always be considered in light of how they conform to well-established divine directives such as "thou shalt not kill" and "love your enemies," as well as how they match up with the perfect love revealed in and through Jesus Christ.[35]

But how are readers to interpret the many scriptural passages in which humans are expressly commanded or allowed by God to commit violence? As a case study, let's consider an oft-quoted pair of verses from the Book of Mormon that feature two otherwise unknown revelations endorsing defensive violence. In the middle of narrating yet another epic battle between Nephites and Lamanites, the prophet-general Mormon pauses the action to note that the Nephite armies

> were doing that which they felt was the duty which they owed to their God; for the Lord had said unto them, and also unto their fathers, that: Inasmuch as ye are not guilty of the first offense, neither the second, ye shall not suffer yourselves to be slain by the hands of your enemies. And again, the Lord has said that: Ye shall defend your families even unto bloodshed.[36]

The source for these two divine commands is not clear from the text—they are not recorded anywhere else in scripture—but their prescriptive quality is both unmistakable and unusual. On its face, these directives appear to *require* violence in the case of self-defense. This is the only place in the Book of Mormon where God seems not only to permit human violence but actually to command it.

Upon closer inspection, the two commands in this passage are more complicated than they appear. Let's look at them in turn. The first command begins by placing a provisional condition on the use of violence: "inasmuch as ye are not guilty of the first offense, neither the second . . ." This echoes both the Sermon on the Mount, with its command to turn the other cheek, and the August 1833 revelation, which requires multiple instances of patient forbearance before violence can be justified. In other words, this is decidedly *not* an allowance for immediate retribution in the face of aggression. Having fulfilled the obligation of forbearance, the command then says, "Ye shall not suffer yourselves to be slain by the hands of your enemies." Two things are worth noting here. First, the command does *not* include an affirmative provision for killing one's enemies; it only says that one should not allow oneself to be killed by them. Second, the provision itself seems curious in light of the long line of righteous martyrs, including many prophets and apostles, who *have* allowed themselves to be slain by their enemies—Paul, Abinadi, and Joseph Smith immediately come to mind. And how does this instruction square with the example of Jesus himself, who consciously decided to allow himself to be killed rather than responding with violence of any kind, and who commanded his followers to be willing to follow him to the cross?

The command in the following verse seems even more straightforward: "Ye shall defend your families even unto bloodshed." This has often been interpreted as the most straightforward rationale for divinely ordained self-defense in the Latter-day Saint tradition.[37] But even this apparently plain statement contains more than meets the eye. First, the verse does not make any provision for *self*-defense, but rather for defense of loved ones in one's care, and specifically one's family. In this regard it echoes the teachings of St. Augustine, the fourth- and fifth-century church father and theologian who stipulated that the Christian law of love allowed a person to use violence in defense of others but not in defense of self. So this is not a stand-your-ground command. Perhaps we can also ask whose blood is being shed here. When an attacker is hell-bent on using violence, it may be impossible to avoid bloodshed. Those committed to loving nonviolence recognize this but affirm that they would rather have their own blood shed than shed the blood of another person. Keep in mind that the Anti-Nephi-Lehies *did* defend their families, even unto bloodshed, but they did so through loving nonviolence and the voluntary shedding of their own blood. On an even broader scale, Jesus chose to defend the entire family of God from evil not through the violent shedding of blood of his "enemies," but rather through voluntarily sacrificing his own body and blood on the cross.

In sum, even the Book of Mormon's most seemingly straightforward divine endorsement of self-defensive violence can actually be read in a way that questions any notion of a standing commandment from God authorizing—even commanding—his children to use violent force. Nothing in the Book of Mormon's war chapters overturns or supersedes Christ's law of love, with its corresponding principles of forbearance and nonviolence.

INTERPRETIVE POSSIBILITIES

The Old Testament famously contains a number of troublesome passages regarding God's apparent commands for his people to use horrific violence in his name. It is difficult for most modern readers to understand what seem to be divine injunctions to commit genocide, such as God commanding King Saul (through the prophet Samuel) to "go and smite Amalek, and utterly destroy all that they have, and spare them not; but slay both man and woman, infant and suckling, ox and sheep, camel and ass."[38] Likewise, Moses's directive for the Israelites to "utterly destroy" the Canaanites is hard to stomach.[39] Such dictates seem incongruous with God's merciful character, and they certainly seem out of harmony with the higher law of love as revealed by and through Jesus in the New Testament and Book of Mormon. Without simply ignoring these passages because they make us uncomfortable, nor taking them as a pattern for how we are to interact with our neighbors, how can we understand what is going on here?

In addition to what we have already outlined, there are multiple interpretive possibilities available to Latter-day Saints grappling with the problem of divine violence while also committed to reading scripture as inherently trustworthy, if still liable to various kinds of imperfection.[40] One such strategy is to recall that all scriptural instances of a direct divine command for humans to commit violence precede Christ's mortal ministry. Thus, we might attribute the statements to a God who is working with people who are living a lesser law; in other words, God meets them where they are and over time tries to get them to do better. This explanation has some merit. God's commands do seem to become less violent over the course of the Hebrew Bible. By the time Micah rolls around, near the end of the book, the message about what God considers "good" behavior is clear: "what doth the Lord require of thee, but to do justly, and to love mercy, and to walk humbly with thy God."[41] Furthermore, in the New Testament Christ explicitly invokes the Mosaic law, "an eye for an eye, and a tooth for a tooth," only to supersede it with the higher law of nonviolence.[42] The challenge with this hermeneutical strategy of upward moral progression is that it could be used to imply that God's own character—rather than the collective capacity of his people—is changing and improving over time, a proposition that is unsettling if not downright heretical for most Christians.

A second possibility is to read scripture intertextually—that is, to read one passage of scripture through others that seem to shed some light on it. For instance, new vistas open up when we read violent Old Testament passages through the lens of the August 1833 revelation to Joseph Smith. Indeed, that particular revelation specifically invites us to read it intertextually since it explicitly states that its provisions, including its preference for forbearance and peace, were given to "Joseph, and Jacob, and Isaac, and Abraham, and all mine ancient prophets and apostles." In this light, Israelite prophets such as Moses, Joshua, and Samuel in some sense possessed the law placing strict limits on their resort to violence. According to the revelation, they would have been aware of God's promises that if they would spare their enemies, even after repeated aggressions, they and their people would "be rewarded for [their] righteousness; and also [their] children and [their] children's children unto the third and fourth generation."[43] In other words, there may have been circumstances in which God's prophets felt justified and even compelled toward violence, but they also knew that the divine command to destroy always existed alongside the standing law to preserve life and proclaim peace. Like Adam and Eve who were given conflicting commandments, prophets (and their people) are never robbed of agency. As free beings in a creative relationship with the divine, they make choices as to which of God's sometimes conflicting or multiple commands to privilege. The August 1833 revelation, not to mention the higher law of nonviolent love taught throughout the scriptures, affirms that while the people of God (including his prophets) may choose violence, and even attribute their choice to a divine directive, in fact it is never their only option.

A third strategy is to interpret the Bible's violent passages using the insights of modern scholarship, which is increasingly skeptical about the historical reliability of the Hebrew Bible's accounts of genocide. Most biblical scholars have concluded that many books of the Hebrew Bible contain textual insertions and other changes by writers who lived many centuries after the events described and who frequently narrated earlier history with their own contemporary interests and dilemmas in mind.[44] Some of those chroniclers may have sought to endorse violence in their own day by adding language to give the appearance of divinely approved genocide by their righteous ancestors. For example, there is little archaeological or genetic evidence of a violent conquest of Canaan by Israelites; to the contrary, the data suggests that the takeover was a slow and relatively peaceful process. Therefore, scholars increasingly believe that significant parts of the military stories recorded in the book of Joshua, including the divine command to utterly destroy the Canaanites, may have been inserted by later scribes to legitimize Israelite occupation of Canaanite lands.[45] Even the scriptural texts themselves state that the people supposedly "destroyed" by Joshua and the Israelite armies not only survived but continued to live on in the land in still large and identifiable communities.[46] In light of this, one scholar suggests that the Bible's record of a divine command to "utterly destroy" is hyperbolic and figurative, similar to a modern sports idiom like "The Yankees completely destroyed the Red Sox last night."[47] In short, seemingly genocidal scriptural language may not be what it appears at first glance, which further erodes any moral authority that might be gleaned from scripture to endorse human violence.[48]

Finally, and most importantly, as we have already established, disciples of Christ already possess an interpretive lens through which they should read and understand the entirety of scripture—namely, Jesus Christ himself. The nonviolence of Jesus's life and example is absolute. His crucifixion offers prophetic judgment on the use of violence for supposedly just purposes. The myth of redemptive or righteous violence is swallowed up in and undermined by the death of the ultimate innocent victim. If an act or statement cannot square with the good news of peace and nonviolence proclaimed by Jesus, disciples of Christ should question whether that act or statement truly reveals the divine will and character—precisely because we know what that divine will and character looks like when embodied in the flesh.

Given the range of interpretive resources available to readers, scriptural episodes in which God commands or commends violence might be read with a certain degree of skepticism that is simultaneously reasonable, ethical, and faithful. Followers of the Prince of Peace can employ a variety of interpretive frameworks that preserve the authority of scripture yet do not simply let violence speak for itself or have the last word. In the end, all readers of scripture are forced to make interpretive choices. No one can give all scriptural passages equal weight, because some of those passages conflict with one another.[49] We affirm that faithful readers can interpret some passages of scripture metaphorically and others literally and can question or even disregard certain passages as being the products of human authors writing with particular perspectives, prejudices, or even traumas. Indeed, this is how most modern Christians, including Latter-day Saints, treat the New Testament texts that forbid women from speaking in church or teaching men.[50]

To affirm that readers have to make interpretive choices should not be confused, however, with giving a green light for readers to choose willy-nilly whatever scriptural passages suit them; scripture reading should never simply be an exercise in confirmation bias. Quite the contrary, it is a call for readers (as individuals and communities) to develop rigorous interpretive frameworks that provide a coherent reading of scripture based on a set of clearly articulated principles. We have asserted that Latter-day Saint theology, ethics, and hermeneutics should be centered on the nonviolent life, teachings, ministry, and atonement of Jesus Christ. Any alternative approach has the burden of explaining why Jesus should be decentered and what ought to be put in his place as the lens through which we should read and evaluate all other scripture.

CHAPTER EIGHT

A Political Theology
of Friendship

I will be your king and watch over you.
Wherefore, hear my voice and follow me,
and you shall be a free people.
—Doctrine and Covenants 38:21–22

I, the Lord, justify you, and your brethren
of my church, in befriending that law which
is the constitutional law of the land.
—Doctrine and Covenants 98:6

ood citizenship makes good sense. It provides social
G stability and undergirds a political order that allows
for humans to live together in community. The two
of us have been fortunate enough to be among the minority of
humans throughout history to live under a democratic regime
that protects fundamental rights and effectively preserves social
harmony. As such, we generally understand government to be a
positive good, while appreciating that citizens will naturally disagree on some of the specifics of how government best does its

work. Precisely because contemporary societies are so diverse, most people recognize that there must be a set of ruling authorities that not only govern but also arbitrate between competing interests. Modern political theory is founded on the notion of a social contract in which individuals surrender some of their personal sovereignty to the government, which in turn promises to keep the peace, prevent violence and anarchy, and offer a range of protections and services that would be difficult to secure on a purely individual basis. Put more positively, the modern nation-state has been a remarkably effective and durable arrangement that at its best has done much to defend its citizens from harm as well as protect and extend their individual rights and liberties.

Yet citizenship can also be tricky. What should people do when they fundamentally disagree with their nation's policies or actions? Citizens in democratic nations have the advantage of being able to use the ballot box as something of a check on their elected officials' decisions and therefore policymaking. But although democracies tend to fight wars less often than do authoritarian states, and rarely with one another, a citizen of any modern democratic nation can point to moments in his or her country's past when it failed to live up to its best ideals, especially in wartime. Americans, for instance, might immediately think of the My Lai massacre or the brutality shown toward Iraqi prisoners in Abu Ghraib prison. Knowing that such abuses have happened and can happen again, people of conscience can and should never assume their nation's moral infallibility.

What about religious individuals and communities who acknowledge a heavenly sovereign in addition to an earthly one? "No one can serve two masters," Jesus said.[1] But believers routinely do. Most of the time there doesn't seem to be a conflict—neither God nor the government is keen on murder or fraud, for instance. Because a basic code of human decency and morality undergirds both civil society and religious life, the obligations to

God and country overlap substantially. For two thousand years, followers of Jesus have generally recognized submission to secular governmental authorities as being fully compatible with Christian discipleship. Indeed, one of the Latter-day Saints' thirteen articles of faith is to be "subject to kings, presidents, rulers, and magistrates, in obeying, honoring, and sustaining the law."[2]

Nevertheless, there are tensions between loyalty to God and loyalty to ruling secular authorities that demand our attention. This is especially true as we consider the type of power and authority wielded by earthly sovereignties versus the model of nonviolent power and influence characteristic of the kingdom of God. As we have seen, divine power is "maintained" by virtue of "persuasion, by long-suffering, by gentleness and meekness, and by love unfeigned."[3] On the other hand, according to Max Weber, one of the founders of modern sociology, the power of the modern nation-state is predicated on the *"monopoly of the legitimate use of physical force* within a given territory. . . . The state is a relation of men dominating men, a relation supported by means of legitimate (i.e. considered to be legitimate) violence. If the state is to exist, the dominated must obey the authority claimed by the powers that be."[4] Most modern political regimes also base their authority on the consent of the governed, but the possibility and reality of force always underlies that relationship. The contrast between the kingdom of God, predicated on the power of love, and the nation-state, predicated on the power of violence, is stark.

Because the kingdom of God has not been fully realized, Christians since the time of Jesus have been forced to determine how their faith commitments relate to their duties as citizens. Early Christians were frequently persecuted by the Roman Empire precisely because of their unwillingness to give their full allegiance to Caesar—in particular, to acknowledge him as a deity and to take up the sword on his behalf. That changed when the empire first recognized and then officially embraced Christianity, which in turn embraced the empire.[5] Since that significant shift in the relationship between Christians and government, there have been times, even long stretches, when subsequent Christians have conflated religion and the state, producing theocracies and religious empires that distorted the integrity of the humble faith taught by Jesus. Through it all, the same questions persist: How much allegiance should followers of Jesus offer to any worldly nation, and what forms should that allegiance take? When the state calls on its citizens to participate in and validate its violence, how should Christians—including Latter-day Saints—respond?

What follows is the basic outline of a political theology predicated on the Restoration's principles of nonviolent power and influence. By "political theology" we simply mean the application of serious religious thinking and commitment to the political sphere.[6] The Church of Jesus Christ of Latter-day Saints is, of course, strictly neutral when it comes to partisan politics. But it has always been concerned with the character of our political communities.[7] Our concern here is not so much with specific policies but rather with the more fundamental question of how Latter-day Saints might rightly "render unto Caesar," especially when the modern nation-state exerts violence. Drawing on Restoration scripture, history, and prophetic teaching, we propose recovering a political theology based less on the principle of subjection than on the concept of friendship.

"Friendship," taught Joseph Smith, "is the grand fundamental principle of Mormonism." Far from being passive or sentimental, true friendship has the power "to revolutionize [and] civilize the world" as it "pour[s] forth love."[8] Accordingly, Restoration theology suggests that the friendship that Latter-day Saints should offer the state is an active, transformative, and sustained relationship that requires substantial interest and investment, and in turn has real force. Precisely because telestial structures of power have a strong natural tilt toward authoritarianism and abuse, it is requisite for people of goodwill not to be passive passengers on the ship of state but rather to be actively involved in navigating, steering, and rowing it in the direction that will serve the interests of peace, justice, and care for all. While living in anticipation of Christ's eventual millennial kingdom, we can still offer our current political communities, from the local to the national and even global level, true friendship and all that it entails—mutual interest, genuine care, commitment, sacrifice, hope, and, yes, love. At the same time, deep friendship includes a willingness, and even a responsibility, to call out bad behavior. Friendship is not blind allegiance. It does not countenance abuse. Even the best of friendships can be betrayed or undermined and consequently suspended or dissolved. Unless and until that happens, however, there is great virtue in demonstrating tremendous and active loyalty to our friends.[9]

In short, while the Restoration articulates the notion of being "subject" to the state—a notion that resonates with traditional Christian political theology—it also offers an alternative political theology of "friendship." Importantly, such friendship does not require the follower of Jesus to condone or participate in the state's violence. Jesus taught that there is no greater love than to *die* for one's friends. This suggests a potency and depth of friendship that we can offer to our political communities, especially as we work to make them communities of care.[10] It even suggests a power of friendship that might extend nonviolent power and influence in ways that could potentially "revolutionize and civilize the world." But note that Jesus never said his disciples should be willing to *kill* for their friends—suggesting a crucial point at which our friendship with the nation-state might reach its limits. A political theology of friendship thus affirms that it is possible for a follower of Christ to be subject to political authority without allowing that authority to become an object of "ultimate concern."

ULTIMATE CONCERN

The principle of "ultimate concern" was first proposed in the 1950s by prominent Protestant theologian Paul Tillich. Noting that modern nation-states had assumed many of the characteristics traditionally associated with religion, Tillich asserted that the nationalisms of the twentieth century, both democratic and authoritarian, had insinuated themselves into "all aspects of human existence, including the smallest concern of one's daily life." The ideology of nationalism, combined with a cradle-to-grave security offered by the modern welfare state, had for many people taken the place of what religious belief and adherence had traditionally provided. The state has thus become an object of "ultimate concern"—meaning something that claims the absolute and total commitment of a person—by promising security and prosperity on the one hand, but on the other hand demanding of its citizens unconditional loyalty and a willingness to die and perhaps even kill on its behalf. Functionally, at least, the state therefore has become the equivalent of a "mortal god."[11]

Of course, no one professes to worship the state, and even in this secular age most religious people would assert that God remains the object of their ultimate concern. Yet consider the following important and telling difference. Many if not most citizens would be willing to die for their country. Similarly, many if not most believers would be willing to die for their faith. But whereas many if not most citizens would be willing to kill for their country, if called upon, how many would be willing to kill for their faith? People are willing to die for many good causes, but the number of things they are willing to kill for is (appropriately) far more limited. When people are willing to kill for one thing but not another, it says something about the nature of their ultimate concern—the thing to which they are willing to make an absolute and total commitment. As theologian William Cavanaugh observed, "It seems clear that, at least among American Christians, the nation-state . . . is subject to far more absolutist fervor than religion. For most American Christians, even public evangelization is considered to be in poor taste, and yet most would take for granted the necessity of being willing to kill for their country, should circumstances dictate."[12] As both Jesus and his brother James taught, one's faith is defined less by what one says than by what one does.[13]

Let us be absolutely clear: we are *not* proposing that believers, including Latter-day Saints, should increase their willingness to kill for their faith to match their willingness to kill for their country. Rather, we *are* proposing that a more sustained reflection on the nonviolent life and atonement of Jesus should lead his followers to think carefully about how far they are willing to go as citizens when their nation summons them to violence. As Latter-day Saints, we rightly and fully honor those who have sacrificed their lives in service to their nation, especially insofar as they made that sacrifice in honest defense of faith, family, and freedom.[14] Yet it is important to recognize that a state musters its armed forces not for the purpose of dying at the enemy's hands—as did the Anti-Nephi-Lehies to protect their families—but rather with the intention of defeating the enemy using overwhelming lethal force. Plus, the objectives of nation-states are usually self-interested. In the nonviolent kingdom of God, the great Jehovah condescended to come to earth and voluntarily give his life, subjecting himself to the unjust violence of the state, for *our* sake. The nation, on the other hand, usually asks its citizens to give their lives—and potentially take the lives of others—for *its* sake. So, while both God and the nation call for our ultimate concern, a key difference between them, in addition to what they can actually promise us, is how they exercise power and influence and to what end.

FROM FRIENDSHIP TO SUBJECTION

A distinctive Latter-day Saint political theology emerged gradually over the first few years of the Restoration and can be traced through the revelations of Joseph Smith and other official statements of the young church. After initially holding the unseemly world of politics at arm's length, when their persecutions in Missouri forced them to engage with the state, the Saints were presented with two basic options: to *befriend* constitutional law and government or to *subject* themselves to "the powers that be."[15] Latter-day Saints have generally privileged the second option, and that has brought significant benefits, including wider acceptance and security for the Church. But it is worth considering the widely forgotten alternative of friendship, as well as some of the notable costs of subjection.

The earliest revelations to Joseph Smith seemed to operate in a political vacuum. They clearly anticipated the imminent return of Jesus Christ to the earth and the advent of a millennial kingdom of God. The revelations barely recognized the presence of earthly political entities, including the United States, treating them as ephemeral placeholders that would soon disappear.[16] A revelation received in January 1831, less than a year after the founding of what was then known as the Church of Christ, referred to a time close at hand when the Saints "shall have no king nor ruler, for I [Christ] will be your king and watch over you. . . . You shall be a free people, and ye shall have no laws but my laws when I come, for I am your lawgiver."[17] The Saints were to behave as if they already lived in the dawn of that millennial day. All that mattered was the kingdom of God; worldly politics were merely an illusion and distraction.

In August 1831, the Sunday after Joseph Smith first arrived in western Missouri to help establish the city of Zion, he received a revelation instructing the Saints to, as noted above, "be subject to the powers that be." This phrase closely paralleled Paul's admonition to the Romans: "Let every person be subject to the governing authorities; for there is no authority except from God, and those authorities that exist have been instituted by God."[18] What seem to be very similar injunctions are actually rather different on closer inspection. The modern revelation does not begin with an endorsement of secular governments, as does Romans 13, but quite the opposite. "Let no man think he is a ruler," the revelation sternly warned. Rather than secular governments being "instituted by God," the revelation to Joseph Smith made clear that God alone is the true ruler of heaven and earth and political authorities are only stewards. Their authority is real, but temporary and limited. At the same time, the revelation counseled the Saints not to break the law of the land, "for he that keepeth the laws of God hath no need to break the laws of the land."[19] In short, the Saints were advised to keep the peace until Jesus, invested with divine authority and power, returned on earth to reign. Temporal laws and governments were merely placeholders until then.

Later that same month, God pronounced through another revelation to Joseph Smith, "I, the Lord, render unto Caesar the things which are Caesar's."[20] This is clearly an echo of the New Testament passage in which Jesus responded to a question of whether he and his followers should pay taxes to Rome.[21] Jesus's declaration to "render unto Caesar" is often read as a divine stamp of approval on, and even license for, the realm of secular statecraft. After all, if the eternal God renders unto Caesar, then shouldn't mortal humans as well? Read carefully, however, these statements offer a critical appraisal, rather than divine endorsement, of Caesar's power. The revelations remind us that God is the Creator and Sovereign of the world and "all things" in it: "For have I not the fowls of heaven, and also the fish of the sea, and the beasts of the mountains? Have I not made the earth? Do I not hold the destinies of all the armies of the nations of the earth?"[22] If *everything* is God's, including the armies of the nations, then there is little room for Caesar's claims to territory, lordship, or sovereignty. Compared to the Lord of creation who holds the whole world, including political dominions, in his hands, "the things which are Caesar's" turn out to be quite limited.

Like that of the first-century Christians, the early Saints' political theology was only a bare sketch, precisely because they thought the world of politics did not matter much when Christ was about to return. But Jesus didn't return to reign in Paul's time, nor in Joseph Smith's. Just as the early Christians were forced to reckon with the power and persecution of the Roman Empire, the early Latter-day Saints had no choice but to engage the state when their fledgling Zion in western Missouri came under attack in the summer of 1833.

In previous chapters we have discussed at length the August 1833 revelation that Joseph Smith received in the wake of the Saints' violent expulsion from Jackson County. Just as this remarkable revelation instructed the Saints how they should respond to violence, and thus serves as a cornerstone of nonviolent Restoration theology, it also provided the basic principles of a Restoration political theology. It went beyond the millennialism of earlier revelations to counsel the Saints how they could maintain their faith in Christ's lordship while orienting themselves to the Leviathan of the modern state.

The revelation opened by acknowledging—and inviting the Saints to acknowledge—that they were in fact members of a political community. Specifically, the Lord told the Saints that he would "justify you, and your brethren of my church, in befriending that law which is the constitutional law of the land," meaning those laws that support "that principle of freedom in maintaining rights and privileges." The wording in this passage is careful and qualified. The Lord would "justify" the Saints in "befriending" constitutional law and its authorized executives, but true obedience was owed to the Lord alone—"it is my will that my people should observe to do all things whatsoever I command them." Secular political authorities are charged with upholding and enforcing laws that protect the rights and privileges of the people, but "whatsoever" the government does that is "more or less than this, cometh of evil."[23] Building on the language of constitutional law, rights, and privileges, another revelation received a few months later singled out the United States Constitution as an inspired document whose principles, when properly implemented, would guarantee "the rights and protection of *all* flesh"—not just the privileged few who happen to live in the United States. Lest the Constitution be hailed as infallible, however, the Lord pointed out one of the document's chief flaws, namely its provisions preserving slavery. In declaring that "it is not right that any man should be in bondage one to another," the revelation affirmed the principle that constitutions, laws, and governments are only as good as the rights they guarantee and extend for the most vulnerable people in their care.[24]

Significantly, these two revelations encouraging the Saints to befriend constitutional law still fell well short of religiously inspired nationalism, or elevating the nation-state to an object of ultimate concern. As historian Mark Ashurst-McGee observes, the Saints "were now 'friends' to the Constitution and to the divine principles of freedom enshrined therein, not subjects to its rule of law."[25] Indeed, in a letter that Joseph Smith sent to Church leaders in Missouri in the summer of 1833, he affirmed that "we are all friends to the Constitution" and "true friends to [the]

Country." Even so, when they peacefully sued for protection and redress from state and federal government officials, the prophet instructed the Saints to present themselves as "Embasadors" from Zion. These ambassadors would be armed only with the power of truth; after all, Joseph mused, "our weapons are not carnal yet mighty."[26] Though the Saints were "justified" by the Lord in offering their true friendship to the nation and its constitutional principles, their primary allegiance was still to Zion.

Over the next few years, the situation in Missouri worsened, climaxing in pitched battles between the Latter-day Saints and other Missourians from August to October 1838. The period from 1833 to 1838—between the revelation to "renounce war and proclaim peace" and the so-called Missouri War—marked a shift in the Saints' political theology in two significant respects. First, the Saints abandoned their earlier commitment to nonviolence and embraced a pragmatic ethic of justified self-defense. Their resort to arms came in spite of a revelation prophesying that if the Saints tried to secure the land of Zion "by blood," their enemies would prevail over them and the Saints would "be scourged from city to city, and from synagogue to synagogue, and but few [would] stand to receive an inheritance."[27] The Saints' armed self-defense was understandable and perhaps even justifiable, but not divinely mandated, sanctifying, or effective.

Second, between 1833 and 1838 the Saints' worldview changed from a millennial outlook in which God was the sole sovereign in the universe and all the nations of the earth merely ephemeral placeholders to a more pliant (and politically compliant) notion of overlapping divine and temporal sovereignties. In 1834 Joseph Smith led "the armies of Israel," better known as Zion's Camp, on a nine-hundred-mile march from Kirtland, Ohio, to Jackson County, Missouri, in order to restore the aggrieved Saints to the homes and farms they had been dispossessed of. He did so partly in response to revelation, but also relying on what turned out to be a false promise of armed protection from Missouri governor Daniel Dunklin. For the "armies of Israel" to accomplish their goals, they needed the state to leverage its monopoly on violence in their favor—an expectation that never materialized. Whereas Enoch's Zion had relied solely on God for its protection, this latter-day would-be Zion mustered arms and appealed to the state to wield its violence on Zion's behalf.

It is true that Zion's Camp formed in response to a revelation promising that "the redemption of Zion must needs come by power." However, the camp militants who interpreted the revelation as an endorsement of holy violence had misunderstood the word of the Lord. The power that would redeem Zion was neither a ragtag frontier militia nor Missouri state troops, but rather the same power that led Moses and the children of Israel out of bondage—the power of God and of angels. What was required of the Saints was their willingness not to inflict suffering but rather to absorb it; for "whoso is not willing to lay down his life for my sake is not my disciple." If the group was to claim victory and glory, it would not be through the force of arms, but rather through "your diligence, faithfulness, and prayers of faith."[28] Nevertheless, by seeking an alliance with the state and not trusting fully in God's promises to fight their battles, the early Saints showed a lack of trust in God's sovereignty and instead affirmed their subjection to the secular political order—precisely the thing that the prophet Isaiah had warned the kingdoms of Israel and Judah against.[29]

A year after Zion's Camp, the Saints adopted and canonized a short treatise, "Of Governments and Laws in General." Penned by Oliver Cowdery, the statement was typical of nineteenth-century American political thought and bore little resemblance to Joseph Smith's earlier revelations about the kingdom of God and Zion. Cowdery wrote that as long as earthly sovereigns preserved the "inherent and inalienable rights" of their citizens, including "freedom of conscience" and the right "to preach the gospel to the nations of the earth," then they could expect the loyalty of their citizens—including the Latter-day Saints, who were "bound to sustain and uphold" their respective governments.[30] This was the moment in which Latter-day Saints struck a grand bargain with the secular state and its monopoly on violence. They would submit themselves to the state in exchange for protection from religious persecution and for freedom to spread the gospel message unfettered. From a worldly political perspective, it was probably the best deal they could reasonably get, and the arrangement has generally worked out well for The Church of Jesus Christ of Latter-day Saints and its members, particularly in the twentieth and twenty-first centuries. It's an arrangement that God had clearly found ways to leverage, as he so often does, to bless his children. But subjection also has a price, part of which is figuring how to be a people of peace when the political leaders to which you have bound yourself now call on you to go to war.

WARRING SOVEREIGNTIES

The dilemma of serving both God and Caesar confronts Christians all over the world, but here we will focus solely on the historical relationship of Latter-day Saints to the United States and its wars. At several points during the Restoration's two-century history, the United States has called on its citizens to demonstrate their loyalty by going to war on its behalf. In the mid-nineteenth century, Latter-day Saints responded to the government's call to arms with reluctance and skepticism, as they rightly felt betrayed by the nation's failure to protect them or provide redress in Missouri and Illinois. By century's end, however, partly in gratitude for Utah's finally being granted statehood in 1896, most Saints enthusiastically embraced the opportunity to prove themselves to be good American citizens, and many volunteered to fight for the nation in the Spanish-American War.[31] Likewise, although initially skeptical of the justice of the "Great War" in Europe, Latter-day Saints exceeded enlistment quotas when the United States eventually joined that tragic and brutal conflict.[32]

Church members fought on both sides of the First World War, but it was not until the dawn of the Second World War that General Authorities thoroughly confronted the dilemma of Latter-day Saints facing one another as military enemies. How could the increasingly global Church "be one" if German and American Saints were firing at one another from opposing battle lines?[33] As the war broke out in Europe, Church leaders initially expressed skepticism about American involvement, partly because the two counselors in the First Presidency, David O. McKay and J. Reuben Clark, had personal sympathies for pacifism.[34] The situation changed after the Japanese attack on Pearl Harbor, which brought the United States into the war. After deliberating about what their official position would be, in the Church's April 1942 general conference the First Presidency delivered a formal message about the Church's position on war.[35]

This ten-page statement, which remains the most detailed official treatment of the subject, articulates four basic principles. First, the Church's primary mission is to preach the gospel to all the earth, and nothing should hinder that divine errand. Second, the Church endorses full separation of church and state, with each carrying out its respective obligations. As a member of the body politic, the Church is interested in the state pursuing successful policies, but it is not responsible for those policies beyond encouraging its members to be good citizens. Third, the Church must, as a church, condemn war. The First Presidency forcefully declared:

> Christ's Church should not make war, for the Lord is a Lord of peace. He has said to us in this dispensation: "Therefore, renounce war and proclaim peace . . ." (D.&C. 98:16)

Thus the Church is and must be against war. The Church itself cannot wage war, unless and until the Lord shall issue new commands. It cannot regard war as a righteous means of settling international disputes; these should and could be settled—the nations agreeing—by peaceful negotiation and adjustment.[36]

In short, war is a violation of the gospel of Jesus Christ. It is always a manifestation of unrighteousness, and the Church of Jesus Christ can never be truly in favor of it.

Notwithstanding this unequivocal denunciation of war, the final principle outlined in the First Presidency's statement is that because Church members are also citizens of sovereign nations, they have the "highest civic duty" to "come to the defense of their country when a call to arms is made."[37] This argument—that Church members have a moral obligation to the nations in which they live, even when the nations participate in wars that the Church itself can never support—is rooted in the Church's twelfth article of faith and the 1835 declaration on government (canonized as Doctrine and Covenants section 134).

The April 1942 First Presidency message has often been interpreted as a full-throated endorsement of Latter-day Saint participation in war, but in fact it presents a far more nuanced view. One of the statement's key passages, referencing the August 1833 revelation (Doctrine and Covenants 98), pragmatically recognizes that "the Church membership are citizens or subjects of sovereignties of which the Church has no control." Therefore, the First Presidency affirmed, if Latter-day Saint soldiers who respond to their nation's call are forced to kill an enemy combatant while acting in the line of duty, "that will not make of them murderers, nor subject them to the penalty that God has prescribed for those who kill."[38]

Four things are crucial to note here. First, recall that in the 1833 revelation approvingly cited by the First Presidency, the

Lord says that he will "justify" the Saints in "befriending" constitutional law. The notion of justification is central here, as it is later in the revelation when the Lord says that he may "justify" a nation's defensive violence under certain strict conditions.[39] The Saints have a sacred obligation to obey the Lord and his commandments; their friendship with the state is justified by the Lord but does not rise to the same level of sacred responsibility. Because, as the First Presidency unequivocally stated, war cannot be "a righteous means of settling international disputes," any state that pursues military action is engaged in inherently unrighteous behavior. The violence might be justified, as the revelation stipulates, and the Saints may be justified in befriending such a state that goes to war to defend constitutional principles. But justified options, for either individuals or the state, should not be confused with sanctifying or holy behaviors.

Second, the First Presidency message affirms that Church members' "highest civic duty" dictates that they heed the government's call into armed military service. However, the statement makes a careful distinction here—such civic duty is invoked only when the government is acting within the framework of constitutional law, namely, "supporting that principle of freedom in maintaining rights and privileges." If a nation's call to arms appears to be motivated by anything "more or less than this" protection of freedom and rights, then it is "evil" and Saints have no obligation to heed it.[40]

Third, if the strict conditions for a "justified" action are met, and Church members do participate in war and kill others while acting under orders, then they will not be held morally liable for their actions. This is a clear application of the doctrine of justification. The soldier's act of killing is not good, righteous, or holy in itself; quite the opposite. But the Lord in his mercy makes allowances for human frailty, and his grace absolves the soldier of ultimate culpability for his actions. Justification does not erase the consequences of the action—a child of God has been killed, his loved ones suffer and grieve his loss, and another child of God has blood on his hands that may cause psychic trauma for years to come. Therefore, even if moral responsibility is assuaged, the practical consequences of the killing remain. Furthermore, the 1942 statement makes clear that the soldier's killing must be done within the chain of command. Presumably the soldier would be fully accountable to God for any violent actions that exceed the necessary and limited prosecution of direct orders. In short, a soldier's duty to the state is qualified, conditional, and contingent, whereas one's duty to God is absolute, inviolable, and eternal.

The final, related point is that while God may justify the individual soldier in committing what would ordinarily be a grave sin, he does not excuse or endorse the sin itself. In a time of war, Church members like all citizens find themselves caught on both sides of a conflict that is not necessarily of their choosing. As the First Presidency noted, these Church members "are the innocent war instrumentalities of their warring sovereignties. On each side they believe they are fighting for home and country and freedom. On each side, our brethren pray to the same God, in the same name, for victory." And echoing Abraham Lincoln's Second Inaugural Address, the First Presidency soberly concluded, "Both sides cannot be wholly right; perhaps neither is without wrong."[41] In other words, in war no one can claim ultimate innocence, although everyone rationalizes their bloody course by saying that they are in the right and supposing that God is on their side. But the universe is not morally relativistic. Humans may "call evil good, and good evil," but God does not.[42] The First Presidency prophetically asserted that "God will work out in His own due time and in His own sovereign way the justice and right of the conflict." The "innocent instrumentalities of war" will not be held accountable for "their work of destruction." But the sin remains, and that sin will condemn the leaders of nations who instigated the conflict, "those rulers in the world who in a frenzy of hate and lust for unrighteous power and dominion over their fellowmen, have put into motion eternal forces they do not comprehend and cannot control. God, in His own due time, will pass sentence upon them." War is not holy. Participation in it is not a godly act. With all the available exceptions and caveats and excuses and contingencies, the First Presidency still affirmed the "universal law" that "force always begets force." They declared that the ultimate authority on the matter came from Jesus Christ, who "laid down a general principle upon which He placed no limitations as to time, place, cause, or people involved." That principle is simple: "all they that take the sword shall perish with the sword."[43]

Six months later, with the "good war" still raging, the First Presidency published a follow-up message. Tellingly, they reinforced their earlier denunciation of war but did not repeat the principles justifying the Saints' individual participation in it. Their tone was forceful and direct, reasserting that "the Church is and must be against war, for war is of Satan and this Church is the Church of Christ, who taught peace and righteousness and brotherhood of man." They called on the leaders of nations to "abandon the fiendishly inspired slaughter" they were engaged in. They renewed their declaration "that international disputes can and should be settled by peaceful means. This is the way of the Lord. . . . In this way only will enduring peace come; it will never be imposed by armed force." This war would end, as all wars eventually do, but "hate-driven militarists and leaders, with murder in their hearts" would simply bring about another conflict unless the people and leaders of the world embraced nonviolent solutions. What role would Church members play in this pursuit of peace and reconciliation? Whatever nation they found themselves in, the First Presidency urged Latter-day Saints to pray and work for peace.[44]

Soon after the Second World War ended and President Heber J. Grant died, the new First Presidency under the leadership of George Albert Smith penned a letter to the Utah congressional delegation in which they formally opposed pending legislation that would institute a peacetime draft and compulsory military training for all American men. In seventeen points, the First Presidency thoroughly rejected the notion of permanent mobilization. Such a policy would "teach our sons not only the way to kill but also, in too many cases, the desire to kill." This would instill "wholly erroneous ideas" of what "manhood" truly consisted of. The letter, published in the Church's official magazine in early 1946, offered a poignant critique of how a permanently mobilized state was a form of structural violence that would inevitably lead to direct violence:

> By the creation of a great war machine, we shall invite and tempt the waging of war against foreign countries, upon little or no provocation; for the possession of military power always breeds thirst for domination, for empire, and for a rule by might not right. . . .
>
> We shall make of the whole earth one great military camp whose separate armies, headed by war-minded officers, will never rest till they are at one another's throats in what will be the most terrible contest the world has ever seen.

The First Presidency concluded by extolling the virtues of diplomacy rather than violence, asserting, "What this country needs and what the world needs, is a will for peace, not war."[45]

RESTORATION POLITICAL THEOLOGY

The August 1833 revelation and the First Presidency statements from the 1940s are the most definitive and prescriptive Restoration texts on the question of how a modern follower of Christ should relate to the state and its violence. When recent

Church leaders such as President Gordon B. Hinckley have spoken on the subject, they have invariably cited these authoritative texts.[46] With these principles in mind, a political theology of the Restoration, particularly on the questions of war and peace, begins to take shape as follows.

GOD IS THE TRUE AND SOLE SOVEREIGN

God is the true and sole sovereign in the universe, and all human beings have eternal worth and dignity as self-existent agents progressing in character and intelligence toward exaltation. God places his children in community during their mortal probation and invites them to create societies characterized by mutual concern, justice, equality, peace, and love.

THE KINGDOM OF CHRIST IS REAL AND COMING

The Saints' primary allegiance—their "ultimate concern"—is to hasten the time when the Messiah "shall judge between the nations, and shall arbitrate for many peoples; they shall beat their swords into plowshares, and their spears into pruning hooks; nation shall not lift up sword against nation, neither shall they learn war any more."[47]

CHRIST'S DISCIPLES ARE CITIZENS OF NATIONS

In the interim, during which Christ's disciples await his return, they are also citizens of nations generally not of their choosing or making. Latter-day Saints can and should exercise active friendship toward political regimes that promote individual freedom and human rights, protect vulnerable populations, and cultivate human dignity. In the course of their normal daily routines, followers of Christ should subject themselves to civil authorities that support these principles as enshrined in constitutional law. As a corollary, Saints are under no obligation to befriend regimes that violate these principles; their friendship can be withdrawn when the other partner in the relationship acts in bad faith. Civil disobedience in the context of an unjust regime—such as the case of Helmuth Hübener, a Latter-day Saint teenager who opposed the Nazi regime in Germany and became the youngest person executed by Hitler's special People's Court—is not a violation of our friendship to constitutional law but rather represents a faithful expression of it.[48] Latter-day Saints may out of necessity still be pragmatically subject to these unrighteous dominions, but their highest loyalties are to God's kingdom and to the creation of a political order that promotes constitutional law as defined above.

WAR IS EVIL

The Church of Jesus Christ opposes war in all its forms and calls nations to repent of their violence and turn to peace. What's more, a duty to "renounce war and proclaim peace" appears to be part of the Latter-day Saints' covenantal relationship with God.[49] Citizen-Saints may be justified in participating in wars that meet the standards outlined in the August 1833 revelation or in which they are enlisted by their government. However, forbearance is always an option and may even be the preferred choice for a disciple of Christ. Conscientious objection, actively seeking noncombatant duty, and other legal forms of nonparticipation are therefore not necessarily a repudiation of the Saints' civic duties. Rather, they can represent deeply moral choices that anticipate the sovereignty of Christ's nonviolent kingdom and demonstrate a sincere personal commitment to constitutional law, especially when a given war violates it.

SECULAR POLITICAL COMMUNITIES DESERVE ACTIVE FRIENDSHIP AND LOYALTY

Secular political communities, including the nation-state, deserve a Christian disciple's active friendship and even loyalty in order to help them fulfill their calling as communities of care. At its best, the nation-state expands our moral boundaries beyond the immediacy of family, clan, tribe, and locality, providing a compassionate social and political framework in which we take into account and address the needs and hurts of people geographically distant from us. In this respect, when the nation is predicated on care rather than violence, it can be a type and shadow of the coming kingdom of Christ and therefore is entitled to his disciples' active friendship and participation. Christians should not withhold their friendship simply because no current political community perfectly embodies the ideals of Zion; rather, our energetic efforts can do much to incrementally transform our communities, "grace for grace."[50]

RENOUNCING FALSE GODS

While acknowledging the transformative potential of actively befriending the modern nation-state, we end this chapter on a cautionary note. At its worst, the modern nation-state can function as an idol. Insofar as the nation-state demands our ultimate loyalty at the expense of our allegiance to God and his kingdom, it is a false god. This is a hard thing to hear, precisely because the modern nation-state occupies so much of our devotion, offers itself to us as an inherent good, and obscures its violence as inevitable, necessary, or redemptive. But the idolatry of the nation-state, particularly in its violence-wielding character, was prophetically condemned in 1976 by President Spencer W. Kimball. The June issue of the Church's magazine *Ensign* was dedicated to celebrating the upcoming bicentennial of the United States. Most of the articles were upbeat, even laudatory, with titles like "A Promised Land" and "Declaration of Independence: Teaching Patriotism in the Home." Most, that is, except for the opening article, the traditional First Presidency message, which Kimball penned himself and titled "The False Gods We Worship."

Kimball expressed gratitude to God for the "people and institutions of America," acknowledging that "there is much that is good in this land, and much to love." Nevertheless, when he looked at the state of the nation, he saw rampant wickedness, with evil "engulf[ing] us like a great wave." Fireworks and flag-waving obscured the corruption at the heart of the nation. Americans had "submitted themselves in one degree or another to the enticings of Satan" and were pursuing "lives of ever-deepening idolatry." "We are, on the whole," Kimball declared, "an idolatrous people—a condition most repugnant to the Lord." This was strong language, but intentional. Speaking to Latter-day Saints and other citizens living in the most militarily powerful nation in the world's history, the Lord's prophet proclaimed:

> We are a warlike people, easily distracted from our assignment of preparing for the coming of the Lord. When enemies rise up, we commit vast resources to the fabrication of gods of stone and steel—ships, planes, missiles, fortifications—and depend on them for protection and deliverance. When threatened, we become antienemy instead of pro-kingdom of God; we train a man in the art of war and call him a patriot, thus, in the manner of Satan's counterfeit of true patriotism, perverting the Savior's teaching:
>
> "Love your enemies, bless them that curse you, do good to them that hate you, and pray for them which despitefully use you, and persecute you;
>
> "That ye may be the children of your Father which is in heaven." (Matt. 5:44–45)
>
> We forget that if we are righteous the Lord will either not suffer our enemies to come upon us—and this is the special promise to the inhabitants of the land of the Americas—or he will fight our battles for us. This he is able to do. . . .
>
> What are we to fear when the Lord is with us? Can we not take the Lord at his word and exercise a particle of faith in him?

Our assignment is affirmative: to forsake the things of the world as ends in themselves; to leave off idolatry and press forward in faith; to carry the gospel to our enemies, that they might no longer be our enemies.[51]

If Latter-day Saints ever had any doubt that Jesus's ethic of nonviolent enemy-love applied to international politics, President Kimball settled the matter in the affirmative. He suggested that it is impossible to fully love one's supposed enemy while building "ships, planes, [and] missiles" to potentially kill him; the violence of the nation-state thus stands in the way of our Christian discipleship. In order to fully worship the God who delivered the Sermon on the Mount, Kimball taught that followers of Christ would first have to recognize and renounce the false gods that compete for their attention and affections. Unfortunately, President Kimball's prophetic lamentation seems to have had little impact on our culture and is seldom referenced. "A prophet is not without honour, save in his own country," Jesus sagely observed.[52] This is especially true when the prophet speaks against his own country.

But such truth-speaking is a form of love. God does not call his people to reject the world but to reform it in his image. Everyone on this planet is subject to the "powers that be," even though those powers are deeply fallen. But as theologian Walter Wink reminds us, "Fallen does not mean depraved. . . . It simply refers to the fact that our existence is not our essence: we are, none of us, what we are meant to be."[53] Once we recognize that the "powers" are fallen but not depraved, we can get to work redeeming them. We are freed from the blind love of dumb idols and instead can love our political communities as God intended them to be loved—as their friends. In offering our nations true friendship, we might then hold them accountable and assist them in becoming communities of care that protect the vulnerable and provide for compassionate and just sharing of goods and opportunities for all. Seeking the redemption of our nations thus entails renouncing the forms of direct, structural, and cultural violence that are too often at their heart and working to transform them with nonviolent love. It will not be easy. It will take creativity and courage, and sometimes conscientious nonconformity. It also may be one of the most significant ways we give real meaning to the Lord's Prayer: "Thy kingdom come. Thy will be done in earth, as it is in heaven."[54] To follow Jesus, we must simultaneously renounce the violence of Caesar and proclaim the positive peace of Zion.

CHAPTER NINE

The Positive Peace of Zion

*There were no contentions and disputations
among them, and every man did deal justly one with
another. And they had all things common among them;
therefore there were not rich and poor, bond and free,
but they were all made free, and partakers of the heavenly gift.*
—4 Nephi 1:2–3

*And the Lord called his people Zion, because they were
of one heart and one mind, and dwelt in righteousness;
and there was no poor among them.*
—Moses 7:18

Zion is the social ideal of the Restoration. Joseph Smith declared, "The salvation of the Saints one and all depends on the building up of Zion. . . . Our hopes, our expectations, our glory and our reward, all depend on our building up Zion. . . . [Without Zion] our hopes perish, our expectations fail, our prospects are blasted, our salvation withers."[1] Restoration scripture repeatedly suggests that Zion is an attainable ideal—here, now. It is created by converted and gathered disciples, transformed through their personal encounters with Christ. Both individually and communally, these disciples renounce all forms of direct, structural, and cultural violence and in their stead "proclaim peace," fostering the conditions for sustainable peace, justice, development, and human flourishing. Thus, Zion collectively declares the advent and joy of the nonviolent kingdom of God.

Zion is often presented in Restoration scripture as the godly alternative to and mirror image of Babylon. If Babylon is characterized by hate, wickedness, violence, selfishness, prejudice, patriarchy, and ecological destruction, Zion is the site of love, righteousness, peace, selflessness, inclusiveness, egalitarianism, and stewardship of creation.[2] Zion therefore offers both a prophetic critique of Babylon and a positive vision of the grand potential of human community. In place of the "vicious triangle" of cultural, structural, and direct violence, Zion fosters a "virtuous triangle" of cultural, structural, and direct peace.[3] While personal holiness is an individual spiritual quest, Zion is the "corporate response to sin," to borrow language from Catholic theologian Lisa Cahill. The building of Zion constitutes neither a withdrawal from the world nor a spiritual elitism, but rather an "active response to evil" predicated on divine principles. Zion is an "antidote to sin" on individual, interpersonal, and communal scales, as it fosters "resistant types of communities and relationships, in which belonging and identity are redefined as love of neighbor, enemy, stranger, and the poor."[4] As Latter-day Saint apostle Jeffrey R. Holland has affirmed, "the gospel of Jesus Christ holds the answer to every social and political and economic problem the world has ever faced."[5] These comprehensive answers are found in Zion.

A person can believe in God as an isolated individual, but building Zion happens only in community. Zion doesn't face inward. The goal is always to gather as many as will come—the whole world if they will put down their arms and heed the call.[6] Zion is an aspirational community that is not yet fully present but is nevertheless attainable, to one degree or another, to anyone who seeks it with purity of heart.[7] As a work in progress, Zion is as much process as product. What it envisions and entails, however, is nothing short of a global revolution of nonviolent love. "I intend to lay a foundation that will revolutionize the whole world," Joseph Smith audaciously proclaimed. "It will not be by sword or gun that this Kingdom will roll on," but by "the power of truth."[8] Zion cannot be established with violence or coercion, "only by persuasion, by long-suffering, by gentleness and meekness, and by love unfeigned."[9]

This chapter and the next offer a vision of what is possible when we extend our individual nonviolent love to a societal level. Restoration scripture is always concerned but never content merely with reforming the heart. The handful of communities that have successfully approximated or achieved Zion share a common recognition that society's structures also require reformation. Collectively these communities attest that the positive peace of Zion can be achieved only when various forms of structural and cultural violence are also transformed. In contrast with ideologies and theories of social change that emphasize either individuals or structures, Zion gives full and equal weight to both. But here most of us run up against the limits of our moral imagination. We generally understand how sin operates on a personal basis but are not as acquainted with how it works on a societal level. So before we can fully appreciate how Zion represents positive peace, a form of redemption that is both personal and structural, we need to explore the inverse of Zion—a concept known as *structural sin*.

STRUCTURES OF SIN

From a Restoration perspective, structures and cultures of violence are not simply unfortunate features of a fallen world akin to "thorns" and "thistles."[10] Rather, they are insidious forms of sin that we collectively inherit, choose, create, and perpetuate; they represent deep alienation from God on both individual and societal levels.

Among the most common forms of structural violence that the scriptures consistently and unflinchingly denounce is the sin of economic injustice, often seen through the lens of inequality. One non–Latter-day Saint scholar was so struck with the Book of Mormon's strident attacks on economic and social inequality that he concluded, "Throughout the book, evil is most often depicted as the result of pride and worldliness that comes from economic success and results in oppression of the poor."[11] This same theme saturates the Doctrine and Covenants. Speaking to the modern Church, the Lord declared that those who "shall take of the abundance which I have made" but fail to share generously with "the poor and the needy" will find themselves "in hell, being in torment."[12] What's more, God commanded that "in your temporal things you shall be equal, and this not grudgingly," and "if ye are not equal in earthly things ye cannot be equal in obtaining heavenly things."[13] In another, earlier revelation, the Lord talked about inequality in the starkest terms, pronouncing that "it is not given that one man should possess that which is above another, wherefore the world lieth in sin."[14] This last phrase is instructive. Inequality is not merely unfortunate or unwise—it is fundamentally unjust, a violation of God's intention for his creation. Accordingly, the world itself, with its violently unequal structures and cultures, "lieth in sin."

The notion of a whole *world*—as compared to simply *individuals*—lying in sin raises fundamental questions about the nature of sin. As an echo and extension of the biblical tradition, the Restoration suggests two interrelated principles regarding the structures of sin: first, that entire groups can be collectively guilty; and second, that the very structures of society can be inherently sinful.

How can entire groups be guilty of sin, especially when not all of the individual members have personally committed the sinful act? Modern notions of the autonomous moral self tend to shrink from this idea, as even some scriptural passages seem to do.[15] And yet, throughout the scriptures, God calls not just individuals but entire nations to repent. God's ancient covenant was with all Israel, not its individual constituents. There seems not to have been either an opt-in or opt-out clause for covenanted Israel—all its members were simply judged together, with blessings and curses given collectively and not meted out person by person. The ancient prophets typically inveighed against the wickedness of entire peoples; for instance, Isaiah directed his prophetic judgments against Israel as a "sinful nation, a people laden with iniquity."[16] Though the notion of individual accountability, connected with personal ethics, emerges as a prominent theme with the later Hebrew prophets and in the New Testament, a sense of collective sin also persisted. This remains true in the modern Church. In revelations to Joseph Smith, God noted that he was at times "speaking unto the church collectively and not individually." He later pronounced that "vanity and unbelief have brought the whole church under condemnation," a judgment that weighed collectively "upon the children of Zion, even all."[17] Thus, in Restoration theology, God holds whole groups, as well as individuals, responsible for their moral choices and collective actions.

The scriptural language of collective sin speaks to the moral interconnectedness of humanity. Although humans are individual spirits endowed with a remarkable degree of agency, our freedom is limited or otherwise shaped by the choices of others. As a result, salvation is a corporate affair, never achieved in splendid isolation. The quality of our exaltation is determined in large part by the relationships we foster within and across the generations.[18] Similarly, individuals can be enmeshed in relational sin through participation in social behaviors and processes that are collectively alienated (and alienating) from God's nature and therefore produce and perpetuate sinful systems.

To borrow a helpful phrase from the Catholic tradition, these systems might be labeled "structures of sin." In introducing this concept, we wish to stress that it does not reduce one's moral responsibility. Indeed, as Pope John Paul II affirmed, "structures of sin" are fundamentally "rooted in personal sin, and thus always linked to the concrete acts of individuals who introduce these structures, consolidate them and make them difficult to remove." In other words, although many of these sinful structures and systems eventually take on a life of their own, at the beginning they originate in individual agency. Structures of sin are likewise perpetuated by individuals who are often motivated by either an "all-consuming desire for profit" or a "thirst for power, with the intention of imposing one's will upon others." Systemic social ills such as poverty, hunger, racism, and war therefore represent types of "moral evil, the fruit of many sins."[19]

The Restoration emphasizes that people are not morally accountable for sins committed by others.[20] Yet it also teaches that individuals can be indirectly complicit in sinful social arrangements. Latter-day Saint prophets and apostles have spoken, for example, of the need to "wash our hands clean of the blood and sins of this generation."[21] Such a statement recognizes that individual moral responsibility is interwoven with social moral responsibility. A person cannot live in society without somehow partaking of its collective sins. All people are constituted by the social relationships in which they participate, even those in which they enter unconsciously or without explicit choice. Indeed, a significant amount of human social identity and participation is inherited or otherwise ascribed rather than fully chosen. People have no say in the families, nations, or cultures into which they are born and raised. Thus, the sins of fathers and mothers have real consequences for their children, and children's children, not only in the opportunities those children are granted or denied from birth but also in the attitudes, behaviors, and systems they inherit unawares. As Latter-day Saint theologian Deidre Green observes, "All are implicated in sin and the suffering that it causes, even though not everyone equally shares culpability for either sinful acts or for social structures."[22]

Restoration scripture persistently denounces the sinful structures of injustice, inequality, and exploitation that characterize our modern world. President Dallin H. Oaks pronounced a similarly prophetic critique when he called out genocide, war, economic inequality, corruption, and the suffering of refugees as the products of sin.[23] These conditions are sinful because they alienate the children of God from one another, repress opportunities for moral growth and progression, inspire resentment and direct violence, and set up power and profit as idols that displace God as the object of worship and love as the defining characteristic of relationships. Thus, while Restoration scriptures encourage disciples of Jesus to strive earnestly to foster personal and interpersonal peace, we should not stop there. Those same scriptures also call us to identify, unmask, root out, and transform structures and cultures of violence, beginning in our own communities. Because the structures of sin are so deeply entrenched and often mask themselves as the way things "naturally" are, transforming structural and cultural violence takes tremendous vision and effort. Peacebuilders quickly learn that addressing direct, structural, and cultural violence is necessarily a simultaneous, not a sequential, process—to neglect the one is to fail to fully attend to the others. So Restoration theology equips peacebuilders with a vision of society committed equally to individual faithfulness, familial harmony, social justice, and systemic peace. God calls it *Zion*.

ZION REVEALED

The reason Latter-day Saints place such hope in Zion as a realistically attainable community—here and now—is because Restoration scripture contains several accounts of communities that realized its core principles. We have already recounted the story of the city of Enoch, which exemplified positive peace—"they were of one heart and one mind, and dwelt in righteousness; and there was no poor among them"—and seems to have been the first to earn the appellation "Zion."[24]

In a similar way, Zion emerges in other biblical stories into which Joseph Smith's revelations breathed new life. Consider the story of Melchizedek, a minor character in Genesis who is mentioned briefly in the New Testament and also has a brief cameo appearance in the Book of Mormon, where we learn that he "did establish peace in the land in his days; therefore he was called the prince of peace" in prophetic anticipation of Christ.[25] We receive even more details in the Joseph Smith translation of Genesis. Even as a child, Melchizedek had such faith that he "stopped the mouths of lions, and quenched the violence of fire." Similar to Enoch, through the power of his faith he controlled nature, "put at defiance the armies of nations," and "subdue[d] principalities and powers." Melchizedek was no conquering hero but rather the paradigmatic servant-leader. Under his kingship, "he obtained peace in Salem" and "his people wrought righteousness," deliberately patterning themselves after the city of Enoch.[26] When Melchizedek received Abram's tithes, he distributed the monies to the poor. Thus, his people achieved positive peace in large part because they successfully reduced economic inequality. As historian Mark Ashurst-McGee observes, "Melchizedek's program for economic redistribution fostered domestic peace."[27]

The Book of Mormon likewise features several narratives about Zion-like communities. The elder Alma, for example, fled the court of the wicked and unjust King Noah and then created a community of disciples in the wilderness. Connecting their faith in Christ to a new social ethic, Alma taught them how to have "no contention one with another" because their hearts were "knit together in unity and in love one towards another." In marked contrast to their prior experience under King Noah, who glutted himself on their labors, "the children of God" practiced economic justice. Each of them, including the priests, labored for their own subsistence, but not in a race to riches. Rather, the members of the church each freely "impart[ed] of their substance, every one according to that which he had," and through their individual and collective surplus they took care of "every needy, naked soul." They pursued this program of economic redistribution as a religious duty, regarding it as a central feature of the covenant they had made with God and with one another. As a result, "they did walk uprightly before God, imparting to one another both temporally and spiritually according to their needs and their wants." This little Zion, eventually consisting of about four hundred and fifty people, survived for a short time before the soldiers of King Noah discovered them and forced them to flee.[28] Reestablishing themselves in a new land, their Zion-like community was eventually threatened again, this time by a Lamanite army. Having established economic equality as one of their guiding principles, Alma and his people also subsequently demonstrated a commitment to loving nonviolent resistance when they fell under the subjection of the former priests of King Noah who ruled them under the authority of the Lamanites. These oppressors made life miserable for the community, even to the point of prohibiting these disciples of Christ from praying aloud. Alma and his people endured such suffering patiently—and engaged in a form of civil disobedience by continuing to pray in their hearts—until God promised that he would deliver them. True to the blessings promised to those who practice nonviolent love, their liberation was achieved without shedding a drop of blood; God put the Lamanite guards into a deep sleep while Alma and his people simply walked out of the city.[29]

The pre-Christ Zion communities led by Enoch, Melchizedek, and Alma foreshadowed the initial Christian community described in the New Testament. Gathered in Jerusalem following the death, resurrection, and ascension of Jesus, these early disciples created a new community under the leadership of the apostles. The fruit of their collective faith in Jesus and transformative encounter with the Holy Spirit was a social ethic pointing toward the positive peace of Zion: "All who believed were together and had all things in common; they would sell their possessions and goods and distribute the proceeds to all, as any had need." Even as the community expanded, they held true to the same principles of social and economic equality: "Now the whole group of those who believed were of one heart and soul, and no one claimed private ownership of any possessions, but everything they owned was held in common." They consecrated their wealth to the community, which the apostles then "distributed to each as any had need." As a result, "there was not a needy person among them," and God blessed the community with "great grace."[30] It is not clear how long the early church retained its commitment to unity through economic redistribution, but we do know that for nearly three centuries the early Christians also embraced loving nonviolence, refusing to take up arms even in self-defense. Peter and Paul, both of whom were eventually martyred, testified that only by suffering along with Christ would his disciples be able to also partake of his glory.[31]

A consistent pattern emerges from these four Zion communities, however briefly they are sketched out in scripture. The people are deeply converted to the good news of Jesus and gather together in unity for both physical protection and spiritual fellowship. They establish a society in which they seek to eliminate all socioeconomic distinctions among them. They do so through a program of economic justice that goes far beyond mere sentiment, charity, or welfare. The fruits of their individual and combined temporal labors are consecrated and redistributed so that the needs and wants of every member of the community are fulfilled. The eradication of inequality in turn eliminates contention and perpetuates internal harmony and peace. They refuse to take up arms against hostile neighbors, either relying on the Lord for protection and deliverance or demonstrating their individual and collective capacity to suffer violence in the name of Christ. The people of God trust in the power of the Resurrection and absorb violence rather than inflict it. They count their nonviolent sufferings as part of their joyful covenant to imitate and follow the Prince of Peace "in all things, and in all places . . . even until death."[32]

THE PEOPLE OF JESUS

Perhaps the most tantalizing vision of Zion comes in the Book of Mormon's account of the Nephites and Lamanites who survived the cataclysmic devastations that preceded the resurrected Jesus's appearance. The unparalleled destruction left the people with a seemingly blank slate on which they could organize a new society from the ground up. With all of the people quickly converted either through the direct ministry of Christ or the subsequent spreading of the word among those not in attendance,

207

the descendants of Lehi cooperatively built a sanctified society based on the principles taught to them by the Savior. Tellingly, one of the first indications that they had completely transformed their former ways of life into something new was the elimination of economic inequality. Whereas only five years earlier Nephite society was predicated on "power, and authority, and riches, and the vain things of the world," now the believers "had all things common among them, every man dealing justly, one with another."[33] Upon that foundation of economic justice, they established a Zion society that lasted a remarkable four generations before gradually losing its way.

At its core, this Zion was a community of dedicated and consecrated Christian disciples. With all the people "converted unto the Lord, upon all the face of the land," they were able to attempt a bold social experiment. They founded their new society not on any political ideology, economic theory, or ethnonational identity, but rather on the teachings of Jesus and his disciples. Their ecclesiastical unity translated into interpersonal harmony, social unity, and economic equality—"there were no contentions and disputations among them . . . ; therefore there were not rich and poor, bond and free, but they were all made free, and partakers of the heavenly gift."[34]

The sequence of events here is noteworthy. The community emerged as a natural outcome of both individual and collective conversion to "the way, the truth, and the life" of Jesus—not simply as accepting a set of truth claims but as a fundamental and radical reorientation of their entire lives.[35] They had faith that God's kingdom was for the poor in spirit, the mourning, the meek, those who hungered and thirsted after righteousness, the merciful, the pure in heart, the peacemakers, and the persecuted. They appreciated that to be faithful disciples they had to avoid anger and eschew violence, seeking paths of reconciliation rather than retribution. They could not lust after each other or divorce for convenience's sake. They trusted that faithful disciples could and should turn the other cheek, give their cloaks, go the extra mile, love their enemies, bless those that cursed and abused them, and pray for their persecutors.[36] These were not sentimental ideals to be merely wished for or applied in easy cases, but expectations for all who took up the name and path of Jesus.

Discipleship of this sort entailed total moral, political, economic, social, cultural, and religious repentance—a change of heart that radiated outward to every aspect of their society. The surviving descendants of Lehi and Mulek had already been rescued from physical calamity. Now their baptism in the name of Jesus became a ritual rebirth into an entirely new way of being, individually and collectively. They renounced evil in all its forms: first their personal sins of "great pride . . . envyings, strifes, malice, persecutions, and murders," then their structural sins of having organized their previous society based on the prideful elevation of rank, riches, learning, and authority.[37] The society they rebuilt was not a parade of piety but a visible community of grace. It reoriented people's lives away from the selfish drive for power and profit and completely swallowed up the alienating logic of structural and cultural violence. They could share all things in common because they saw one another as sisters and brothers in Christ, fellow children of God—not as a constituency, a labor force, or a rival ethnic bloc, nor as competition for resources. Every vestige of their pre-Christian (and anti-Christian) society—with its violence, ranks and classes, disparate opportunities, amassing of wealth, elitist and exclusivist education, and jockeying for power—now vanished. Social distinctions based on race, ethnicity, nationality, and class melted away. There was no other side of the tracks. Only then, fully in communion with one another, were they "made free"—individually and collectively—from the alienating bondage of sin and violence in all its forms. Only then, fully in communion with one another, did they become "partakers of the heavenly gift" and fully encounter and embody the power of God.[38]

It is one thing to build Zion, quite another to maintain it. Alas, the precise formula for doing so remains something of a mystery, at least in terms of practical details. In one of our few complaints against Mormon's editorial sensibilities, we wonder why he dedicated twenty whole chapters in the book of Alma to fourteen years of war, whereas in 4 Nephi he reduced 165 years of peace to a mere twenty-two verses. Mormon's beautiful but general depiction of this Zion leaves the reader begging for more. What do politics look like in Zion? How exactly do you reorganize an entire economy to provide for all and not create unequal classes? How do you create and maintain an identity that is entirely positive and inclusive, not predicated on opposition to the "other"? What educational structures and pedagogies allow a Zion society to effectively transmit its values across the generations? Mormon answers none of our questions about the *particularities* of life in Zion, but he does paint an evocative portrait of the *quality* of life in Zion:

> And it came to pass that there was no contention in the land, because of the love of God which did dwell in the hearts of the people. And there were no envyings, nor strifes, nor tumults, nor whoredoms, nor lyings, nor murders, nor any manner of lasciviousness; and surely there could not be a happier people among all the people who had been created by the hand of God. There were no robbers, no murderers, neither were there Lamanites, nor any manner of -ites; but they were in one, the children of Christ, and heirs to the kingdom of God.[39]

Notice Mormon's stylistic decision here. Zion is described almost wholly in apophatic, or negative, terms. It is almost as if Mormon, in comparing this Zion to his own age of civilizational apocalypse, was impressed primarily with what was *not* happening—no contention, no violence, no sexual depravity, and no ethnic, racial, or national fracture and hatred. It is through the lens of all that was blessedly *missing* in this Zion that we get a taste of what was actually present in abundance—"the love of God which did dwell in the hearts of the people."

The gospel delivered by Christ and his disciples and confirmed by the Holy Spirit gave the converted descendants of Lehi and Mulek eyes to see things "as they really are."[40] Their heightened moral perceptions cut through the deception of sin, bringing into focus the previously invisible (or ignored) dynamics of cultural and structural violence. This once-normal state of affairs was now unmasked in its true depravity, and the people could see how their violence had alienated them from God and their fellow humans. The very categories that had defined them— Lamanite and Nephite, rich and poor—were revealed as artificial constructs unnecessarily creating schisms among the children of God. Greater awareness and sympathy for others—or as Pope John Paul II describes it, "a feeling of vague compassion or shallow distress at the misfortunes of so many people"—were not sufficient on their own. Deep conversion led beyond such sympathy to embrace authentic and deep-seated solidarity, "a firm and persevering determination to commit oneself to the common good; that is to say to the good of all and of each individual, because we are all really responsible for all." This Zion was a concrete demonstration that the structures of sin, as John Paul II taught, are overcome only through "a commitment to the good of one's neighbor with the readiness, in the gospel sense, to 'lose oneself' for the sake of the other instead of exploiting him, and to 'serve him' instead of oppressing him for one's own advantage."[41] In short, this Zion overcame the structures of sin through a fundamentally religious response by committed human beings, filled with the love of God and humanity, who as individuals and together in community produced new and divinely graced structures of justice, peace, and the common good.

There is yet another way to think about "the love of God which did dwell in the hearts of the people." In Enoch's Zion, "the Lord came and dwelt with his people."[42] This language invokes the central Christian doctrine of the Incarnation, which Nephi calls "the condescension of God."[43] God does not reign remotely in a distant heaven but enters the world and meets humanity in all its grime, sin, and violence. As theologian Lisa Cahill writes, in his incarnation Christ "enters into every aspect of human suffering," including victimization, oppression, forsakenness, and death. His suffering in Gethsemane and on the cross reveals his "willingness to enter into the human condition of guilt as well as of innocent suffering in order to restore relationships and communities that have been perverted by human sin."[44] Zion is an extension and collective embodiment of God's incarnation, wherein his love became fully expressed in a body that experienced pain, suffering, abuse, and even torture. Zion is the living body of Christ, with all its wounds, encompassing, embracing, and even experiencing the victimization of those who are suffering from violence, then working to transform their suffering and heal their wounds through love.

The account in 4 Nephi offers powerful testimony that Zion is characterized not only by negative peace but also by the durable and comprehensive presence of positive peace. Operating on the same principles that guided other Zion communities, the economy was based on radical voluntary redistribution. Occupation, class, and wealth did not define the worth of a soul. Each member of the community consecrated and applied her or his distinctive gifts and talents, recognized they were all given by God, and received just compensation for honest effort. What's more, because of their unity in Christ, the people discarded previous tribal and political identities. Their individual and collective identity was constructed in entirely positive terms, as "children of Christ, and heirs to the kingdom of God."[45] Every other distinction was incidental rather than inhibiting, and the natural aspects of human diversity became cause for celebration, not division. The inhabitants of Zion were not robots or clones. To the contrary, they were truly free—free from the enslavements of caste, class, nation, race, ethnicity, neighborhood, profession, partisanship, ideology, and every other artificial divide that alienates members of the human family from one another. Being "made free," they could be "partakers of the heavenly gift" of human identity and community in all its richness. As a result, "there could not be a happier people among all the people who had been created by the hand of God."[46]

Alas, although it lasted for nearly two hundred years, this remarkable Zion came to an end. The denouement came slowly, as individuals dismantled the positive peace of Zion piece by piece. First a group of dissenters rebranded themselves as Lamanites, in one fell swoop shattering the spiritual and ethnonational unity of the people. Even then, the now-Nephite Zion seems to have remained intact for several years, more or less immune from the influence of those who chose to go their own way. Zion's eventual demise came from within. Mormon attributes the collapse of the nearly two-century-old Christian society to the reintroduction of inequality—"there began to be among them those who were lifted up in pride, such as the wearing of costly apparel, and all manner of fine pearls, and of fine things of the world. And from that time forth they did have their goods and their substance no more common among them." Economic inequality created socioeconomic classes and renewed the old fissures of their pre-Zion society. Within the space of only a few years, classism and sectarianism reigned supreme. Now alienated from one another, viewing others as members of competing groups rather than as sisters and brothers in Christ, their society reintroduced cultural, structural, and direct violence. Those who remained committed to the gospel ethic of Christian nonviolence and justice were targeted in particular, as they represented a reminder of Christ's alternative path and thus a threat to the rekindled systems of power and profit. At times the disciples were miraculously delivered from harm like the people of Enoch, but for the most part they had to endure their sufferings like the people of Alma and the early New Testament Christians. "And they did smite the people of Jesus," Mormon records, "but the people of Jesus did not smite again." The "true worshipers of Christ" did not forget the words of his sermon at the temple.[47] Having lost influence within mainstream culture, "the people of Jesus" once again became the counterculture. Society had changed, but the way of Jesus had not.

Although the Book of Mormon narrative ultimately ends with the complete abandonment of Zion principles and a descent into genocidal warfare, these few verses in 4 Nephi, along with the other scriptural accounts of other Zion communities, beckon readers to attempt similar efforts. Representing the practical fruit of its nonviolent theology, Zion is the ultimate goal that the Restoration consistently points to and encourages us to pursue. Restoration scripture amply testifies that anytime we seek to distribute the world's wealth and resources more equitably, we build Zion. Anytime we work to overcome debilitating cultures of racism or sexism or classism or any other form of systemic violence, we build Zion. Anytime we work to ensure wise stewardship of the earth and the natural beauty and life it encompasses, we build Zion. Anytime we expand the borders of our communities to better embrace those who are overlooked or forgotten, and anytime we extend our reach to include and embrace our enemies, we build Zion. Such efforts will naturally be imperfect and ongoing. But insofar as we strive to create societies in which cultural, structural, and direct forms of violence are eliminated and transformed, establishing in their stead communities where everyone's "hearts [are] knit together in unity and in love one towards another," we build Zion.[48]

CHAPTER TEN

Just Ward Theory

Verily I say, men [and women] should be anxiously engaged in a
good cause, and do many things of their own free will, and bring
to pass much righteousness; for the power is in them, wherein
they are agents unto themselves.
—Doctrine and Covenants 58:27–28

The kingdom of heaven is like yeast.
—Matthew 13:33 (NRSV)

Do you love Jesus? If so, you are called to be a peace-builder. Are you part of a covenant Christian community? If so, your community is called to peacebuilding. Peacebuilding is a staple of the Christian diet, a central element—or "prime priority," as President Russell M. Nelson has called it—for both individuals and groups who have pledged to follow Jesus Christ.[1]

It's tempting to think of peacebuilding as something done by diplomats, generals, and heads of state participating in elaborate ceremonies to sign treaties ending major conflicts. Although those formalities are important, they represent only the very tip of a peacebuilding pyramid, while most of the foundational work is done at lower levels. Sometimes peace comes from the top down, but more often than not it emerges from the bottom up. Latter-day Saint apostle John A. Widtsoe taught this principle in 1943 amid the ravages of the Second World War, when peace truly had been taken from the earth. He instructed the Church, "Each individual . . . holds in his own hands the peace of the world. That makes me responsible for the peace of the world, and makes you individually responsible for the peace of the world. The responsibility cannot be shifted to someone else. It cannot be placed upon the shoulders of Congress or Parliament, or any other organization of men with governing authority."[2] Peace can't simply be something that other people pursue on our behalf.

In recent decades, scholars, practitioners, political leaders, and religious leaders have all given greater attention to the importance of local and community actors in transforming conflict and building sustainable peace.[3] Beginning in the early 1990s, the United Nations recognized community-level efforts as essential, not merely ornamental, in global peacebuilding efforts.[4] These efforts include but go well beyond the cessation of violence (negative peace) to focus on a wide range of practices that contribute to a sustainable and just peace (positive peace) adapted to local circumstances. These practices include but are by no means limited to peace education, conflict prevention, establishing a rule of law that is applied equitably and justly for all citizens, interreligious (and often intrareligious) dialogue, promoting women's and children's rights, economic development and microenterprise, trauma healing and psychosocial work, reintegration of former combatants and convicts, racial reconciliation initiatives, and democratization efforts such as voter education and elections monitoring. The prominent conflict transformation theorist and practitioner John Paul Lederach emphasizes that peacebuilding is largely about relationships, and while macro structural forces must always be accounted for, the key relationships for building sustainable peace exist primarily at the local and community level.[5] While community efforts may not be able to correct global economic inequities, or eliminate the results of centuries of racism and misogyny, or end large-scale armed conflict, they can do much to alleviate or transform the local and personal effects of such systems.

So what does this mean for members of The Church of Jesus Christ of Latter-day Saints? It means you are part of a potentially powerful but often overlooked resource for community-based peacebuilding. Even experts on religious peacebuilding have barely noticed the possibilities of what this particular Christian community could (and already does) accomplish.[6] The preceding chapters having laid out a Restoration theology of nonviolence, this concluding chapter turns toward application. What might you, as a covenanted follower of Jesus, do to build peace? How might you address the cultural violence, structural injustices, and sometimes outright direct expressions of violence that occur in your community? Beyond individual impact, what might Latter-day Saint wards and stakes do to renounce war, proclaim peace, and build Zion? There exists no blueprint that works for every Church member or congregation (although people can benefit from consulting existing handbooks for peace practitioners).[7] Instead, this chapter offers illustrations and insights that we hope may inspire you to contemplate what *you* might do within your own context. We somewhat playfully refer to applied principles of Latter-day Saint peacebuilding as "just ward theory" because the peacebuilding potential of the Restoration is most fully realized when our local congregations—from branches and wards to stakes and missions—are mobilized to build the positive peace of Zion.

PEACEBUILDING POTENTIAL

Although The Church of Jesus Christ of Latter-day Saints is now truly global, with more members outside the United States than inside, its membership is not equally distributed across the world. As of 2020, the vast majority of Church members (82 percent) and congregations (77 percent) resided in North, Central, and South America—in other words, in the Western Hemisphere where there is little to no intrastate or interstate war.[8] In a real way, then, the general security and relative prosperity that most Latter-day Saints enjoy means that the revelation that Zion and "her stakes" would be "a refuge from the storm" is more true for the twentieth- and twenty-first-century Church than it was in the volatile (and violent) year of 1838, when the revelation was received.[9]

Given their relative distance from major armed conflict, it may be difficult for most Latter-day Saints to think of peacebuilding as a "prime priority." It is easy to be lulled into thinking that if our nation is not at war, or if direct violence does not affect our daily life, then peacebuilding is not a pressing concern. This is why it is essential to think about violence in broader terms—identifying it not just as war but as the whole range of behaviors and attitudes that constitute direct, structural, and cultural violence and that are present in every community. Thinking more broadly about the problem and pervasiveness of violence in its multiple forms opens up a wider array of potential contributions by peacebuilders. Indeed, the purposes of peacebuilding are to transform the structures and cultures of violence precisely so that direct violence in its various forms is avoided, reduced, transformed, and reconciled. One way to visualize this is through a conflict curve.[10]

This curve was created to illustrate the patterns that define large-scale direct violence such as war, but it has broader appli-

CURVE OF CONFLICT

PEACE   routine diplomacy   reconciliation

CONFLICT   preventive   post-conflict
           diplomacy   peacebuilding

VIOLENCE

WAR   crisis   peace-
                 diplomacy   keeping

                        peacemaking

cation as we think about various forms of violence in our local communities, from school shootings to domestic violence. No matter the form direct violence takes, most of the work of peacebuilding occurs either before or after the actual incidence of violent conflict—in other words, on the left and right sides of the curve. Arguably the most important work takes place above the line of direct violence, addressing the structures and cultures of violence that, if left unchecked, eventually precipitate direct violence. In other words, the peacebuilder strives to transform conflict before it becomes directly violent and to work toward long-term healing and reconciliation when transitioning out of direct violence.

Latter-day Saints already engage in a number of peacebuilding activities that fall on the left or right sides of the conflict curve, even if we and others do not recognize them as such. A bishop counseling a couple in a troubled marriage; young women and men engaging in meaningful community service activities; mothers and fathers raising children "to love one another, and to serve one another";[11] people extending forgiveness and reconciliation to those who have transgressed against them; missionaries teaching the gospel of peace and inviting people to reform their personal behavior—all of these are quiet examples of Christian peacebuilding that already occur every day throughout the

Church. In addition, as President Dallin H. Oaks has taught, there are many individual Church members who actively work to "reduce human suffering" or to "promote understanding among different peoples." Latter-day Saints around the world are engaged in interreligious dialogue, refugee resettlement, various forms of diplomacy, and sustainable development initiatives. Acting from their deepest religious convictions, Latter-day Saints are seeking to prevent or end human trafficking, persecution of religious minorities, and gender-based violence. All of these actions, rooted in "basic goodness" and a desire to love one's neighbor, are powerful avenues of peacebuilding.[12]

So Latter-day Saints do not need to wait for the Church to create a Peacebuilding Department in Salt Lake City. We already have a clear commandment to "proclaim peace."[13] Now it is simply our responsibility to "be anxiously engaged in a good cause, and do many things of [our] own free will, and bring to pass much righteousness."[14] The best place to start is where we are. Rather than waiting for the introduction of a new Churchwide program, with creativity and inspiration we can mobilize existing Church structures and resources at the local level to become more intentional peacebuilders in our communities. Consider the following possibilities.

Inspired by the thought that his stake could do more to serve the community, several years ago the president of a Brigham Young University student stake asked each ward to form a partnership with a social service provider in the county. As the stake president made his rounds at sacrament meetings in each ward, he delivered a talk designed to awaken the members from their slumber (figuratively and literally):

> Brothers and sisters, I bear you my testimony that were the Lord Jesus Christ to be physically present in Provo today, He would not attend a single meeting of the BYU Ninth Stake. Why not?

. . . The Lord I know would be at the state mental hospital, the battered women's shelter, the prison, and in south Provo with a recently arrived family from Central America. . . . If those are the places our Lord would be, then that is where we need to be.

Under the stake president's direction, bishops called some of the spiritually strongest women and men in the ward to lead the "Pure Religion Committee," which coordinated each ward's work with its selected social service provider. These initiatives were not designed as one-off projects, but rather as sustained relationship-building endeavors with vulnerable populations in the community. The stake presidency told bishops that the work of each Pure Religion Committee was the principal work of the ward outside Sunday meetings, replacing dances and other social activities that students could readily find elsewhere on campus. They kicked off the school year with a stake fireside featuring a segment from a documentary on Mother Teresa, followed by talks using Matthew 25—Jesus's injunction to serve "the least of these"—as their main text. Not all of the wards or ward members caught the vision, but for those who participated it was transformative, not only for them but also for the community members with whom they worked.[15]

It is probable that few (perhaps none) of the members of the BYU Ninth Stake believed they were involved in the vocation of peacebuilding. So to some degree this lack of awareness represents a simple semantic gap—what one person calls community service another might call peacebuilding. We shouldn't get hung up on the language—it is entirely possible to constructively transform structural and cultural violence without labeling them as such. Yet intentionality does matter, not only for the proper diagnosis of issues but also for a person's or organization's notion of what is at stake. Peacebuilding would lose utility as a term if it was applied so broadly as to encompass all good and desirable actions, but neither should it be limited only to the cessation or mediation of direct violent conflict. It is valuable and motivating for people—especially disciples of Christ—to recognize they can be grassroots peacebuilders in their immediate context.

Another enormous and already-existing resource for Latter-day Saint peacebuilding is the Church's unparalleled missionary program. For many reasons, missionaries and peacebuilders haven't always gotten along. One of the authors will never forget being in a graduate seminar when the professor, who as an anthropologist had long experience seeing the negative effects of colonialism around the world, started pounding on the table shouting, "I hate missionaries!" Latter-day Saints need to become more aware of the ways that the global expansion of Christianity has been historically connected with forms of structural and cultural violence such as colonialism and imperialism, which has left a sour taste in many people's mouths for the work that missionaries do. But missionaries don't have to be agents of cultural imperialism. Using the example of Ammon as their paradigm, missionaries can be remarkable bridges between cultures. Their sincere love and selfless service can be vehicles of reconciliation that touch hearts and even transform communities—whether or not people get baptized. This is already the case with thousands of worldwide humanitarian missionaries who have done wonders in bringing the good news of Jesus's love to the poor, healing the brokenhearted, ministering to the mentally ill, helping the blind recover their sight, feeding the hungry, giving clean water to the thirsty, clothing the naked, visiting the imprisoned, providing medical care, assisting refugees, saving vulnerable newborns, and providing wheelchairs to the immobilized.[16] Some have even developed curricula about human rights for public school classrooms around the world. All of this is the work of peacebuilding.

But it's not just humanitarian missionaries who can be— and already are—peacebuilders. Every missionary on a full-time proselytizing mission is expected to "learn to be a disciple of Jesus Christ by serving as He did," and doing so "with a sincere desire to help others without any expected outcomes."[17] All full-time missionaries dedicate hours each week to community service. Many of these young disciples, with just a little awareness and training, might choose to direct their service toward a wide range of intentional peacebuilding-related activities, including but not limited to teaching basic literacy skills; offering conflict resolution workshops for children, juveniles, and adults; visiting and helping to reintegrate former prisoners; assisting community-based refugee resettlement efforts; or offering invitations and providing support for people to participate in the Church's self-reliance and addiction recovery programs. Of course, most eighteen- to twenty-one-year-olds don't have any particular expertise in these areas—but neither are they theologians or linguists before leaving on their missions. They can be trained, and they can partner with existing community-based organizations—many of which are faith-based—that are already doing this kind of work but often suffer from a labor shortage.

Latter-day Saint missionaries already come home with remarkable life skills that help them in their careers and make them attractive to a wide range of employers. In the United States various government agencies have long recognized how missions, with their promotion of foreign-language fluency and intercultural literacy, are excellent preparation for valuable service to the nation. Those same language skills and cultural sensitivities, as well as discipline and personal sense of calling, are also tremendously useful to a wide range of nonprofit peacebuilding and development organizations that do crucial work in communities around the world. Returned missionaries thus represent a large—and largely untapped—pool of potential peacebuilders.

The Church's existing programs to combat the structural violence of socioeconomic inequality already represent important peacebuilding efforts. However, like so many elements of the Restoration, their full potential has not yet been realized. Consider the Church's addiction recovery, self-reliance, and refugee assistance programs. These programs are not designed solely for Church members, nor are they limited to the scope of ward or stake boundaries. With greater outreach and increased volunteer efforts, they could have a far greater impact on our communities, especially among our most vulnerable populations. What's more, in addition to the Church's existing programs, wards could be even more anxiously engaged in partnering with non–Latter-day Saint community service providers that work on issues related to homelessness, restorative justice, conflict resolution, violence prevention, adult literacy, after-school programs, reduction of gender-based violence and domestic abuse, addiction recovery, interfaith understanding, food insecurity, and job retraining. Don't know where to start? Read your local newspaper, talk to social workers or local politicians. Find out where people are suffering or struggling in your community. If you are lucky enough to live in a place with little to no direct violence, discover where structural and cultural violence may be lurking, and go there. Sometimes Christ had problems come to him, but he also went to the places where he would find the poor, the marginalized, and the victimized. Peacebuilding is proactive.

With inspired vision, appropriate training, and the signature Latter-day Saint qualities of love-based commitment and voluntarism, our wards and stakes might do this type of work with nothing more than an imaginative rearrangement of existing resources. A 2013 study showed that Latter-day Saint Americans give an average of 336.5 hours of volunteer labor per year, roughly nine times more than the average American volunteer.[18] The Church's new emphasis on ministering and the flexibility of the new youth program, two signatures of the administration of President Russell M. Nelson, have freed us to more effectively apply our efforts in cultivating Christian discipleship toward transforming our societies by responding to the real needs around us. We can be peacebuilders not *in addition* to being members of The Church of Jesus Christ of Latter-day Saints, but rather *because* we are Latter-day Saints who belong to the Church of Jesus Christ.

LEAVENING SOCIETY

Over the last two centuries, Latter-day Saints have done an extraordinary job of producing an intensive congregational structure with relationships characterized by trust, cohesion, strong organization, and genuine affection and solidarity. As we approach our third century, one of the challenges facing The Church of Jesus Christ of Latter-day Saints may be how to mobilize our existing structures and resources for maximum impact. The Church's primary mission is to bring people to Christ. That mission necessarily focuses on saving and transforming individuals. But we hope that by now you are convinced (if you weren't already) that a call to Zion should also inspire disciples of Christ to embrace ambitious goals for saving and transforming our society. God gifted us this Church not to be merely a club for members, but as a means of structuring and scaling up Christ's injunction to "love one another." The Church may not be Zion per se, but it is one of the principal means God has ordained for building Zion.

Another Restoration faith tradition, the Community of Christ, has adopted a vocabulary that describes local congregations as "signal communities of justice and peace that reflect the vision of Christ."[19] This is similar to what Gandhi called "cells of good living."[20] Andrew Bolton, formerly a member of the Council of Twelve Apostles in the Community of Christ, describes what it takes to build a Christian signal community:

> The vision necessary for forming a signal community is God's vision for a saved, redeemed world where no child anywhere

225

goes to bed hungry, cold or afraid. God's vision is a world where
God's peace is fully restored on earth. . . . As a Christ-centered
community, our mission is to promote communities that signal
the Peaceful Reign of God on Earth (the cause of Zion).

Inspired by scriptural examples of Zion, Bolton outlines the
threefold mission of a signal community: (1) to provide compassionate ministries to feed the hungry, heal the sick, and attend
the grieving; (2) to provide Christian witness and foster discipleship, recognizing the infinite worth of all persons in the sight of
God; and (3) to work for peace and justice in our societies—in
other words, as Jesus proclaimed in the synagogue, to proclaim
good news to the poor, liberate the captives, and set at liberty the
bruised and oppressed.[21] This notion of a signal community—of
being a light to the world—should resonate with most Latter-day
Saints. Its tripartite formulation parallels many of the "divinely
appointed responsibilities" of The Church of Jesus Christ of
Latter-day Saints: (1) living the gospel of Jesus Christ, (2) car-
ing for those in need, (3) inviting all to receive the gospel, and
(4) uniting families for eternity.[22] Our congregations may likewise reflect and embody these responsibilities to signal the paths
of peace to a weary world.

Of course, mobilizing our wards as signal communities of
intentional peacebuilding is not really a radical innovation. Such
work has been done before. In the early twentieth century, for
example, the Church endorsed the worldwide peace movement
and adopted peace as a central component of annual ward activities. At those events, the Saints decorated their meetinghouses
in the colors of the international peace movement (gold, purple,
and white). Ward choirs sang anti-war songs, and ward members
wrote their own peace-related poems and composed and signed
peace resolutions that renounced war and called for international
institutions to peacefully arbitrate conflict. While most members

and leaders were involved, local Relief Society sisters led these peace efforts, seeing the pursuit of peace as integral to their organization's mission to relieve human suffering.[23]

In recent years Church leaders have also summoned another aspect of our collective history—a pattern of fleeing persecution—to inspire contemporary peacebuilding efforts to support, resettle, and integrate refugees from war-torn countries. The "I Was a Stranger" refugee assistance program—initiated by the First Presidency and Relief Society General Presidency in 2016—mobilized the resources of both the Church's worldwide humanitarian program as well as local wards and members. Comparing current refugees' harrowing predicaments to the plight of the early Latter-day Saints, repeatedly driven from their homes and forced to settle in a strange land, Elder Patrick Kearon has noted, "Their story *is* our story, not that many years ago."[24] Inspired by these shared histories of sorrow, local wards have opened their arms and hearts to these vulnerable populations, working to mitigate the cultural, structural, and direct violence that has done such harm. These efforts demonstrate that peacebuilding initiatives are effective and sustainable when they are rooted in a person's or group's deepest values, leading to concrete steps toward transformative social action.[25]

President Joseph F. Smith once prophetically observed that "peace comes only by preparing for peace."[26] One crucial component of "preparing for peace" is peace education, which is now formally instituted at the Church's three main universities. The vanguard for these efforts has been Brigham Young University–Hawaii, where the David O. McKay Center for Intercultural Understanding sponsors both a certificate program and undergraduate major in intercultural peacebuilding. The program builds on the prophetic mandate that President McKay gave when establishing the university over a half century ago, saying, "From this school . . . will go men and women whose influence will be felt for good towards the establishment of peace internationally." Students learn theories of conflict resolution, conflict transformation, and intercultural understanding, then put those theories to work through applied training in mediation.[27] Similar efforts have been initiated at the Provo campus, where the J. Reuben Clark Law School at Brigham Young University hosts the Center for Peace and Conflict Resolution, and at Brigham Young University–Idaho, which recently introduced an undergraduate minor in peace and conflict transformation.[28] Students who receive such training—in areas such as mediation, arbitration, negotiation, and conflict resolution—are prepared for a wide variety of careers in government, the private sector, and nonprofit organizations. Yet think about the impact such graduates, numbering at first in the dozens but now in the hundreds and eventually in the thousands and beyond, will also have in their families, wards, and communities. Of course, it doesn't take a college degree to be a peacebuilder. But these highly trained students will likely be important catalysts for helping the Latter-day Saints fulfill their mission as a peacebuilding people.

It is true that in most places Latter-day Saints probably do not yet have sufficient numbers, even acting collectively as congregations, to represent a critical mass of transformative peacebuilders. But we shouldn't let that deter us. Wards and stakes that want to be "signal communities" may have to be strategic—not to mention prayerful—about what they can realistically achieve in their sphere of influence with the skills, resources, and connections they have. No one ward or stake can do it all, so to more intentionally "proclaim peace" each may have to be selective about where and how it can make the greatest impact. It is doubtful that a ward in Springville will bring peace to Syria. The bumper sticker adage "Think global, act local" is useful here.

Furthermore, when it comes to peacebuilding, numbers do not always matter. In a conversation one day with Somalis about how local communities could ever address the violent power of the warlords, someone suggested to the prominent international peacebuilder John Paul Lederach that they needed "a critical mass of opposition," perhaps even an outside military force that could intervene. In a moment of inspiration, Lederach responded, "It seems to me that the key to changing this thing is getting a small set of the right people involved at the right places. What is missing is not the critical mass. The missing ingredient is the *critical yeast.*" This metaphor, emerging from Lederach's familiarity with Jesus's teachings about Christians being the leaven (or yeast) in society, shifts the conversation from being about critical mass to thinking creatively about what Lederach calls "the strategic who": "Who, though not like-minded or like-situated in this context of conflict, would have a capacity, if they were mixed and held together, to make other things grow exponentially, beyond their numbers?"[29] Latter-day Saints have proved that even as a small percentage of the general population they can have a disproportionate political impact when they unite and mobilize around a specific goal.[30] Wards and stakes may never provide sufficient critical mass for local peacebuilding efforts, but they can be the critical yeast, so long as they are fully kneaded into the social mixture.

In aspiring to build Zion here and now we should not get too heady. Peacebuilding requires patience and humility. The city of Enoch took centuries to build and cultivate as a peacebuilding Zion. Yes, Jesus calls us to be salt and yeast, but we should remember not only the disproportionate influence of those substances but also their smallness. The leaven never actually becomes the loaf—it is merely an activating agent. The gathered community of Saints will always be a minority in the world, and in some places a negligible presence. For much of scriptural and early Latter-day Saint history, Zion was a place set apart from the rest of the world, where believers could worship God and build their intentional community at least somewhat separate from the outside world. Withdrawal was the modus operandi. But in the twentieth and twenty-first centuries, the possibility of finding new land beyond the reach of any outside entity is no longer feasible. Saintly gathering and Zion building are thus forced to take on a localized dimension, with the creation of many mini-Zions throughout the world rather than one centralized Zion.

This lack of critical mass is a real challenge for many Latter-day Saint wards and branches. Outlying units struggle just to survive, let alone have any larger impact in places where they represent a tiny percentage of the population. However, the establishment of mini-Zions at the local level, embedded in rather than separate from society, may in fact be advantageous to signaling, and eventually bringing about, the peaceable kingdom of God. More Zions mean the influence of Zion can be spread wider, though perhaps in less concentrated form, around the globe. Being in the minority also increases the chances that a group hasn't been corrupted by power or isn't hobbled by entanglements with the status quo. It is almost always from the margins of society, rather than the courts of power, that prophetic voices emerge.

WHAT DO WE SAY?

Some Latter-day Saints may see peacebuilding as unnecessarily burdensome for congregations or a distraction from more pressing matters. Certainly, bishops, Relief Society presidents, and elders quorum presidents already have more than enough on their plates, and many wards and especially branches struggle just to meet basic organizational needs. But as the president of the BYU Ninth Stake implicitly recognized, mobilizing our congregations around the concept of pure religion—which overlaps substantially with peacebuilding—may be one of the best ways to reenergize spiritually comatose members and even whole units. In his 1955 classic *God in Search of Man*, Rabbi Abraham Joshua Heschel wrote, "It is customary to blame secular science and anti-religious philosophy for the eclipse of religion in modern society. It would be more honest to blame religion for its own defeats. Religion declined not because it was refuted, but because it became irrelevant, dull, oppressive, insipid."[31] The Christian theologian and civil rights activist Howard Thurman similarly observed, "The masses of men live with their backs constantly against the wall. They are the poor, the disinherited, the dispossessed. What does our religion say to them? . . . The search for an answer to this question is perhaps the most important quest of modern life."[32]

We live in an era when people are leaving organized religion—including The Church of Jesus Christ of Latter-day Saints—in droves. In such a time, the audacious call of Zion, rooted in Jesus's ministry of nonviolent love, may thus produce two secondary goods, in addition to the primary outcomes of reducing violence and building communities of sustainable peace and justice. First, integrating peacebuilding into our ward- and stake-level ministries will give Latter-day Saints a vision that the Restoration is not "irrelevant, dull, oppressive, insipid," but rather relevant, ambitious, liberating, and irrepressibly meaningful. Second, an active peacebuilding agenda will demonstrate, in real terms and concrete initiatives, how the Restoration truly does have something to say to those whose backs are against the wall, those who suffer from not only direct violence but also the insidious forces of structural and cultural violence that dominate the lives of "the poor, the disinherited, the dispossessed." At a time when many people are questioning the role of religion in modern society, the moment may be ripe for Latter-day Saints to develop and apply a "just ward theory."

Epilogue

Let Zion in her beauty rise;
Her light begins to shine.
—*Hymns*, no. 41

The Restoration is an ongoing process;
we are living in it right now.
—Dieter F. Uchtdorf

In 1833 Joseph Smith directed his scribe Frederick G. Williams to draw what he called the "plat of the city of Zion." This rendering of Zion's physical layout was no more than a rough sketch with a few accompanying notes, but it has inspired Saints and city builders ever since.[1] In many ways this plat is a metaphor for the entirety of the Restoration. Joseph Smith and his associates provided the outline and began to fill it in, but it would fall to later generations, including ours, to flesh out that vision and bring it to life in the contemporary world. This is what current Church leaders have called the "ongoing Restoration."[2]

This book is our attempt to participate in the ongoing Restoration by roughly (and imperfectly) sketching out the contours of its distinctive theology of peace and nonviolence. We do not see this effort as the final word on the subject, but rather an early chapter in an unfolding narrative. We invite readers to fill in the empty spaces in our sketch and other scholars and practitioners to erase, extend, or correct some of the lines we have drawn. Nothing would delight us more than for others to come along and help us all better understand what a peace-loving God intends for his children.

We believe that the positive peace of Zion represents the full embodiment and realization of the Restoration's nonviolent theology. But we do not live in Zion, yet. By *we*, we mean ourselves, the authors, as well as the communities and broader world we inhabit. Although personally committed to loving nonviolence, we have not discovered a way—or have not tried hard enough— to disentangle ourselves from the structures and cultures of violence that are embedded in our twenty-first-century society. We demonstrate "friendship" to our national government in part by paying taxes that support ongoing military actions and other structurally violent policies we morally oppose. We participate in an economic system that we know exacerbates inequality and contributes to ecological degradation even while it has brought prosperity to many. We benefit from the long-standing privileges associated with being white heterosexual males and wonder if we are doing enough to create an equitable and just society for those who are not, including our own daughters.

We deeply admire those who strive to model themselves after the early disciples of Jesus and have created intentional communities based on Christian nonviolence, economic redistribution or sharing all things in common, and love for all God's children. Communities like the Catholic Workers and the Bruderhof demonstrate that even in our complex modern world it is possible to build "signal communities" that try to approximate Zion.[3] Without relinquishing our own personal convictions and our full allegiance to The Church of Jesus Christ of Latter-day Saints, we celebrate the profound witness of these Christians, along with so many others throughout history and from other faith traditions, who have much to teach us.

If "Rome wasn't built in a day," as the saying goes, then it's important to remember that Zion won't be built overnight. In some aspects our covenant community of Latter-day Saints seems closer to realizing Zion than it has ever been. Still, as prophets and apostles constantly attest, in many areas we still falter. God is truly working in and through the contemporary Church, but there remains significant work for us to do. After all, one way that the devil "cheateth [our] souls" is by whispering in our ears, "All is well in Zion; yea, Zion prospereth, all is well."[4] So we "meet together oft," whether in weekly sacrament meetings or semi-annual general conferences, to repent—to hear and feel where our current path of discipleship, both individually and collectively, can be straightened and refined.[5]

One effect of learning about structural and cultural violence is that we begin to recognize that this fallen world is saturated with such insidious and destructive forces. There are no human institutions and communities that are untouched or immune, including ours. Many early readers of this manuscript—especially younger ones—immediately recognized historical and contemporary Latter-day Saint attitudes and practices that fall well short of the positive peace of Zion. It is good to acknowledge such shortcomings. As individuals and as a community, we want to do and be better, and that begins with recognizing precisely where we need to improve, or what the Book of Mormon calls exercising "faith unto repentance."[6] Our hope is that we have given you a few tools to not only see various forms of violence in your sphere of influence, but to also work toward constructively and lovingly transforming yourself and your community. It is not enough to "renounce" or condemn; we are also called to "proclaim" and build.[7]

As far as our covenant community goes, here is the good news: never before have there been more Latter-day Saints attuned to the possibilities of Jesus Christ's "good news." Over the last few decades, our community has increasingly focused on Jesus Christ, in part because of improved interactions with other Christian communities, but mostly owing to a renewed and prophetic emphasis on the Book of Mormon. As we (re)discover Jesus in our Restoration scriptures, we will (re)discover the social, political, economic, cultural, and ecological implications of his teachings. Like so many Saints in former days, Latter-day Saints are being transformed by their encounter with Jesus Christ and his perfect atonement and are thinking actively about how being "peaceable followers of Christ" translates into the promise and potential of Zion.[8]

Readers may be frustrated that we—similar to Mormon's all-too-brief account in 4 Nephi—have not provided a more detailed blueprint for a personal life of Christian nonviolence or how to build a Zion society. It is true that the preceding chapters have been long on principles and short on concrete steps and tactics, leaving so much unsaid and undone. But we know God's grace to be boundless. We've felt a portion of that grace lifting and transforming us as we've tried to sketch the barest outline of the Restoration's theology of peace. And we trust his grace will be with all of us as we seek to fill in that picture, both individually and collectively. We leave it to you to determine what a theology of peace means concretely in your individual life. But, in the end, we know this is a collective endeavor. And, along with President Russell M. Nelson, we believe "peace is possible"—which means Zion is achievable—in *this* world, *before* Christ returns.[9] We likewise affirm that the Restoration has much to teach a world full of conflict and violence. Applying its principles will help establish more sustainably peaceful, just, loving, and equitable societies. Positive peace is within our reach—or maybe the reach of our children or our children's children. It begins now as we heed Jesus's call to truly "renounce war and proclaim peace."[10]

Notes

INTRODUCTION

1. *Hymns of The Church of Jesus Christ of Latter-day Saints* (Salt Lake City: The Church of Jesus Christ of Latter-day Saints, 1985), no. 129.
2. *Hymns*, no 129.
3. Doctrine and Covenants 45:26–27; Matthew 24:6, 12; see Doctrine and Covenants 63:33; 87:1–2.
4. Matthew 5:9; 3 Nephi 12:9. Quotations from the Bible are from the King James Version unless otherwise noted.
5. Moses 6:38.
6. Genesis 5:24 (New Revised Standard Version).
7. Moses 6:27–28.
8. Moses 7:16, 33.
9. Moses 7:13, 18.
10. See Moses 7:68–69.
11. Martin Luther King Jr., *I Have a Dream: Writings and Speeches That Changed the World*, ed. James Melvin Washington (San Francisco: HarperSanFrancisco, 1992), 195.

12. For a Latter-day Saint theology of creation, see George B. Handley, *The Hope of Nature: Our Care for God's Creation* (Provo, UT: Neal A. Maxwell Institute for Religious Scholarship, Brigham Young University, 2020).

13. See Grant Hardy, *Understanding the Book of Mormon: A Reader's Guide* (New York: Oxford University Press, 2010). This approach is also exemplified in Elizabeth Fenton and Jared Hickman, eds., *Americanist Approaches to The Book of Mormon* (New York: Oxford University Press, 2019).

14. Adam S. Miller, "A Manifesto for Mormon Theology," in *Rube Goldberg Machines: Essays in Mormon Theology* (Salt Lake City: Greg Kofford Books, 2012), 59–60.

15. Boyd K. Packer, "Little Children," *Ensign*, November 1986, 17.

16. Otis Moss III, *Blue Note Preaching in a Post-Soul World: Finding Hope in an Age of Despair* (Louisville, KY: Westminster John Knox, 2015), 105.

17. Doctrine and Covenants 98:16.

18. Psalm 119:165.

19. Romans 12:18 (NRSV).

20. Mosiah 4:13.

21. Isaiah 2:4; 2 Nephi 12:4.

22. A foundational article in this regard is Johan Galtung, "Violence, Peace, and Peace Research," *Journal of Peace Research* 6, no. 3 (1969): 167–91.

23. Dallin H. Oaks, "World Peace," *Ensign*, May 1990.

24. The phrase has been attributed to several people. For one prominent example, see Pope John Paul II, "No Peace without Justice; No Justice without Forgiveness," message for the celebration of World Day of Peace, January 1, 2002, https://w2.vatican.va/content/john-paul-ii/en/messages/peace/documents/hf_jp-ii_mes_20011211_xxxv-world-day-for-peace.html.

25. John Paul Lederach and R. Scott Appleby, "Strategic Peacebuilding: An Overview," in *Strategies of Peace: Transforming Conflict in a Violent World*, ed. Daniel Philpott and Gerard F. Powers (New York: Oxford University Press, 2010), 23–24.

26. Galtung, "Violence, Peace, and Peace Research," 171.

27. See Johan Galtung, "Cultural Violence," *Journal of Peace Research* 27, no. 3 (August 1990): 291–305.

28. The Church of Jesus Christ of Latter-day Saints, "Locking arms for racial harmony in America," June 8, 2020, https://medium.com/@Ch_Jesus Christ/locking-arms-for-racial-harmony-in-america-2f62180abf37.

29. Mormon 7:4.

30. Matthew 26:52, in Thomas A. Wayment, *The New Testament: A Translation for Latter-day Saints—A Study Bible* (Provo, UT: Religious Studies Center, Brigham Young University; Salt Lake City: Deseret Book, 2019).

31. See Mosiah 29:32; Alma 28:13; 32:2–3; 3 Nephi 6:12–15.

32. Mosiah 15:18 (see vv. 14–18).

33. Moroni 7:4.

34. For just a few examples, see R. Scott Appleby, *The Ambivalence of the Sacred: Religion, Violence, and Reconciliation* (Lanham, MD: Rowman & Littlefield, 2000); Mohammed Abu-Nimer, *Nonviolence and Peace Building in Islam: Theory and Practice* (Gainesville: University of Florida Press, 2003); David Little, ed., *Peacemakers in Action: Profiles of Religion in Conflict Resolution* (New York: Cambridge University Press, 2007); David Whitten Smith and Elizabeth Geraldine Burr, *Understanding World Religions: A Road Map for Justice and Peace* (Lanham, MD: Rowman & Littlefield, 2007); John Howard Yoder, *Christian Attitudes to War, Peace, and Revolution*, ed. Theodore J. Koontz and Andy Alexis-Baker (Grand Rapids, MI: Brazos Press, 2009); Robert J. Schreiter, R. Scott Appleby, and Gerard F. Powers, eds., *Peacebuilding: Catholic Theology, Ethics, and Praxis* (Maryknoll, NY: Orbis Books, 2010); Atalia Omer, R. Scott Appleby, and David Little, eds., *The Oxford Handbook of Religion, Conflict, and Peacebuilding* (New York: Oxford University Press, 2015); Susan Hayward and Katherine Marshall, eds., *Women, Religion, and Peacebuilding: Illuminating the Unseen* (Washington, DC: United States Institute of Peace Press, 2015); Joyce S. Dubensky, ed., *Peacemakers in Action: Profiles in Religious Peacebuilding—Volume II* (New York: Cambridge University Press, 2016); and Lisa Sowle Cahill, *Blessed Are the Peacemakers: Pacifism, Just War, and Peacebuilding* (Minneapolis: Fortress Press, 2019).

35. Bruce Springsteen, "Nebraska," *Nebraska* (Columbia Records, 1982).

36. See John 1:4; 3:17.

37. Russell M. Nelson, "'Blessed Are the Peacemakers,'" *Ensign*, November 2002.

38. Valerie Johnson, "Elder Uchtdorf encourages all to become 'a people of peace and reconciliation' during Volkstrauertag event," *Church News*, November 18, 2019.

39. Sydney Walker, "President Oaks gives universal 'formula' for peace," *Church News*, December 8, 2019.

40. Emma Lou Thayne, "How Much for the Earth? A Suite of Poems: About Time for Considering," *Dialogue: A Journal of Mormon Thought* 17, no. 4 (Winter 1984): 118, 138. See Casualene Meyer, "Emma Lou Thayne and the Art of Peace," *BYU Studies Quarterly* 53, no. 3 (2014): 181–91.

CHAPTER ONE

1. Alexander McRae, as quoted in Richard Lyman Bushman, *Joseph Smith: Rough Stone Rolling* (New York: Knopf, 2005), 375.

2. B. H. Roberts, *A Comprehensive History of the Church of Jesus Christ of Latter-day Saints* (Salt Lake City: Deseret News Press, 1930), 1:526.

3. Doctrine and Covenants 121:1–5. This revelation was excerpted (and later canonized) from a long letter written in two parts by Joseph Smith to Bishop Edward Partridge and the Church at large. For the full text, see "Letter to the Church and Edward Partridge, 20 March 1839," The Joseph Smith Papers, https://www.josephsmithpapers.org/paper-summary/letter-to-the-church-and-edward-partridge-20-march-1839/ and "Letter to Edward Partridge and the Church, circa 22 March 1839," The Joseph Smith Papers, https://www.josephsmithpapers.org/paper-summary/letter-to-edward-partridge-and-the-church-circa-22-march-1839/.

4. See Doctrine and Covenants 121:7–10.

5. Doctrine and Covenants 121:39, 41–42.

6. *True to the Faith: A Gospel Reference* (Salt Lake City: The Church of Jesus Christ of Latter-day Saints, 2004), s.v. "Priesthood"; emphasis added. On the development of Mormon ideas about priesthood, see Jonathan Stapley, *The Power of Godliness: Mormon Liturgy and Cosmology* (New York: Oxford University Press, 2018).

7. Doctrine and Covenants 121:36.

8. Doctrine and Covenants 93:29.

9. See Abraham 3:16–19. This theology was most fully developed by Joseph Smith shortly before his death. See Stan Larson, "The King Follett

Discourse: A Newly Amalgamated Text," *BYU Studies* 18, no. 2 (Winter 1978): 193–208.

10. See Revelation 12:7–9.

11. Thomas Paine, *The Age of Reason*, as quoted in Boyd Jay Petersen, "'One Soul Shall Not Be Lost': The War in Heaven in Mormon Thought," *Journal of Mormon History* 38, no. 1 (Winter 2012): 11.

12. See Abraham 3:23–26.

13. Doctrine and Covenants 130:2.

14. Doctrine and Covenants 78:7.

15. Terryl Givens and Fiona Givens, *The God Who Weeps: How Mormonism Makes Sense of Life* (Salt Lake City: Ensign Peak, 2012), 20.

16. "Know This, That Every Soul Is Free," *Hymns* (Salt Lake City: The Church of Jesus Christ of Latter-day Saints, 1985), no. 240. See *A Collection of Sacred Hymns for the Church of the Latter Day Saints*, sel. Emma Smith (Kirtland, OH: F. G. Williams & Co., 1835), no. 1. Words quoted from the modern version.

17. Abraham 3:27; Moses 4:2.

18. Moses 4:1–2.

19. Moses 4:3.

20. God's honor was central to the thinking of the influential eleventh-century Christian theologian Anselm of Canterbury, who thought of it as being akin to the honor of a feudal lord. This led to the development of Anselm's influential "satisfaction theory" of atonement, which has increasingly come to be questioned in modern times. See J. Denny Weaver, *The Nonviolent Atonement*, 2nd. ed. (Grand Rapids, MI: William B. Eerdmans, 2011), 16–17, 228–35.

21. Doctrine and Covenants 121:36–37, 41; emphasis added.

22. Doctrine and Covenants 121:42.

23. See Ether 3:12; 1 John 4:19; Moroni 10:19.

24. Various scriptural passages suggest that this is the principle on which the natural world responds to God's command. See Mark 4:36–39; Helaman 12:7–13; Abraham 4.

25. Doctrine and Covenants 29:36; emphasis added.

26. See Bernard Bailyn, *The Ideological Origins of the American Revolution*, enl. ed. (Cambridge, MA: Belknap Press of Harvard University Press, 1992), 368–79; Matthew S. Holland, *Bonds of Affection: Civic Charity and*

the *Making of America—Winthrop, Jefferson, and Lincoln* (Washington, DC: Georgetown University Press, 2007); and Richard Dagger, *Civic Virtues: Rights, Citizenship, and Republican Liberalism* (New York: Oxford University Press, 1997).

27. Doctrine and Covenants 121:45–46.

28. Doctrine and Covenants 121:43–44.

29. Dallin H. Oaks, "Free Agency and Freedom," Brigham Young University devotional, October 11, 1987, https://speeches.byu.edu/talks/dallin-h-oaks /free-agency-freedom/.

30. Victor Frankl, *Man's Search for Meaning* (New York: Washington Square Press, 1985), 86.

31. See Moses 7:28–37. See also Byron R. Merrill, "Agency and Freedom in the Divine Plan," in *Window of Faith: Latter-day Saint Perspectives on World History*, ed. Roy A. Prete (Provo, UT: Religious Studies Center, Brigham Young University, 2005), 161–74.

32. Leon Trotsky, "The Danger of Thermidor," *The Militant* 6, no. 5 (February 4, 1933): 1.

33. Doctrine and Covenants 121:36.

34. As quoted in Larson, "King Follett Discourse," 206.

35. Abraham 3:27–28; Doctrine and Covenants 29:36.

36. Doctrine and Covenants 29:37.

37. John Milton, *Paradise Lost*, bk. 6, lines 824–26; spelling modernized.

38. Dante Alighieri, *Inferno*, canto 3, line 5.

39. Moses 4:3; Doctrine and Covenants 29:37.

40. 2 Nephi 2:17; Doctrine and Covenants 76:27

41. This is repeatedly portrayed in the Church's illustrated scripture videos for children. See "Before the Old Testament," https://www.churchofjesus christ.org/children/videos/scripture-stories/old-testament/1-before -the-old-testament?; "Introduction: Our Heavenly Father's Plan," https:// www.churchofjesuschrist.org/children/videos/scripture-stories/new -testament/introduction-our-heavenly-father's-plan?;and"Introduction: Before the Doctrine and Covenants," https://www.churchofjesuschrist .org/children/videos/scripture-stories/doctrine-and-covenants. An ana- logous narrative can be found in the Book of Mormon; see Alma 46.

42. Doctrine and Covenants 76:26–27, 29.

43. Articles of Faith 1:10.

44. Doctrine and Covenants 45:55. See 1 Nephi 22:26.
45. Doctrine and Covenants 123:7, 9, 13.
46. Ether 8:19.
47. Ether 12:11.
48. Ether 8:26.
49. Ether 12:27.
50. Cornel West and George Yancy, "Power Is Everywhere, but Love Is Supreme," *New York Times*, May 29, 2019.
51. 3 Nephi 13:10.

CHAPTER TWO

1. 3 Nephi 27:27.
2. See 2 Peter 1:2–4. For an example of how following Jesus leads to a contemporary social ethic, see Richard A. Burridge, *Imitating Jesus: An Inclusive Approach to New Testament Ethics* (Grand Rapids, MI: William B. Eerdmans, 2007).
3. The concept of Christ's "infinite atonement" is introduced in the Book of Mormon first by Jacob in 2 Nephi 9:7.
4. "I Stand All Amazed," *Hymns* (Salt Lake City: The Church of Jesus Christ of Latter-day Saints, 1985), no. 193.
5. Deidre Nicole Green, *Jacob: a brief theological introduction* (Provo, UT: Neal A. Maxwell Institute for Religious Scholarship, Brigham Young University, 2020), 100.
6. Daniel Becerra, *3rd, 4th Nephi: a brief theological introduction* (Provo, UT: Neal A. Maxwell Institute for Religious Scholarship, Brigham Young University, 2020), 68.
7. John 13:34.
8. Matthew 5:44. See Preston Sprinkle, *Fight: A Christian Case for Nonviolence* (Colorado Springs: David C. Cook, 2013), 142.
9. Martin Luther King Jr., "Pilgrimage to Nonviolence," in *I Have a Dream: Writings and Speeches That Changed the World*, ed. James M. Washington (San Francisco: HarperSanFrancisco, 1992), 59. See also Martin Luther King Jr., "Loving Your Enemies," in *A Knock at Midnight: Inspiration from the Great Sermons of Reverend Martin Luther King Jr.*, ed. Clayborne Carson and Peter Holloran (New York: Warner Books, 2000), 37–60.

10. See Bible Dictionary, Latter-day Saint edition of the King James Version of the Bible, s.v. "Atonement," https://www.churchofjesuschrist.org/study/scriptures/bd/atonement.
11. Acts 4:32–33.
12. 4 Nephi 1:15, 17.
13. Mark 10:21.
14. Mark 10:42 (42–45). This passage is rendered especially bluntly in the New Revised Standard Version (NRSV), in which Jesus describes political power among the Gentiles thus: their "rulers lord it over them, and their great ones are tyrants over them."
15. Luke 4:18–19 (NRSV).
16. On the importance of the jubilee in Jesus's ministry, see John Howard Yoder, *The Politics of Jesus*, 2nd ed. (Grand Rapids, MI: William B. Eerdmans, 1994), 28–33, 60–75.
17. John 6:15.
18. Luke 9:22–23, 51.
19. Luke 4:5–6. Matthew records this as the third temptation.
20. See Yoder, *Politics of Jesus*, 32.
21. Matthew 5:43–48 (NRSV).
22. Robert W. Brimlow, *What about Hitler? Wrestling with Jesus's Call to Nonviolence in an Evil World* (Grand Rapids, MI: Brazos Press, 2006), 11, 111.
23. See Matthew 5:43–48; John 13:34–35; 15:12; Matthew 6:12, 14–15; 18:32–33; John 13:1–17; Mark 10:42–45; Matthew 5:10–12; Luke 14:27–33; John 15:20–21; Matthew 5:38–39; 26:52.
24. See Walter Wink, *Naming the Powers: The Language of Power in the New Testament* (Minneapolis: Fortress, 1984); *Unmasking the Powers: The Invisible Forces That Determine Human Existence* (Minneapolis: Fortress, 1986); and *Engaging the Powers: Discernment and Resistance in a World of Domination* (Minneapolis: Fortress, 1992). For a one-volume digest of the trilogy, see *The Powers That Be: Theology for a New Millennium* (New York: Galilee, 1999).
25. Wink, *Powers That Be*, 101–2.
26. Wink, *Powers That Be*, 101–2.
27. Wink, *Powers That Be*, 103.
28. See Matthew 26:51–53; Luke 22:50–51; John 18:3–11.

29. James E. Talmage, *Jesus the Christ: A Study of the Messiah and His Mission according to the Holy Scriptures Both Ancient and Modern* (Salt Lake City: Deseret News, 1915), 613.

30. Luke 22:44; see also Doctrine and Covenants 19:18–19.

31. Bruce R. McConkie, "The Purifying Power of Gethsemane," *Ensign*, May 1985, 9. See McConkie, *Doctrinal New Testament Commentary*, 1:774–75, quoted in *The Life and Teachings of Jesus and His Apostles* (Salt Lake City: The Church of Jesus Christ of Latter-day Saints, 1978), 172.

32. Jeffrey R. Holland, "Atonement of Jesus Christ," *Encyclopedia of Mormonism*, https://eom.byu.edu/index.php/Atonement_of_Jesus_Christ. See also S. Kent Brown, "Gethsemane," *Encyclopedia of Mormonism*, https://eom.byu.edu/index.php/Gethsemane, especially quotations therein by Marion G. Romney and Ezra Taft Benson.

33. See John Hilton III and Joshua P. Barringer, "The Use of *Gethsemane* by Church Leaders, 1859–2018," *BYU Studies Quarterly* 58, no. 4 (2019): 49–76; and John Hilton III, Emily K. Hyde, and McKenna Grace Trussel, "The Teachings of Church Leaders Regarding the Crucifixion of Jesus Christ, 1852–2018," *BYU Studies Quarterly* 59, no. 1 (2020): 49–80. For a dramatic graphic representation of the increase of references to Gethsemane from the pulpit in general conference in recent decades, see the Latter-day Saint General Conference Corpus (https://www.lds-general-conference.org/), with keyword search "Gethsemane." On the ongoing significance of the cross in Latter-day Saint teaching, see Robert L. Millet, *What Happened to the Cross? Distinctive LDS Teachings* (Salt Lake City: Deseret Book, 2011); and Eric D. Huntsman, "Preaching Jesus, and Him Crucified," in *His Majesty and Mission*, ed. Nicholas J. Frederick and Keith J. Wilson (Provo, UT: Religious Studies Center, Brigham Young University; Salt Lake City: Deseret Book, 2017), 55–76.

34. See Helaman 14:15–18.

35. Given the focus on Christ's suffering in the garden, some Latter-day Saint authors have struggled to explain the necessity or meaning of the cross. Both Elders Talmage and McConkie surmised that "all the agonies and merciless pains of Gethsemane recurred" on Golgotha (see McConkie, "Purifying Power of Gethsemane," and Talmage, *Jesus the Christ*, 613). While certainly possible, such an explanation leads to yet another question—if Christ's agonizing vicarious and sacrificial suffering in the

garden was "infinite and eternal" (Alma 34:10), why would it need to be repeated?

36. See Matthew 16:21–24.

37. See Luke 22:42; John 18:11. In Luke the "cup" is related to his suffering in the garden, whereas in John it refers to the path he would take thereafter.

38. Matthew 20:16.

39. Matthew 20:25–26.

40. John 18:36; emphasis added.

41. See Yoder, *Politics of Jesus*, 107.

42. Matthew 22:21.

43. Doctrine and Covenants 104:14–15; 117:6.

44. Luke 23:38.

45. See Mark 15:6–13.

46. See Doctrine and Covenants 121:37–46.

47. Colossians 2:15 (New International Version).

48. See Alma 7:11–12.

49. 3 Nephi 27:14.

50. Isaiah 53:5.

51. Luke 23:34.

52. 2 Nephi 10:3. Jesus illustrated the downward spiral of violence in his parable of the wicked husbandmen (Matthew 21:33–39), who were given the run of the vineyard and used their power to abuse their fellow servants, whom they attacked with successively more violence until finally they killed the lord of the vineyard's own son and heir.

53. See Wink, *Powers That Be*, 42–48.

54. John D. Caputo, *What Would Jesus Deconstruct? The Good News of Postmodernism for the Church* (Grand Rapids, MI: Baker Academic, 2007), 82, 84.

55. Mark 8:31 (KJV) and 34–36 (NRSV).

56. John 10:1; Luke 9:22–23. See Dietrich Bonhoeffer, *The Cost of Discipleship* (1937; repr., New York: Touchstone, 1995), 86–87.

57. Mosiah 16:8; see also 1 Corinthians 15:54–57.

58. See 1 Corinthians 15:19.

59. Martin Luther King Jr., "Where Do We Go from Here?," in Washington, *I Have a Dream*, 179.

60. Martin Luther King Jr., *Why We Can't Wait* (1963; repr., New York: Signet Classics, 2000), 69.

61. See Revelation 6:1–8.

62. Doctrine and Covenants 121:41. As John Howard Yoder writes, "The triumph of the right, although it is assured, is sure because of the power of the resurrection and not because of any calculation of causes and effects, nor because of the inherently greater strength of the good guys. The relationship between the obedience of God's people and the triumph of God's cause is not a relationship of cause and effect but one of cross and resurrection." Yoder, *Politics of Jesus*, 232.

63. 1 Corinthians 1:23.

64. Alma 34:10.

65. Doctrine and Covenants 88:75; see 112:33.

66. 1 Nephi 11:32–33.

CHAPTER THREE

1. Jared Hickman, "*The Book of Mormon* as Amerindian Apocalypse," *American Literature* 86, no. 3 (September 2014): 436; note that here we are appropriating and reapplying Hickman's argument, which was about the Book of Mormon's apparent racism. For a similar approach, see Kimberly M. Berkey and Joseph M. Spencer, "'Great Cause to Mourn': The Complexity of *The Book of Mormon*'s Presentation of Gender and Race," in *Americanist Approaches to* The Book of Mormon, ed. Elizabeth Fenton and Jared Hickman (New York: Oxford University Press, 2019), 306.

2. See Mosiah 15:15–18.

3. See 2 Nephi 26:16.

4. We are not the first authors to grapple with how to read the Book of Mormon's many violent passages. For a variety of perspectives, see the essays in Patrick Q. Mason, J. David Pulsipher, and Richard L. Bushman, *War and Peace in Our Time: Mormon Perspectives* (Salt Lake City: Greg Kofford Books, 2012). For a contrary view, see Duane Boyce, *Even unto Bloodshed: An LDS Perspective on War* (Salt Lake City: Greg Kofford Books, 2015).

5. 1 Nephi 1:1.

6. 1 Nephi 1:19.

7. 1 Nephi 1:20.
8. See 1 Nephi 3:29–31. A similarly nonchalant description of an encounter with heavenly messengers is found in Genesis 18:1–2.
9. See 1 Nephi 3:31; 4:1–2.
10. 1 Nephi 4:1, 4.
11. 1 Nephi 4:9–10.
12. 1 Nephi 4:10.
13. See Genesis 18:16–33; 32:24–30; Exodus 32:7–14; Jacob 5:26–28, 49–51.
14. No doubt removing Laban's clothing would have been easier and cleaner had he not been decapitated and his vestments presumably soaked in blood.
15. See Mosiah 22:6–11; Alma 55:8–23.
16. 1 Nephi 4:13.
17. 1 Nephi 4:18. Other interpretations of this story include Fatimah Salleh with Margaret Olsen Hemming, *The Book of Mormon for the Least of These, Volume 1: 1 Nephi–Words of Mormon* (Salt Lake City: By Common Consent Press, 2020), 11–13; and Joseph Spencer, *1st Nephi: a brief theological introduction* (Provo, UT: Neal A. Maxwell Institute for Religious Scholarship, Brigham Young University, 2020), chap. 4.
18. Doctrine and Covenants 98:16, 32 (see vv. 23–32).
19. The classic formulation of the imitative (or "mimetic") quality of violence is René Girard, *Violence and the Sacred*, trans. Patrick Gregory (Baltimore, MD: Johns Hopkins University Press, 1977). For Girardian readings of the Nephi and Laban account, see Eugene England, *Making Peace: Personal Essays* (Salt Lake City: Signature Books, 1995), 131–54; Mack C. Stirling, "Violence in the Scriptures: Mormonism and the Cultural Theory of Rene Girard," *Dialogue: A Journal of Mormon Thought* 43, no. 1 (Spring 2010): 59–105; and Joseph M. Spencer, "Rene Girard and Mormon Scripture: A Response," *Dialogue: A Journal of Mormon Thought* 43, no. 3 (Fall 2010): 6–20.
20. See 1 Nephi 4:19–26. For "God of truth," see Deuteronomy 32:4; Psalm 31:5; Isaiah 65:16. For "Prince of Peace," see Isaiah 9:6, reproduced by Nephi in 2 Nephi 19:6.
21. See 1 Nephi 4:31–38; see also 2 Nephi 1:30–32. For another perspective, see Salleh and Hemming, *Book of Mormon for the Least of These*, 13–14.

22. 1 Nephi 5:9. See S. Kent Brown, "What Were Those Sacrifices Offered by Lehi?," in *From Jerusalem to Zarahemla: Literary and Historical Studies of the Book of Mormon* (Provo, UT: Religious Studies Center, Brigham Young University, 1998), 1–8; and Grant Hardy, *Understanding the Book of Mormon: A Reader's Guide* (New York: Oxford University Press, 2010), 16–23.

23. See 1 Nephi 5:21–22.

24. See 2 Nephi 4:17–27. Eugene England interprets this question as remorse for the killing of Laban, a position that Duane Boyce effectively critiques. See England, "'Thou Shalt Not Kill' : An Ethics of Non-Violence," in *Making Peace*; and Boyce, *Even unto Bloodshed*, 176–77.

25. For a moving account by a contemporary General Authority reminiscent of the mature Nephi's realization, see Robert C. Gay, "Taking upon Ourselves the Name of Jesus Christ," *Ensign*, November 2018.

26. See 1 Nephi 7:7–15.

27. See 1 Nephi 7:16–21.

28. See Doctrine and Covenants 121:41–43.

29. See 1 Nephi 11–14; quotation from 11:22.

30. 1 Nephi 8:37.

31. See 1 Nephi 15:9–21; quotation from v. 20.

32. 1 Nephi 16:1, 5.

33. 1 Nephi 2:22.

34. See 1 Nephi 17:17–48; quotation from v. 44.

35. See 1 Nephi 17:48–54; emphasis added.

36. See 1 Nephi 17:55; 18:1–22.

37. 1 Nephi 17:45.

38. 2 Nephi 4:17.

39. 2 Nephi 5:3, 6.

40. See 2 Nephi 5:14.

41. See 2 Nephi 5:17–19.

42. 2 Nephi 5:34; Jacob 1:10.

43. 2 Nephi 12:4.

44. 2 Nephi 26:2–9; quotation from v. 9.

45. 2 Nephi 26:33.

46. 2 Nephi 33:7–9.

47. 2 Nephi 33:12.

48. See 2 Nephi 25:23–26.
49. Regina M. Schwartz, *The Curse of Cain: The Violent Legacy of Monotheism* (Chicago: University of Chicago Press, 1997), 23.
50. Amin Maalouf, *In the Name of Identity: Violence and the Need to Belong*, trans. Barbara Bray (New York: Penguin Books, 2003), 27.
51. Mormon 8:8.
52. Jacob 3:3–5; 7:24. See Salleh and Hemming, *Book of Mormon for the Least of These*, 116.
53. See Omni 1:12–30.
54. On the complicated legacy of King Benjamin, see Patrick Q. Mason, "King Benjamin's Statebuilding Project and the Limits of Statist Religion," forthcoming.
55. See Alma 17–26.
56. See Omni 1:10–11.
57. See Words of Mormon 1:10–11. Rebecca A. Roesler has traced how some of the consequential doctrine recorded on the small plates seems to disappear from subsequent Nephite memory and theology; see her "Plain and Precious Things Lost: The Small Plates of Nephi," *Dialogue* (Summer 2019): 85–106.
58. See Words of Mormon 1:3–7.
59. 2 Nephi 4:17, 19.
60. See 2 Nephi 33:9–10.

CHAPTER FOUR

1. 3 Nephi 11:29.
2. Doctrine and Covenants 38:27.
3. Letter from Joseph Smith to Israel Daniel Rupp, 5 June 1844, The Joseph Smith Papers, https://www.josephsmithpapers.org/paper-summary/letter-to-israel-daniel-rupp-5-june-1844/1; spelling modernized.
4. 2 Nephi 2:11.
5. See Russell M. Nelson, "Lessons from Eve," *Ensign*, November 1987; Moses 2:31.
6. For an overview of Latter-day Saint temple rituals, see Patrick Q. Mason, *What Is Mormonism? A Student's Introduction* (New York: Routledge, 2017), 199–204. See also Jonathan A. Stapley, *The Power of Godliness:*

Mormon Liturgy and Cosmology (New York City: Oxford University Press, 2018).

7. Genesis 1:18; Moses 2:18.
8. Matthias Cowley, in Conference Report, April 1901, 16.
9. Genesis 2:24; Moses 3:24.
10. Genesis 1:31; Moses 2:31; Abraham 4:21.
11. See Moses 5:11.
12. See 2 Nephi 2:15–25. See also Boyd Jay Petersen, "'Redeemed from the Curse Placed upon Her': Dialogic Discourse on Eve in the *Woman's Exponent*," *Journal of Mormon History* 40, no. 1 (Winter 2014): 135–74.
13. Genesis 1:28; Moses 2:28. In game theory, this is called a "coordination problem."
14. See Moses 4:12; 5:4–5.
15. For an overview of the Restoration theology of the Fall, see Daniel K. Judd, "The Fortunate Fall of Adam and Eve," in *No Weapon Shall Prosper: New Light on Sensitive Issues*, ed. Robert L. Millet (Provo, UT: Religious Studies Center, Brigham Young University; Salt Lake City: Deseret Book, 2011), 297–328.
16. See 3 Nephi 11:28–30.
17. See, for example, Gordon B. Hinckley, "Excerpts from Recent Addresses of President Gordon B. Hinckley," *Ensign*, August 1996; Barack Obama, keynote address at 2004 Democratic National Convention, https://www.pbs.org/newshour/show/barack-obamas-keynote-address-at-the-2004-democratic-national-convention; Quentin L. Cook, "We Follow Jesus Christ," *Ensign*, May 2010; and Dallin H. Oaks, "Love Your Enemies," *Ensign*, November 2020.
18. See 4 Nephi 1:15–17; emphasis added.
19. Galatians 2:9–16 (New Revised Standard Version); see Acts 9–15 for background.
20. This section builds on insights in J. David Pulsipher, *When We Don't See Eye to Eye* (American Fork, UT: Covenant Communications, 2014).
21. Luke 22:42.
22. Rush, "Freewill," *Permanent Waves* (Mercury Records, 1980).
23. John Paul Lederach, *The Moral Imagination: The Art and Soul of Building Peace*, reprint ed. (New York: Oxford University Press, 2010), 42; emphasis in original. For an introduction to Lederach's theory of conflict

transformation, see Lederach, *The Little Book of Conflict Transformation* (Intercourse, PA: Good Books, 2003).

24. Martin Luther King Jr., *Why We Can't Wait* (1963; repr., New York: Signet Classics, 2000), 67.

25. See Terry C. Warner, "The Path to Peace Is a Peaceful Path," lecture delivered at "Blessed Are the Peacemakers: Peace Is Possible," 26th Annual Conference of the LDS International Society, April 6, 2015, Brigham Young University, Provo, Utah. For more on principles of self-deception and collusion, along with practical ways to escape their cycles, see Arbinger Institute, *The Anatomy of Peace: Resolving the Heart of Conflict*, 2nd. ed. (New York City: Berrett-Koehler, 2015).

26. See Terry C. Warner, *Bonds That Make Us Free: Healing Our Relationships, Coming to Ourselves* (Salt Lake City: Shadow Mountain, 2001).

27. Richard Lyman Bushman, "The Lamanite View of Book of Mormon History," in *Believing History: Latter-day Saint Essays*, ed. Reid L. Neilson and Jed Woodworth (New York: Columbia University Press, 2004), 79–92.

28. See 1 Nephi 16:38.

29. See 2 Nephi 1:24–29.

30. 2 Nephi 5:3.

31. Subsequent instances of sudden or secret departures with records, heirlooms, or property—especially those of the first Mosiah (Omni 1:12–13), Limhi (Mosiah 22:11–12), and the elder Alma (Mosiah 24:18–20)—may have also contributed to the Lamanite's (inaccurate but understandable) perception that the people of Nephi were inherently liars and robbers.

32. Alma 20:13.

33. Alma 43:8.

34. See Alma 54:16–24.

35. 1 Nephi 17:44.

36. Enos 1:20. See Fatimah Salleh with Margaret Olsen Hemming, *The Book of Mormon for the Least of These, Volume 1: 1 Nephi–Words of Mormon* (Salt Lake City: By Common Consent Press, 2020), 138.

37. Alma 26:25.

38. See Alma 50:7–15; 51:9, 22–27.

39. See Michael A. Sells, *The Bridge Betrayed: Religion and Genocide in Bosnia* (Berkeley: University of California Press, 1996), esp. chap. 2.

40. 2 Timothy 1:7.

41. For an excellent primer on creative conflict transformation rooted in love, see Chad Ford, *Dangerous Love: Transforming Fear and Conflict at Home, at Work, and in the World* (Oakland, CA: Berrett-Koehler, 2020).

42. Moroni 7:48.

43. Romans 12:14–21 (NRSV).

44. Mosiah 27:9–10 and 28:4.

45. Mosiah 27:11–16.

46. Alma 26:17.

47. Mosiah 28:1–2.

48. See Alma 21:11–13.

49. See Alma 17–19.

50. See Alma 20:9–23.

51. Alma 20:24–26.

52. Alma 22:3.

53. Alma 22:15–18.

54. The designation "Anti-Nephi-Lehi" might be read to signify "children of Lehi who are *not* the descendants of Nephi." If so, the people's new name was thus a rebuke of their ancestor Laman—whom they now perceived as an unworthy model—and a way of distinguishing themselves from unbelievers with whom they shared an ethnic history but no longer a religious or political identity. At the same time, it would also distinguish them from fellow Lehite believers, the Nephites, with whom they had common origins but no shared history except that of war.

55. Alma 23:18.

56. Alma 27:27.

57. Alma 26:32–34.

58. Alma 62:27–29.

59. See Duane Boyce, *Even unto Bloodshed: An LDS Perspective on War* (Salt Lake City: Greg Kofford Books, 2015), esp. chaps. 4–5. For an overview of how Latter-day Saints have interpreted the Anti-Nephi-Lehite narrative, see J. David Pulsipher, "Buried Swords: The Shifting Interpretive Ground of a Beloved Book of Mormon Narrative," *Journal of Book of Mormon Studies* 26 (2017): 1–47.

60. See Peter Ackerman and Jack Duvall, *A Force More Powerful: A Century of Nonviolent Conflict* (New York: St. Martin's, 2000).

61. Martin Luther King Jr., *A Testament of Hope: The Essential Writings and Speeches of Martin Luther King, Jr.*, ed. James M. Washington (San Francisco: HarperCollins, 1986), 594.

62. King Jr., *Testament of Hope*, 291.

63. "The King Philosophy," The Martin Luther King, Jr. Center for Nonviolent Social Change, https://thekingcenter.org/king-philosophy/.

64. See John Paul Lederach, *Building Peace: Sustainable Reconciliation in Divided Societies* (Washington, DC: United States Institute of Peace, 1997); see also Ford, *Dangerous Love*, chaps. 5–6.

CHAPTER FIVE

1. Matthew 5:44; 3 Nephi 12:44.

2. Mosiah 3:19.

3. Preston Sprinkle, *Fight: A Christian Case for Nonviolence* (Colorado Springs, CO: David C. Cook, 2013), 202.

4. Romans 12:14, 17, 19–21.

5. Doctrine and Covenants 121:43.

6. 1 Corinthians 12:31.

7. Janne M. Sjodahl, *An Introduction to the Study of the Book of Mormon* (Salt Lake City: Deseret Book, 1927), 270.

8. Alma 26:33.

9. See Alma 24:12–16.

10. Alma 24:10; Helaman 15:9. See, for example, Joseph Fielding McConkie and Robert L. Millet, *Doctrinal Commentary on the Book of Mormon* (Salt Lake City: Bookcraft, 1991), 170.

11. Alma 26:32.

12. See Alma 24:6–8, 12, 16 for the inclusive way the Anti-Nephi-Lehies employ this term.

13. American journalist Webb Miller witnessed firsthand this attempt to resist an oppressive British monopoly on salt, and he reported how it played out: "Not one of the marchers even raised an arm to fend off the blows. They went down like ten-pins. From where I stood I heard the sickening whacks of the clubs on unprotected skulls. . . . The survivors without breaking ranks silently and doggedly marched on until struck down. . . . Group after group walked forward, sat down, and submitted to being beaten into insensibility without raising an arm to fend off the

blows." *I Found No Peace* (New York City: Simon and Schuster, 1936), 446.

14. See Alma 24:18–21.

15. See Mark 8:34.

16. See Alma 24:21–27.

17. As a narrator, Mormon is sometimes quite precise in his death tallies, noting, for example, that in one battle the Nephites lost "six thousand five hundred sixty and two souls" (Alma 2:19), and in another they killed "three thousand and forty-three" Lamanites (Mosiah 9:18). Most of the time he utilizes round numbers, such as "thousands" or "tens of thousands."

18. Deseret Sunday School Union, *The Quorum Bulletin and Gospel Doctrine Sunday School Quarterly* 6, no. 1 (January–March 1939), 12–13.

19. J. Karl Wood, *Outline Study of the Book of Mormon* (Salt Lake City: LDS Department of Education, 1950), 143.

20. Pierre Teilhard de Chardin, SJ, *Les directions de l'avenir* (Paris: Éditions du Seuil, 1973), 92.

21. Romans 1:31; 2 Timothy 3:3. Some readers have interpreted the King James phrase "natural affection" to mean heterosexual desire. Modern translations, however, render the KJV phrase "without natural affection" as "heartless" (New Revised Standard Version) or "inhuman" (New International Version). See also Thomas A. Wayment, *The New Testament: A Translation for Latter-day Saints—A Study Bible* (Provo, UT: Religious Studies Center, Brigham Young University; Salt Lake City: Deseret Book, 2019), Romans 1:31 and note for Romans 1:26–27.

22. See 1 Corinthians 11:11; Doctrine and Covenants 128:18.

23. See Jonathan Haidt, *The Righteous Mind: Why Good People Are Divided by Politics and Religion* (New York: Pantheon Books, 2012).

24. See Lt. Col. Dave Grossman, *On Killing: The Psychological Cost of Learning to Kill in War and Society* (Boston: Little, Brown, 1995), 160–67.

25. Genesis 6:11; Moses 7:33.

26. See Matthew 5:21–22.

27. Diego Muro-Ruiz, "The Logic of Violence," *Politics* 22, no. 2 (May 2002): 109–17.

28. Mosiah 10:12; Alma 26:24–25.

29. Dallin H. Oaks, "Bible Stories and Personal Protection," *Ensign*, November 1992.

30. Julio Diaz, "As he's walking away, I'm like 'Hey, you forgot something . . . ,'" StoryCorps interview, originally aired March 28, 2008, on NPR's Morning Edition, https://storycorps.org/listen/julio-diaz/.

31. Angie O'Gorman, "Defense through Disarmament: Nonviolence and Personal Assault," in *The Universe Bends Toward Justice: A Reader on Christian Nonviolence in the U.S.*, ed. Angie O'Gorman (Philadelphia: New Society, 1990), 242–43.

32. Antoinette Tuff and Alex Tresniowski, *Prepared for a Purpose: The Inspiring True Story of How One Woman Saved an Atlanta School under Siege* (Bloomington, MN: Bethany House Publishers, 2014).

33. Sjodahl, *Introduction*, 270. For more on the dynamics, theories, and science of love, see Ford, *Dangerous Love*, and Lewis, Amini, and Lannon, *General Theory of Love*.

34. See Alma 17–26.

35. See Helaman 4–6, quotations from 5:46, 50–51; 6:7.

36. Alma 31:5.

37. For more examples than we can list here, see Peter Ackerman and Christopher Kruegler, *Strategic Nonviolent Conflict: The Dynamics of People Power in the Twentieth Century* (Westport, CT: Praeger, 1994); and Peter Ackerman and Jack DuVall, *A Force More Powerful: A Century of Nonviolent Conflict* (New York: Palgrave, 2000).

38. See John P. Burgess, "Church-State Relations in East Germany: The Church as a 'Religious' and 'Political' Force," *Journal of Church and State* 32, no. 1 (Winter 1990): 17–34; and Wolfgram Nagel, "From Hope, a Movement: The Role of Churches in the Fall of the GDR," November 6, 2014, https://www.dw.com/en/from-hope-a-movement-the-role-of-churches-in-the-fall-of-the-gdr/a-18035129.

39. David Cortright, *Peace: A History of Movements and Ideas* (New York: Cambridge University Press, 2008), 310–11.

40. See S. L. A. Marshall, *Men Against Fire: The Problem of Battle Command* (New York: William Morrow, 1947), 77; see also Grossman, *On Killing*.

41. Bernard Lafayette, in *A Force More Powerful*, directed by Steve York (Washington, DC: York Zimmerman, 2000), DVD.

42. John Lewis, *Walking with the Wind: A Memoir of the Movement* (New York: Simon and Schuster, 1998), 93; emphasis in original.
43. Lewis, *Walking with the Wind*, 85–86.
44. This is already done on a small scale by groups such as Christian Peacemaker Teams. See https://www.cpt.org/.
45. See Amanda Trejos, "Why Getting Rid of Costa Rica's Army 70 Years Ago Has Been Such a Success," *USA Today*, January 5, 2018.
46. Doctrine and Covenants 121:41.
47. Erica Chenoweth and Maria J. Stephan, *Why Civil Resistance Works: The Strategic Logic of Nonviolent Conflict* (New York: Columbia University Press, 2011).
48. See John Paul Lederach, *Building Peace: Sustainable Reconciliation in Divided Societies* (Washington, DC: United States Institute of Peace, 1997); and Daniel Philpott and Gerard F. Powers, eds., *Strategies of Peace: Transforming Conflict in a Violent World* (New York: Oxford University Press, 2010).
49. Victor Frankl, *Man's Search for Meaning* (New York: Washington Square Press, 1985), 86.
50. Mohandas K. Gandhi, *Young India*, June 30, 1920, 3.
51. 1 Peter 3:14, selected phrasing from both the King James Version and the New Revised Standard Version.
52. See John 15:13.
53. Martin Luther King Jr., "The Power of Nonviolence," in *I Have a Dream: Writings and Speeches That Changed the World*, ed. James M. Washington (San Francisco: HarperSanFrancisco, 1992), 30.
54. Daniel 3:17–18.
55. Ephesians 4:19; 1 Nephi 17:45; Moroni 9:20.
56. See 1 Corinthians 15:54–55; Mosiah 16:8.
57. See, for example, Thomas Lewis, Fari Amini, and Richard Lannon, *A General Theory of Love* (New York: Vintage Books, 2001).
58. Abraham Lincoln, First Inaugural Address, https://avalon.law.yale.edu/19th_century/lincoln1.asp.

CHAPTER SIX

1. Jeffrey R. Holland, "Of Souls, Symbols, and Sacraments," Brigham Young University devotional, January 12, 1988, http://www.familylifeeducation .org/gilliland/procgroup/Souls.htm. Elder Holland delivered a revised version of this address in the October 1998 general conference under the title "Personal Purity."

2. Holland, "Of Souls, Symbols, and Sacraments"; Alma 39:5. Latter-day Saints would fill in the blank by saying, "God has commanded that the sacred powers of procreation are to be employed only between a man and woman who are legally and lawfully wedded."

3. See 3 Nephi 12:28; Matthew 5:28.

4. See Valerie M. Hudson et al., *Sex and World Peace* (New York: Columbia University Press, 2012).

5. See 3 Nephi 12:22 and Matthew 5:22; Isaiah 33:14.

6. Deuteronomy 30:19.

7. See John 3:16–17.

8. See Doctrine and Covenants 84:23–26.

9. See Doctrine and Covenants 119. On consecration, see Neal A. Maxwell, "'Swallowed Up in the Will of the Father,'" *Ensign*, November 1995.

10. See Mosiah 13:29–32.

11. William Shakespeare, *Julius Caesar*, act 3, scene 1.

12. See Doctrine and Covenants 98:1, 11–16.

13. Doctrine and Covenants 98:23–24.

14. See Leviticus 24:19–21.

15. Doctrine and Covenants 98:25–26.

16. See Doctrine and Covenants 98:28–31.

17. Doctrine and Covenants 134:11.

18. See Kenneth Appold, "Justification," in *The Cambridge Dictionary of Christian Theology*, ed. Ian A. McFarland et al. (New York: Cambridge University Press, 2011), 257–59.

19. Bible Dictionary (in the Latter-day Saint edition of the King James Version of the Bible), s.v. "Saint."

20. See Doctrine and Covenants 20:30–31.

21. Doctrine and Covenants 98:30.

22. Doctrine and Covenants 58:27.

23. See Doctrine and Covenants 98:33–36.
24. Doctrine and Covenants 98:37.
25. Matthew 26:52.
26. See Doctrine and Covenants 98:39–47.
27. Cheap grace is "the grace which amounts to the justification of sin without the justification of the repentant sinner who departs from sin and from whom sin departs." Dietrich Bonhoeffer, *The Cost of Discipleship* (New York: Touchstone, 1937; repr., 1995), 44.
28. See Daniel K. Judd, "'Resist Not Evil': The Supreme Test of Christian Discipleship," in *The Sermon on the Mount in Latter-day Scripture*, ed. Gaye Strathearn, Thomas A. Wayment, and Daniel L. Belnap (Provo, UT: Religious Studies Center, Brigham Young University; Salt Lake City: Deseret Book, 2010), 1–23.
29. Mark 9:42.
30. See Lisa Sowle Cahill, *Blessed Are the Peacemakers: Pacifism, Just War, and Peacebuilding* (Minneapolis: Fortress, 2019); and Michael Walzer, *Just and Unjust Wars: A Moral Argument with Historical Illustrations*, 4th ed. (New York: Basic Books, 1977; repr. 2006).
31. United States National Conference of Catholic Bishops, "The Challenge of Peace: God's Promise and Our Response: A Pastoral Letter on War and Peace by the National Conference of Catholic Bishops," May 3, 1983, https://www.usccb.org/resources/statement-challenge-peace-gods-promise-and-our-response-may-3-1983, 18–22.
32. Book of Mormon passages that uphold just war principles include Alma 55:6–24 and 3 Nephi 3:20–21. To see how Latter-day Saint thinkers have reflected on the just war tradition, see John Mark Mattox, "YES—The Book of Mormon as a Touchstone for Evaluating the Theory of Just War," and Mark E. Henshaw, "NO—Murder to Get Gain: LDS Thoughts on U.S. Elements of National Power," in *Wielding the Sword While Proclaiming Peace: Views from the LDS Community on Reconciling the Demands of National Security with the Imperatives of Revealed Truth*, ed. Valerie M. Hudson and Kerry M. Kartchner (Provo, UT: David M. Kennedy Center for International Studies, Brigham Young University, 2004), 57–77; Mark Henshaw et al., "War and the Gospel: Perspectives from Latter-day Saint National Security Practitioners," in *War and Peace in Our Time: Mormon Perspectives*, ed. Patrick Q. Mason, J. David Pulsipher,

and Richard L. Bushman (Salt Lake City: Greg Kofford Books, 2012), 235–66; Mark Henshaw, "My Brother's Keeper, and *Jus in Bello* Ideals in War," in *A Time of War, a Time of Peace: Latter-day Saint Ethics of War and Diplomacy*, ed. Valerie M. Hudson, Eric Talbot Jensen, and Kerry M. Kartchner (Provo, UT: David M. Kennedy Center for International Studies, Brigham Young University, 2015), 149–65; and Duane Boyce, *Even unto Bloodshed: An LDS Perspective on War* (Salt Lake City: Greg Kofford Books, 2015), esp. 271–73.

33. "Message of the First Presidency," *Semi-Annual Conference Report*, October 1942 (Salt Lake City: The Church of Jesus Christ of Latter-day Saints), 15.

34. "Message of the First Presidency," *Annual Conference Report*, April 1942 (Salt Lake City: The Church of Jesus Christ of Latter-day Saints), 94, 95.

35. Moroni 10:30.

36. "Message of the First Presidency," April 1942, 90.

37. Two divine commands recorded in Alma 43:46–47 may initially seem to be exceptions. But, as we discuss in the next chapter, they ultimately support this fundamental principle.

38. See Doctrine and Covenants 98:28–31.

39. Brown v. United States 256 U.S. 335, 343 (May 16, 1921).

40. See Doctrine and Covenants 98:33–36.

41. "Message of the First Presidency," April 1942, 94, 95; see Doctrine and Covenants 98:5–6.

42. For historical examples of conscientious objection and other forms of nonparticipation by those within the Restoration tradition, see Patrick Q. Mason, "'When I Think of War I Am Sick at Heart': Latter Day Saint Nonparticipation in World War I," *Journal of Mormon History* 45, no. 2 (April 2019): 1–21.

43. Charles D. Tate Jr., "Conscientious Objection," in *Encyclopedia of Mormonism* (New York: MacMillan, 1992), 311. See also lesson 39 in *Doctrine and Covenants Instructor's Guide: Religion 324–325* (Salt Lake City: The Church of Jesus Christ of Latter-day Saints, 1981).

44. Tate Jr., "Conscientious Objection," 312.

45. See Doctrine and Covenants 130:20–21. This brief teaching by the prophet Joseph Smith does not fully account for unmerited divine grace, but it does offer a basic Latter-day Saint framework for moral law.

46. See Alma 43:53–54; 44:19–20; 55:6–24; 58:12–29; 3 Nephi 3:20–21.
47. Ezekiel 33:11.
48. Alma 48:23.
49. See Dallin H. Oaks, "Love Your Enemies," *Ensign*, November 2020.
50. *True to the Faith: A Gospel Reference* (Salt Lake City: The Church of Jesus Christ of Latter-day Saints, 2004), s.v. "War"; emphasis added.
51. Matthew 5:44.
52. Doctrine and Covenants 121:43.
53. At their best, the Nephites provided useful examples of how this principle of increased love might be applied in a time or aftermath of war. See Alma 44:1–20; 50:36; 62:27–29; 3 Nephi 6:3–4.
54. Alma 48:15–16.
55. See 1 Nephi 2:1–2; 2 Nephi 5:2–7; Omni 1:12; Mosiah 23:1; 24:16–17; Alma 27:11–12.
56. See Alma 16:5–6; 43:23–24.
57. This is an especially strong theme in the books of Mormon and Ether.
58. Interestingly, although Mormon sometimes attributes Nephite victories to the "strength of the Lord" (see, e.g., Words of Mormon 1:14), he more often than not describes battles without comment or allows other narrators such as Zeniff (Mosiah 9:17), Moroni (Alma 44:4–5), Helaman (Alma 56:56), and Gidgiddonni (3 Nephi 3:21) to make those claims.
59. See Acts 10; Official Declaration 2. See also Romans 8:26.
60. See Ether 2:23-25; Doctrine and Covenants 9:8.
61. Isaiah 28:10.
62. Matthew 5:45.

CHAPTER SEVEN

1. 1 John 4:8.
2. 2 Nephi 26:33.
3. Galatians 3:28.
4. See Ephesians 4:13–19.
5. Luke 4:18 (New Revised Standard Version).
6. Scriptural accounts of God's violence are frequently an aspect of atheists' critiques of religion. For two prominent examples, see Sam Harris, *The End of Faith: Religion, Terror, and the Future of Reason* (New York:

Norton, 2005); and Christopher Hitchens, *God Is Not Great: How Religion Poisons Everything* (New York: Twelve, 2007).

7. For just a few examples, see Philip Jenkins, *Laying Down the Sword: Why We Can't Ignore the Bible's Violent Verses* (New York: HarperOne, 2011); Eric A. Seibert, *The Violence of Scripture: Overcoming the Old Testament's Troubling Legacy* (Minneapolis: Fortress, 2012); and John Dominic Crossan, *How to Read the Bible and Still Be a Christian: Is God Violent? An Exploration from Genesis to Revelation* (New York: HarperOne, 2016).

8. See 3 Nephi 8:5–23.

9. 1 Nephi 19:12.

10. 3 Nephi 9:3–12.

11. That is, Latin *con* means "with" and *descendere* means "come down." See 1 Nephi 11:26.

12. See Isaiah 7:14; 2 Nephi 17:14.

13. 3 Nephi 27:27.

14. Matthew 5:48; compare 3 Nephi 12:48.

15. Russell M. Nelson, "Perfection Pending," *Ensign*, November 1995.

16. Mormon 8:20; see Mormon 3:15; Romans 12:19. There is considerable debate on exactly who is speaking in the scriptures when a given passage refers to "God" or "the Lord." The dominant view among Latter-day Saints is that it is usually Christ, in either his premortal role as Jehovah or his postmortal role as the glorified Savior and Redeemer. Even if it is Christ, rather than the Father, who speaks these words, the distinction remains between the mortal Jesus, living on earth as a human, and the glorified members of the eternal Godhead.

17. Isaiah 55:8.

18. Mosiah 4:9.

19. John 13:34 (NRSV).

20. Doctrine and Covenants 64:10.

21. 1 Nephi 11:17.

22. Doctrine and Covenants (1835 edition), 36.

23. See Genesis 7:11–24; 19:24–25; 3 Nephi 8:5–19.

24. See 2 Samuel 6:6–7; Acts 5:1–11; Jacob 7:13–21.

25. 2 Nephi 2:11.

26. Adam S. Miller, *Grace Is Not God's Backup Plan: An Urgent Paraphrase of Paul's Letter to the Romans* (CreateSpace, 2015), 5.

27. See Moses 7:28–40.
28. See Doctrine and Covenants 138 as a revelatory expansion on 1 Peter 3:18–20 and 4:6.
29. Doctrine and Covenants 121:43–44.
30. 3 Nephi 9:13–14.
31. See Revelation 21:4; 1 Corinthians 15:55–57; Mosiah 16:7–8.
32. Michael Walzer argues, for instance, that the Hebrew Bible provides no "theory of war and peace," offering instead only narratives of wars that were commanded by God (mostly associated with the conquest of the land) and those that were permitted (as "a concession to Israel's kings"). See Michael Walzer, "War and Peace in the Jewish Tradition," in *The Ethics of War and Peace: Religious and Secular Perspectives*, ed. Terry Nardin (Princeton, NJ: Princeton University Press, 1998), 95–114.
33. The story of Jesus cleansing the temple is told in all four Gospels, though its chronological placement differs between the Synoptics and John. Matthew, Mark, and Luke all describe Jesus overturning the tables of the money changers. In John he fashions a whip, but modern translations agree that he used the whip not against the money changers themselves but rather to drive their animals from the area—an important distinction that is obscured in the King James Version. See Matthew 21:12–17; Mark 11:15–19; Luke 19:45–48; John 2:13–16.
34. See Alma 48:11–18; and Grant Hardy, *Understanding the Book of Mormon: A Reader's Guide* (New York: Oxford University Press, 2010), 109, 112, 148.
35. See Exodus 20:13 (also Genesis 4:10–11; 9:5–6); 3 Nephi 12:21–22 (Matthew 5:21–22); 3 Nephi 12:44–45 (Matthew 5:44–45).
36. Alma 43:46–47.
37. This verse provides the title for Duane Boyce, *Even unto Bloodshed: An LDS Perspective on War* (Salt Lake City: Greg Kofford Books, 2015).
38. 1 Samuel 15:3.
39. Deuteronomy 7:2; see Regina M. Schwartz, *The Curse of Cain: The Violent Legacy of Monotheism* (Chicago: University of Chicago Press, 1997).
40. While retaining a high view of scripture, Restoration theology does not endorse the notion of scriptural inerrancy as advocated by fundamentalist and many evangelical Protestants. See Articles of Faith 1:8; 1 Nephi 13:25–29; Mormon 9:31–33.

41. Micah 6:8.
42. See Matthew 5:38–39.
43. Doctrine and Covenants 98:30–32.
44. See Michael D. Coogan et al., eds., *The New Oxford Annotated Bible*, 4th ed. (New York: Oxford University Press, 2010), 4–6, 313–16.
45. See Marc Haber et al., "Continuity and Admixture in the Last Five Millennia of Levantine History from Ancient Canaanite and Present-Day Lebanese Genome Sequences," *The American Journal of Human Genetics* 101, no. 2 (July 2017): 274–82; and Karen Armstrong, *The Great Transformation: The Beginning of Our Religious Traditions* (New York: Anchor, 2007), 43–57.
46. For example, see 1 Samuel 15:8 and 2 Samuel 1:1 for the persistence of the Amalekites even after their supposed annihilation.
47. Preston Sprinkle, *Fight: A Christian Case for Nonviolence* (Colorado Springs, CO: David C. Cook, 2013), 73–92.
48. Unfortunately, this is not merely a theoretical concern. For instance, English colonists invoked the Bible's genocide texts to help justify mass violence against Native Americans, and "the imagery of Amalek was imported into writing about Mormons, Jews, Jehovah's Witnesses, Muslims, Catholics, and an assortment of other religious groups." See John Corrigan, "New Israel, New Amalek: Biblical Exhortations to Religious Violence," in *From Jeremiad to Jihad: Religion, Violence, and America*, ed. John D. Carlson and Jonathan H. Ebel (Berkeley: University of California Press, 2012), 111–27, quotation from p. 112.
49. This is part of what is meant by one scholar when he refers to "the ambivalence of the sacred." See R. Scott Appleby, *The Ambivalence of the Sacred: Religion, Violence, and Reconciliation* (Lanham, MD: Rowman and Littlefield, 2000).
50. See 1 Corinthians 14:34; 1 Timothy 2:11–12.

CHAPTER EIGHT

1. Matthew 6:24 (New Revised Standard Version).
2. Articles of Faith 1:12.
3. Doctrine and Covenants 121:41.
4. Max Weber, *Politics as a Vocation*, trans. H. H. Gerth and C. Wright Mills (Philadelphia: Fortress, 1965), 1–2.

5. See David Chidester, *Christianity: A Global History* (New York: Harper-One, 2000), 75–76, 91–95; and Lisa Sowle Cahill, *Blessed Are the Peacemakers: Pacifism, Just War, and Peacebuilding* (Minneapolis: Fortress, 2019), chaps. 3–4.

6. See Craig Hovey and Elizabeth Phillips, eds., *The Cambridge Companion to Christian Political Theology* (New York: Cambridge University Press, 2015).

7. For the Church's position on various current issues, see https://news room.churchofjesuschrist.org/.

8. "Discourse, 23 July 1843, as Reported by Willard Richards," p. [13], *The Joseph Smith Papers*, https://www.josephsmithpapers.org/paper -summary/discourse-23-july-1843-as-reported-by-willard-richards/3; spelling standardized. These notes by Willard Richards were the source for the more familiar expanded quotation in the *History of the Church*, which reads: "Friendship is one of the grand fundamental principles of Mormonism; [it is designed] to revolutionize and civilize the world, and cause wars and contentions to cease and men to become friends and brothers. Even the wolf and the lamb shall dwell together" (5:517).

9. Special thanks to Jeannie Johnson, who was instrumental in shaping the thinking in this paragraph, and the chapter more broadly.

10. See John 15:13.

11. Paul Tillich, *Dynamics of Faith* (New York: Harper and Brothers, 1957), 2. For "mortal god," see Thomas Hobbes, *Leviathan*, ed. Marshall Missner (New York: Pearson, 2008), 116.

12. William T. Cavanaugh, *The Myth of Religious Violence: Secular Ideology and the Roots of Modern Conflict* (New York: Oxford University Press, 2009), 55–56. See also Carolyn Marvin and David W. Ingle, *Blood Sacrifice and the Nation: Totem Rituals and the American Flag* (New York: Cambridge University Press, 1999), 9.

13. See Matthew 7:21; James 2:14–16.

14. See Alma 46:12–16.

15. See Doctrine and Covenants 98:6; 58:22.

16. See Richard Lyman Bushman, *Joseph Smith: Rough Stone Rolling* (New York: Alfred A. Knopf, 2005), 168. See also Grant Underwood, *The Millenarian World of Early Mormonism* (Urbana: University of Illinois Press, 1993); and Christopher James Blythe, *Terrible Revolution:*

Latter-day Saints and the American Apocalypse (New York: Oxford University Press, 2020), chap. 1.

17. Doctrine and Covenants 38:21–22.
18. Doctrine and Covenants 58:22; Romans 13:1 (NRSV). For illuminating commentary on Romans 13:1–7, see John Howard Yoder, *The Politics of Jesus*, 2nd ed. (Grand Rapids, MI: William B. Eerdmans, 1994), chap. 10.
19. See Doctrine and Covenants 58:19–23.
20. Doctrine and Covenants 63:26.
21. See Matthew 22:21.
22. Doctrine and Covenants 117:6. See 104:14.
23. Doctrine and Covenants 98:4–7.
24. See Doctrine and Covenants 101:77–80; emphasis added.
25. Mark Ashurst-McGee, "Zion Rising: Joseph Smith's Early Social and Political Thought" (PhD diss., Arizona State University, 2008), 374.
26. Joseph Smith, "Letter to Church Leaders in Jackson County, Missouri, 18 August 1833," p. 2, The Joseph Smith Papers, https://www.josephsmith papers.org/paper-summary/letter-to-church-leaders-in-jackson-county -missouri-18-august-1833/2.
27. Doctrine and Covenants 63:31. See Patrick Q. Mason, *Mormonism and Violence: The Battles of Zion* (New York: Cambridge University Press, 2019), 25–35; and Mason, "Zionic Nonviolence as Christian Worship and Praxis," in *How and What You Worship: Christology and Praxis in the Revelations of Joseph Smith*, ed. Rachel Cope, Carter Charles, and Jordan T. Watkins (Provo, UT: Religious Studies Center, Brigham Young University; Salt Lake City: Deseret Book, 2020), 249–70.
28. Doctrine and Covenants 103:15, 28, 36. For a fuller interpretation of Zion's Camp along these lines, see Mason, "Zionic Nonviolence," 262–67.
29. See Isaiah 7–8, esp. 8:11–13.
30. See Doctrine and Covenants 134:5–7, 12.
31. See D. Michael Quinn, "The Mormon Church and the Spanish-American War: An End to Selective Pacifism," *Pacific Historical Review* 43, no. 3 (August 1974): 342–66; and Ronald W. Walker, "Sheaves, Bucklers, and the State: Mormon Leaders Respond to the Dilemmas of War," in *The New Mormon History: Revisionist Essays on the Past*, ed. D. Michael Quinn (Salt Lake City: Signature Books, 1992), 267–301.

32. See J. David Pulsipher, "'We Do Not Love War, But . . .': Mormons, the Great War, and the Crucible of Nationalism," in *American Churches and the First World War*, ed. Gordon L. Heath (Eugene, OR: Pickwick, 2016), 129–48.
33. Doctrine and Covenants 38:27.
34. See D. Michael Quinn, "Pacifist Counselor in the First Presidency: J. Reuben Clark Jr., 1933–1961," in *War and Peace in Our Time: Mormon Perspectives*, ed. Patrick Q. Mason, J. David Pulsipher, and Richard L. Bushman (Salt Lake City: Greg Kofford Books, 2012), 141–60.
35. Privately, J. Reuben Clark remained adamantly opposed to any American involvement in the war. Only days after his own son-in-law had been killed on the battleship *West Virginia*, Clark wrote an early draft of the proposed First Presidency message condemning those young Americans who wanted to "go out with commissions to kill their fellow men. . . . It is not the Master's way. It is the jungle law of the beasts." In light of the nation's war fever, President Heber J. Grant opted for a more moderate and patriotic statement. Quoted in Quinn, "Pacifist Counselor in the First Presidency," 151.
36. "Message of the First Presidency," *One Hundred Twelfth Annual Conference of the Church of Jesus Christ of Latter-day Saints* [April 1942] (Salt Lake City: The Church of Jesus Christ of Latter-day Saints, 1942), 94.
37. "Message of the First Presidency," 93, 94.
38. "Message of the First Presidency," 94.
39. Doctrine and Covenants 98:6, 36.
40. "Message of the First Presidency," 94. See Doctrine and Covenants 98:5–7.
41. "Message of the First Presidency," 95.
42. Isaiah 5:20.
43. "Message of the First Presidency," 95–96; Matthew 26:52.
44. James R. Clark, *Messages of the First Presidency* (Salt Lake City: Bookcraft, 1975), 6:170–85.
45. "Letter of the First Presidency," December 14, 1945; reprinted in *Improvement Era*, February 1946, 76–77.
46. See Gordon B. Hinckley, "War and Peace," *Ensign*, May 2003.
47. Isaiah 2:4 (NRSV).

48. See Blair R. Holmes and Alan F. Keele, eds., *When Truth Was Treason: German Youth Against Hitler, The Story of the Helmuth Hübener Group* (Urbana: University of Illinois Press, 1995).
49. See Doctrine and Covenants 98:3, 16.
50. Doctrine and Covenants 93:12.
51. Spencer W. Kimball, "The False Gods We Worship," *Ensign*, June 1976, 4–6.
52. Matthew 13:57.
53. Walter Wink, *The Powers That Be: Theology for a New Millennium* (New York: Galilee, 1998), 33–35.
54. Matthew 6:10.

CHAPTER NINE

1. "History, 1838–1856, volume B-1 [1 September 1834–2 November 1838] [addenda]," pp. 8–9 [addenda], The Joseph Smith Papers, https://www.josephsmithpapers.org/paper-summary/history-1838-1856-volume-b-1-1-september-1834-2-november-1838/312.
2. The contrast between Zion and Babylon is a recurrent theme in Hugh Nibley, *Approaching Zion*, ed. Don E. Norton (Salt Lake City: Deseret Book; Provo, UT: Foundation for Ancient Research and Mormon Studies, 1989).
3. Johan Galtung, "Cultural Violence," *Journal of Peace Research* 27, no. 3 (August 1990): 302.
4. Lisa Sowle Cahill, "A Theology for Peacebuilding," in *Peacebuilding: Catholic Theology, Ethics, and Praxis*, ed. Robert J. Schreiter, R. Scott Appleby, and Gerard F. Powers (Maryknoll, NY: Orbis, 2010), 306.
5. Jeffrey R. Holland, "A Handful of Meal and a Little Oil," *Ensign*, May 1996, 31.
6. See Doctrine and Covenants 45:68–69.
7. See Doctrine and Covenants 97:21.
8. "History, 1838–1856, volume F-1 [1 May 1844–8 August 1844]," p. 18, The Joseph Smith Papers, https://www.josephsmithpapers.org/paper-summary/history-1838-1856-volume-f-1-1-may-1844-8-august-1844/24.
9. Doctrine and Covenants 121:41.
10. See Moses 4:22–24.

11. Nathan O. Hatch, *The Democratization of American Christianity* (New Haven, CT: Yale University Press, 1989), 117.
12. Doctrine and Covenants 104:18.
13. Doctrine and Covenants 70:14; 78:6.
14. Doctrine and Covenants 49:20.
15. See, e.g., Ezekiel 18:20.
16. Isaiah 1:4.
17. See Doctrine and Covenants 1:30; 84:54–57.
18. See Doctrine and Covenants 128:18; 131:1–4.
19. John Paul II, *Sollicitudo Rei Socialis* [On social concern], December 30, 1987, papal encyclical on the twentieth anniversary of *Populorum Progressio*, http://w2.vatican.va/content/john-paul-ii/en/encyclicals/documents/hf_jp-ii_enc_30121987_sollicitudo-rei-socialis.html, quotations from pp. 36–37. For background and analysis, see Gregory Baum and Robert Ellsberg, eds., *The Logic of Solidarity: Commentaries on Pope John Paul II's Encyclical "On Social Concern"* (Maryknoll, NY: Orbis, 1989); see esp. Gregory Baum, "Structures of Sin," 110–26.
20. Articles of Faith 1:2.
21. George F. Richards, in Conference Report, October 1937, 27, https://content.ldschurch.org/chpress/bc/media/GFR/George-F-Richards-1937-10-01.pdf. Richards connected this sentiment with temple ceremonies and made a novel suggestion that this proxy work could be done by "employing men and women whose financial conditions are such that otherwise they are obligated to labor for a mere pittance." He thus connected salvation of the dead with correcting the collective sin of inequality in this world. Latter-day Saint temple ceremonies reinforce this notion of collective sin, as the ordinances are designed in part to purify covenanting members from the blood and sins of their generation. The necessity of the ordinance suggests that a condemnation is in place that requires expiation of at least a ritual sort.
22. Deidre Nicole Green, *Jacob: a brief theological introduction* (Provo, UT: Neal A. Maxwell Institute for Religious Scholarship, Brigham Young University, 2020), 30.
23. See Dallin H. Oaks, "World Peace," *Ensign*, May 1990. See also Sydney Walker, "President Oaks Gives a Universal 'Formula' for Peace," *Church News*, December 8, 2019.

24. Moses 7:18.
25. See Alma 13:14–19; Genesis 14:18–20; Hebrews 7:1–4.
26. See Joseph Smith Translation, Genesis 14:26–39.
27. Mark R. Ashurst-McGee, "Zion Rising: Joseph Smith's Early Social and Political Thought" (PhD diss., Arizona State University, 2008), 199.
28. See Mosiah 18:17–29.
29. See Mosiah 23–24.
30. Acts 2:44–45; 4:32–35 (New Revised Standard Version).
31. See Acts 5:41; Romans 8:17; 2 Timothy 2:12; 3:12; 1 Peter 3:14–18; 4:13.
32. Mosiah 18:9.
33. 3 Nephi 6:15; 26:19.
34. 4 Nephi 1:2–3.
35. John 14:6.
36. See 3 Nephi 12.
37. Helaman 13:22. See 3 Nephi 6:10–15.
38. 4 Nephi 1:3. See Daniel Becerra, *3rd, 4th Nephi: a brief theological introduction* (Provo, UT: Neal A. Maxwell Institute for Religious Scholarship, Brigham Young University, 2020), chap. 4.
39. 4 Nephi 1:15–17.
40. Jacob 4:13.
41. John Paul II, *Sollicitudo Rei Socialis*, 38–39.
42. Moses 7:16.
43. See 1 Nephi 11:16, 26–33.
44. Cahill, "Theology for Peacebuilding," 314–15. See Alma 7:11–12.
45. 4 Nephi 1:17.
46. 4 Nephi 1:3, 16.
47. See 4 Nephi 1:20–41; quotations from vv. 24–25, 34, 37.
48. Mosiah 18:21.

CHAPTER TEN

1. Russell M. Nelson, "'Blessed Are the Peacemakers,'" *Ensign*, November 2002.
2. John A. Widtsoe, in *One Hundred Fourteenth Semi-Annual Conference of The Church of Jesus Christ of Latter-day Saints* [October 1943] (Salt Lake City: The Church of Jesus Christ of Latter-day Saints, 1943), 113.

3. See John Paul Lederach, *Building Peace: Sustainable Reconciliation in Divided Societies* (Washington, DC: United States Institute of Peace, 1997), esp. chap. 4; Thomas Bamat and Mary Ann Cejka, eds., *Artisans of Peace: Grassroots Peacemaking among Christian Communities* (Maryknoll, NY: Orbis, 2003); Daniel Philpott and Gerard F. Powers, eds., *Strategies of Peace: Transforming Conflict in a Violent World* (New York: Oxford University Press, 2010); Cecelia Lynch, "Religious Communities and Possibilities for Justpeace," in *The Oxford Handbook of Religion, Conflict, and Peacebuilding*, ed. Atalia Omer, R. Scott Appleby, and David Little (New York: Oxford University Press, 2015), 597–612; and Susan Hayward and Katherine Marshall, eds., *Women, Religion, and Peacebuilding* (Washington, DC: United States Institute of Peace, 2015).

4. See Boutros Boutros-Ghali, *An Agenda for Peace: Preventive Diplomacy, Peacemaking and Peacekeeping* (New York: Department of Public Information, United Nations, June 17, 1992).

5. See Lederach, *Building Peace*. See also Lederach, *The Little Book of Conflict Transformation* (Intercourse, PA: Good Books, 2003); Lisa Schirch, *The Little Book of Strategic Peacebuilding* (Intercourse, PA: Good Books, 2004); and Lederach, *The Moral Imagination: The Art and Soul of Building Peace* (New York: Oxford University Press, 2005).

6. In nearly seven hundred pages of expert analysis, *The Oxford Handbook of Religion, Conflict, and Peacebuilding*, cited above, contains only one passing reference to Latter-day Saints. An early attempt to begin the conversation was made by Patrick Q. Mason, "The Possibilities of Mormon Peacebuilding," *Dialogue: A Journal of Mormon Thought* 37, no. 1 (Spring 2004): 12–45.

7. See John Paul Lederach and Janice Moomaw Jenner, eds., *A Handbook of International Peacebuilding: Into the Eye of the Storm* (San Francisco: John Wiley and Sons, 2002); and Roger Mac Ginty, ed., *Routledge Handbook of Peacebuilding* (New York: Routledge, 2015).

8. Official Church statistics state that as of December 2020 the Americas had 13,597,682 members and 23,826 congregations out of global totals of 16,565,036 members and 30,940 congregations; see http://www .mormonnewsroom.org/facts-and-statistics#. On the ending of war in the Western Hemisphere, see Steven Pinker and Juan Manuel Santos,

"Colombia's Milestone in World Peace," *New York Times*, August 26, 2016.

9. Doctrine and Covenants 115:6.

10. Adapted from United States Institute of Peace, https://www.usip.org /public-education/students/curve-conflict.

11. Mosiah 4:15.

12. Dallin H. Oaks, "World Peace," *Ensign*, May 1990.

13. Doctrine and Covenants 98:16.

14. See Doctrine and Covenants 58:26–27.

15. Personal communication with Thomas Griffith, September 18, 2016; and speech by Thomas Griffith at the J. Reuben Clark Law Society Annual Conference, Tempe, Arizona, February 15, 2008, copy in possession of the authors.

16. See Luke 4:18; Matthew 25:34–40; and https://www.ldsphilanthropies .org/humanitarian-services.

17. *Missionary Standards for Disciples of Jesus Christ*, 2.7, https://www .churchofjesuschrist.org/study/manual/missionary-standards-for -disciples-of-jesus-christ.

18. See Van Evans, Daniel W. Curtis, and Ram A. Cnaan, "Volunteering among Latter-Day Saints," *Journal for the Scientific Study of Religion* 52, no. 4 (December 2013): 827–41.

19. Community of Christ, *Book of Doctrine and Covenants* (Independence, MO: Herald Publishing House, 2007), 163:5a.

20. Tom Cornell, "The Future of Christian Nonviolence: Should Every Church Be a Peace Church?," *Plough Quarterly* (Summer 2015): 43.

21. See Andrew Bolton, "Congregations as Signal Communities: Transforming the World," 5, 17, http://www.cofchrist-gpnw.org/documents /Congregations%20as%20Signal%20Communities.pdf. See also Luke 4:18–19.

22. *General Handbook: Serving in The Church of Jesus Christ of Latter-day Saints* (Salt Lake City: Intellectual Reserve, 2020), section 1.2.

23. See David Pulsipher, "When Mormon Women Led Out for Peace," *Juvenile Instructor*, March 20, 2012, http://juvenileinstructor.org/when -mormon-women-led-out-for-peace; and Leonard J. Arrington, "Modern Lysistratas: Mormon Women in the International Peace Movement," *Journal of Mormon History* 15 (1989): 89–104.

24. Patrick Kearon, "Refuge from the Storm," *Ensign*, May 2016; emphasis in original. See https://www.churchofjesuschrist.org/refugees.

25. See Bolton, "Congregations as Signal Communities," 23.

26. Joseph F. Smith, "The Great War," *Improvement Era*, September 1914, 1074.

27. https://mckaycenter.byuh.edu/davidomckaycenter/about.

28. See https://cpcr.byu.edu and https://www.byui.edu/catalog#/programs /SJODzdwYL?bc=true&bcCurrent=Peace.

29. Lederach, *Moral Imagination*, 91; emphasis in original. This notion also builds on the broader theory of conflict transformation elaborated by Lederach in *Building Peace*. See also Matthew 13:33.

30. See David E. Campbell, John C. Green, and J. Quin Monson, *Seeking the Promised Land: Mormons and American Politics* (New York: Cambridge University Press, 2014), chap. 6.

31. Abraham Joshua Heschel, *God in Search of Man: A Philosophy of Judaism* (1955; repr., New York: Farrar, Straus and Giroux, 1976), 3.

32. Howard Thurman, *Jesus and the Disinherited* (Boston: Beacon, 1996), 3.

EPILOGUE

1. "Plat of the City of Zion, circa Early June–25 June 1833," The Joseph Smith Papers, https://www.josephsmithpapers.org/paper-summary/plat -of-the-city-of-zion-circa-early-june-25-june-1833/1.

2. See Dieter F. Uchtdorf, "Are You Sleeping through the Restoration?," *Ensign*, May 2014; Gary E. Stevenson, "The Ongoing Restoration," Brigham Young University devotional, August 20, 2019, https://speeches.byu .edu/talks/gary-e-stevenson/the-ongoing-restoration/; and LeGrand R. Curtis Jr., "The Ongoing Restoration," *Ensign*, April 2020.

3. See https://www.catholicworker.org/ and https://www.bruderhof.com/en.

4. 2 Nephi 28:21.

5. Moroni 6:5.

6. See Alma 34:15–17.

7. See Doctrine and Covenants 98:16.

8. Moroni 7:3.

9. Russell M. Nelson, "'Blessed Are the Peacemakers,'" *Ensign*, November 2002.

10. Doctrine and Covenants 98:16.

Subject Index

A

Aaron, 85–86, 87–88
Abu Ghraib prison, 172
abuse, serial, 134
accountability, 140–41
Adam and Eve, 70–71
agency
    and choosing violence, 136–41,
        167
    and divine power and influence,
        8–9
    versus freedom, 10–13
    in plan of salvation, 6–7
    of souls, 4–5
Alma the Elder, 205–6
Ammon, 86–88, 89, 97, 98
angel, appears to Laman and
        Lemuel, 47–48
anger
    and destructive conflict, 72–73
    and emotional distance, 105

Anselm of Canterbury, 244n20
Anti-Nephi-Lehies, 88–91, 97–102,
        109, 257n54
antisocial personality disorder,
        122–23
Ashurst-McGee, Mark, 181, 205
Atonement, 19–23
    and dynamic of kingdom of God,
        23–30
    as fulfillment of Christ's nonvio-
        lent political ethic, 37–42
    impact of, 34–35
    as nonviolent, 30–36
    and questions on necessity of
        crucifixion, 248–49n35
    and social aspect of redemption,
        20–21, 22–23
    transformation through, 20,
        21–22
Augustine, Saint, 164
authoritarian states, 11–12
authority, abuse of, 3–4

B

Babylon, 198
backhanding, 27–28
Barabbas, 34
Becerra, Daniel, 21
Bolton, Andrew, 225–26
Bonhoeffer, Dietrich, 134
Book of Mormon
  conflict in, 90–93
  nonviolent reading of, 45–46
  violence in, 43–45
  Zion-like communities in,
    205–6, 207–14
Bountiful, 56–57
brass plates, 47–53
Brigham Young University, 228
BYU Ninth Stake, 220–21
Brigham Young University–Hawaii,
  227–28
Brigham Young University–Idaho,
  228
Brimlow, Robert, 26
Bushman, Richard, 78
BYU Ninth Stake, 220–21

C

Caesar, 33–34, 35, 39, 173–74,
  179–80
Cahill, Lisa, 198, 212
Caputo, John, 39
Cavanaugh, William, 177
chastisement, divine, 10
cheap grace, 134, 263n27
cheek, turning, 27–29
Chenoweth, Erica, 120
choice, violence as, 136–41, 167
Christianity
  and peacebuilding, 215
  and Roman Empire, 173–74
  structural violence and expan-
    sion of, 222, 269n48
Christians, early, as Zion commu-
    nity, 206–7

Church of Jesus Christ of Latter-day
  Saints, The
  and community-based peace-
    building, 217
  and conscientious objection,
    139–40
  endorses peace movement,
    226–27
  friendship as fundamental prin-
    ciple of, 270n8
  increased focus on Jesus Christ,
    236
  integrating peacebuilding into
    local ministries of, 230–31
  LDS involvement in US wars,
    184–90
  missionary program of, 222–23
  peacebuilding potential of,
    218–25
  political involvement of, 174
  position on war, 185–86, 192,
    272n35
  and signal communities, 225–26,
    228
  social assistance programs of,
    224
  and transforming society, 225
citizenship. *See* political theology
city of Enoch, xviii, 204, 212
civil disobedience, 192
civil rights movement, 91–92
Clark, J. Reuben, 185, 272n35
collective sin, 200–204, 274–75n21
colonialism, 222, 269n48
commandment(s)
  to be perfect, 154
  to renounce war and proclaim
    peace, 50–51
  violence as, 160–65
communities
  and justified violence, 132–33
  redemption for, 42
Community of Christ, 225–26
competition, impulse for, 104

Nephites
    choose justified violence, 145–47
    Christ appears to, 151–52
    conflict between Lamanites and,
      62–64, 78–82, 90–91
noncombatant duty, 139–40
nonviolence
    advantages of, 121–22
    of Anti-Nephi-Lehies, 89–90,
      97–102
    and Church's position on war,
      185–86, 192, 272n35
    difficulty of, 145
    examples of, 113–19
    as ideal, 131–32
    Webb Miller on, 258n13
    success of, 119–20
    training in, 116–18
    transition from violence to,
      118–19

O

Oaks, Dallin H., xxii, xxvi, 10–11,
    109–12, 203, 220
Oaks, June, 109–10
"Of Governments and Laws in
    General," 183–84
Old Testament, divine violence in,
    165–68
opposition, 68–69. *See also* conflict
oppression, resisting, 27–29
others. *See also* enemies
    awareness and sympathy for, 211
    defense of, 164

P

Packer, Boyd K., xx
parenting, 11
patriotism, 193–94
Paul, 73, 96
peace
    defining, xxi–xxiv
    intercommunal, xxi–xxii
    interpersonal, xxi

    negative, xxii
    positive, xxii
    possibility of, xxiv–xxvi, 236–37
    preparing for, 227–28
    proclaiming, xxiv, 50–51
    Restoration scriptures and theol-
      ogy and practice of, xix–xx
    through Jesus Christ, xv–xvi
    through love, 114
peacebuilding, xvi, 126, 215–24,
    226–31
    Church's potential for, 218–25
    and conflict curve, 219
    Restoration's potential for, xvi–xvii
    and transforming society, 225–30
peace education, 216, 227–28
peace movement, 226–27
perfection, 154–55
persecution of Saints, xxi, 1–3, 129–30,
    178, 180–81, 182–83, 227
Peter, Apostle, 29, 40, 73, 138
Pilate, Pontius, 32–33, 34
plan of salvation, 5–7, 13
political theology, 171–76
    of early Saints, 178–84
    and Latter-day Saint involvement
      in US wars, 184–90
    and renouncing false gods, 193–96
    of Restoration, 190–93
    and secular authority as object of
      ultimate concern, 176–78
positive peace
    as embodiment of Restoration's
      nonviolent theology, 234,
      236–7
    defined, xxii
    following Jesus Christ and, xxiv
    goal of global peacebuilding
      efforts, 216
    preceded by negative peace, 103,
      108
    recognizing need to work
      toward, 235, 237

Scripture Index

287

BOOK OF MORMON

DOCTRINE AND COVENANTS

PEARL OF GREAT PRICE

About the Authors

Patrick Q. Mason holds the Leonard J. Arrington Chair of Mormon History and Culture at Utah State University, where he is an associate professor of religious studies and history. He is the author or editor of several books for academic and Latter-day Saint audiences, including the recent titles *Mormonism and Violence: The Battles of Zion* (Cambridge University Press, 2019) and *Restoration: God's Call to the 21st-Century World* (Faith Matters Publishing, 2020). He and his wife, Melissa, live in Logan, Utah, with their four children.

J. David Pulsipher is a professor of history at Brigham Young University–Idaho, where he leads its program in peace and conflict transformation and is also a practicing mediator. He is the author of *When We Don't See Eye to Eye: Using the Weapon of Love to Overcome Anger and Aggression* (Covenant Communications, 2014) and editor, with Patrick Mason and Richard Bushman, of *War and Peace in Our Time: Mormon Perspectives* (Greg Kofford Books, 2012). He and his wife, Dawn, live in Rexburg, Idaho, and they are the parents of six children.